Praise for

"Sensational."
— Joey Tannenbaum, leading industrialist; philanthropist; supporter of the Canadian Opera, the Art Gallery of Ontario, and various hospitals

"Thank you for giving me a copy of your book about your mother. I picked up the volume to leaf through it after dinner and I could not put it down until midnight. It is truly outstanding and you deserve enormous credit on many, many fronts—which this letter is far too short to enumerate. Thank you, once more, and very best wishes for your publication."
—Peter Munk, Chair, Barrick Gold Corporation; Philanthropist; Companion of the Order of Canada; Recipient of the Woodrow Wilson Award for Corporate Citizenship; Inductee into the Canadian Business Hall of Fame; the Peter Munk Charitable Foundation dispersed over $50 million to a variety of organizations to improve the health, learning, and international reputation of Canadians; he holds honorary degrees from five universities

"Michael Fekete has written a brilliant, poignant, very personal description of the extraordinary life of his mother, Ilona Deutsch, and her family, while in the process of covering the 300 years of the history of the Austro-Hungarian Empire prior to World War II, in an erudite, compelling narrative. This book is a must-read for anyone interested in the impact of the Holocaust on Eastern European Jewry and the historical context through which it emerged."
—Allan S. Kaplan, MSc, MD, FRCP(C), Loretta Anne Rogers Chair in Eating Disorders, Toronto General Hospital; Senior Clinician/Scientists, Centre for Addiction and Mental Health; Vice-Chair Research and Professor of Psychiatry, University of Toronto, Faculty of Medicine

"This is a fabulous read. It is more than a memoir, more than history, and more than a love story. *The Times and Life of Ilona Deutsch* relates a beautiful story of the life of the Deutsch family starting from the Holy Roman Empire, through the Austro-Hungarian Monarchy and birth of Nazism, up to the Stalinist regime, during which the author was born. The description of the times that shaped the lives and characters of her ancestors and later Ilona's own life is vivid and engaging. The main thread in the book, the mother's love, struggle, and efforts to protect her children and to instill in them her values, takes us through charming episodes that add colour and taste to the main narrative and appears and disappears like a brook flowing through fields and forests."

—Rose Wolfe, former two-term Chancellor of the University of Toronto; Companion of the Order of Canada; philanthropist; fighter for social justice

From School to Prison and Down the River

OTHER TITLES BY MICHAEL FEKETE

The Times and Life of Ilona Deutsch

From School to Prison and Down the River

Michael Fekete

Copyright © 2017 Michael Fekete

All rights reserved. No part of this publication may be reproduced or transmitted in any form or by any means, or stored in a data base or retrieval system, without the prior written permission of the authors.

From School to Prison and Down the River
ISBN 978-0-9782295-3-5

Design and Print Production: Beth Crane, WeMakeBooks.ca

Printed and bound in Canada

I dedicate this book to the memory of my Mother whose loving wisdom not only helped me endure, but made me stronger and wiser. Like no one else in the world, with her knowing and patient ways, she formed the person I am. Everything that's good in me comes from her.

Memory is that most paradoxical of the senses—at the same time so powerful that even the most fleeting impressions can be stored, forgotten completely, and then reproduced in perfect detail years later.
—Peter Fenwick, *Past Lives*

As we know, time moves back and forth.
—Roberto Calasso, personal letter from

Question: "What would you do if you had a time machine?"
Paul McCartney: "Go back and spend time with my Mum."

▪

We sit in the car in the hospital parking lot, engine running. The warm air flowing from the vents feels good on my knees and on my hands. As I gaze at the snowflakes tumbling about outside, my thoughts drift back to a spring day in 1968.

I was in the library in Szeged, reading for my Latin colloquium. I had just finished collecting quotes from the selected orations of Cicero to illustrate the use of irregular verbs—*facio, facere, feci, factum*, and the like—when the closing bell rang. I gathered my notes, shut the parched, musty book, and was just getting up to return it to the librarian when I caught sight of two men I had not noticed before. They didn't look like students. Moving without a word between them and without looking at each other, as if everything had been agreed on in advance, they folded their newspapers and stood up in unison. They were wearing black leather jackets—uncommon garb for students.

I returned Cicero, said good night to the librarian, and walked to the door. Once outside, I headed straight to the café across the street, a gathering place for students. Out of the corner of my eye, I saw that the leather jackets were following me. I pushed the door open, stepped into an acrid fog of cigarette smoke, and made my way through the crowd of young people talking loudly and all at once about Jack Kerouac, Allen Ginsberg, samizdat literature, and—above all—the Prague Spring. These were not hippies or acid heads. Unlike the Beat Generation, they didn't have access to LSD. They didn't need it—they were they own drug: empty talk. (They would have balked at any proposal for serious action or anything of consequence.) I liked them, regardless. I also liked the music coming from the record player: Marvin Gaye, Otis Redding, Steppenwolf.

I found an empty table and laid out my notes, but Cicero and his irregulars were quickly pushed out of my mind by the two leather jackets who showed up at the door, eyes darting across the noisy crowd until they found me. They took a table next to mine and sat stiffly, pretending to read their newspapers and appearing just as out of place here as they had in the library. I was certain they were plainclothes police—and I knew that they were not here by accident.

I had to shake them. Leaving my pen and my notes on the table, I moved through the crowd to the washroom in the back, where I took off and discarded my too easily recognizable grey Harvard sweatshirt. I returned immediately, but my men were not at their table. Through the café window, I spotted one standing on the sidewalk and the other inside a telephone booth.

A small group of students was leaving the café, and I ducked out among them. Once out on the street, I began to run, turning at the first side street and dashing into the darkness of an alley without looking back. My escape plan, hatched as I ran, was to gather a few belongings and documents from my dormitory, take the streetcar to the canoe club, stuff my knapsack into the hull of a kayak, and paddle downriver to Yugoslavia in the dark of night.

I was not far from my dorm when two unmarked Moskvitch cars pulled up to the curb, tires screeching. The doors flew open before the cars had even come to a halt, and five or six leather jackets jumped out and surrounded me, guns drawn. There was nowhere to run. Two of them grabbed my arms and twisted them behind my back, forcing my wrists together. I felt a cold pinch and heard the metallic click of locking handcuffs. The leather jackets pushed me into the back seat of one of the Moskvitches, where I sat pressed between two goons, who gripped my arms tightly.

It all happened in a flash. One minute, I was running free; the next, I was a captive.

It's past noon. We move slowly, almost crawling, through the heavy slush that covers Kossuth Street. A small convoy of transport trucks passes us, and each time we find ourselves in the trajectory of the grey mud rising in the wake of their enormous wheels our windshield is plastered. The wipers screech and bend as they struggle with the heavy mess. The trucks disappear where the road curves at Ady Street, and Alexandra stops the car at the intersection.

In the angle of the sun's rays, the fresh snow covering the rooftops is pale blue rather than white. The last flakes lingering in the air tumble like cabbage butterflies, fall onto the pavement one by one, and are swallowed by the slush. Looking to my right, I see the steeple of the old Calvinist church rising above the smaller buildings that hug the ground. As though showing their solidarity with this sleepy town by having no concern for the passage of time, the two faces of the clock tower are even further behind than they were yesterday. Completely out of whack, the one on the west is half an hour behind the one facing north, the arms of which are about to close at the top. I glance at my watch. It is 12:18 p.m., February 26, 2006.

Through the car window, now opaque with a film of salt, I see someone standing on the corner, his feet planted in the snow. He is the same old, heavily bearded man who was feeding the pigeons yesterday. The hands that distributed food to his feathered flock are now held aloft, as if in exhortation to the birds huddling side by side on the ledge above the church door. Motionless, as if frozen in a frieze, they are fluffed up into little balls against the cold. The sun falls squarely against the side of the church and lights up the snow-covered grounds. The man's gaze is steady, and as he looks skyward, his face appears gripped by some profound revelation. He reminds me of a painting I once saw in a gallery. However, I'm certain that the title of the painting was *The Praying Saviour* and not *The Prophet*.

Except for me, no one seems to pay attention to him. Not the people crossing the intersection, nor the feathered flock he is so intent on drawing under his spell. Palms raised, he lifts his hands even higher, then drops them against his sides in a gesture of helpless resignation. The shadow he casts on the snowbank appears larger than life.

There is a loud peal, followed by a brief silence, as though the rest of the bells weren't sure whether they should go with the clock on the north, now showing twelve, or wait for the west face, still at half past eleven. The birds throw themselves into the air and rise above the trees. When the bell rings a second time, they whirl and change the direction of their flight. The old man raises an arm to shield his eyes from the sun and follows them with a transfixed stare.

While we wait for the last pedestrian to make his way through the slush, the old man steps up onto the snowbank. With his eyes shut and a look of rapture on his face, he chants with complete devotion and concentration, as if repeating the same incantations would protect him from the terrifying clarity of rational thought. I can relate to that. His pigeons soar high in the vault of the winter sky, the sun's rays piercing through the feathers of their outstretched wings. They retreat in the distance. The ringing of the church bells fades into a tinkle so faint that I'm not sure whether it's ringing only in my head.

We inch onto Attila Street. Out of the corner of my eyes I see the man only vaguely as he waves, but his transfigured countenance remains clear in my head, sharp as a photograph.

Impatiently, I check my watch, then look over at the speedometer a few times, but time is not going to move slower and the car is not going to move faster. "What time is your flight?" my daughter asks. I shake my head as if I had just surfaced from some cavernous depth.

"Mother must think I'm abandoning her," I say, ignoring her question. I think of her lying in bed, soon to be delivered from suffering, delivered from awareness, and I am not there to provide sheltering care.

"She is happy you came to see her." Alexandra turns her wanting-to-please face in my direction.

"I should call the hospital and postpone my surgery," I say, as though thinking aloud.

"Don't even think it." Alexandra rolls her eyes. "Of course, you shouldn't." Her voice is earnest. But it sounds to me as if my daughter is using the pitiful alibi of my surgery to absolve me of the sad fact that I am leaving Mother, the mainstay of my youth, to attend to my own health rather than remain with her to the end. We stare ahead, each in our own silence, and let our thoughts hang unspoken between us. As if we had agreed that this is not the time to turn the car into a parrot cage of mindless chatter. Silence is better than speaking words that glide off us, or talking without hearing each other.

My mind drifts in memories. As I look at the snowbank, peppered with grey dabs of mud, I imagine tiny green heads poking out of it, and in my head, they turn into white, bell-shaped flowers seeking the sun. I hear Mother singing her welcome song in the kitchen: "There was a curious snowdrop. ..." I admired her vibrant, joyous spirit, her happy industrious nature. She was always doing something—or rather, many things at the same time: cooking our dinner, sweeping the kitchen floor, feeding the fire, singing a song.

Sometimes she would stop in the middle of whatever she was doing, and at such times her face looked like a portrait or a profile on a coin: distant, as though she was dreaming of a completely different life than the one she was living. (As a child, I didn't like her having thoughts and reveries of her own. They distracted her from caring for me with instant and constant attention to my needs. I would make stupid noises or ask silly questions.) Or in the middle of reading, she would close her book and gaze into the distance, as if she wanted to understand some hidden meaning. A certain page could bring so much sadness and terror to her eyes, as though the words on it had opened a door in her mind and made her recoil at what she saw. Whenever I caught her in such a state, I wanted to step between her and that faceless threat.

Growing up, I was often the one who made her freeze in anguish with my rash and reckless acts. By age nine, rebellion had become the main thread in my personality. At twelve, it was an obsession, stronger than the love of reading or the love of nature, both implanted in me by Mother. By fourteen, I embraced it as my raison d'être. Attracted to the dangerous and deaf to her pleas for normalcy, I let the tug of mutinous adventures win out over her appeals for safety. Most boys have some rebellious thoughts. Some even commit token acts of revolt, defiance, and daring. But when it comes to a serious act that would have serious consequences, most of us realize that the odds of getting away with it are small. As common sense prevails, the sharp edges of defiance fall away. But not with me. I became a rebel without a pause. By eighteen, defiance had become an irrational inner force, independent of my conscious choices. The more extreme an idea sounded, the more obsessed I became with it.

Mother never complained. She never even mentioned how difficult I was; perhaps if she did, I might not have had the heart to have children of my own.

I remember how I felt when my son David was arrested for one of his teenage slips. My chest was empty, my head full of bad thoughts, as I drove south on the Bayview Extension to 51 Division. After talking to the police who would not let me see him, I paced the sidewalk in front of the station, feeling helpless and useless, and wished I had a rocket launcher. At the thought of my son locked in a cell, my heart felt like lead. It did not matter that I was certain he would not be treated all too badly—the absolute worst bullies inside that station were mere learners compared to the ones who had once interrogated me—but this was the first time I had a glimpse of how Mother must have felt upon hearing the news of my arrest, when the agents of the Political Police descended on her home with a search warrant. Although she was a lot stronger than me, able to take everything in a tranquil, serene manner, the thought of her son in handcuffs must have devastated her.

I was sitting on my cot and watching the rays of the morning sun straining through the clouds, moving up and down on the vertical bars of the tiny window high in the wall.

To find myself locked up in the interrogation cell of the Political Police should not have been a surprise. It was the logical outcome of my deep-seated antagonism to the regime, a hostility that led to a series of reckless acts. If anything, my arrest should have happened earlier, but it was shocking in its finality, regardless. I had lost my freedom. Gone was my dream of the Olympics, together with my plans to escape from Hungary. My reality had become that six-by-ten block of concrete with a steel door and a small, barred window a foot or so up above my head, showing a small piece of blue, May sky behind the opaque glass.

Mother used to call me "the whirlwind." Restless, always on the move. One moment I was reading, the next running to the swimming pool. School was hardly over and I was on my bike to the river. That whirlwind was now captured and bottled up between walls of concrete, but unlike the genie, not about to be set free by any fisherman.

I heard the echo of distant footsteps on the corridor. They became louder and louder, then died right outside my cell. After a moment of silence, there was a faint metallic sound and the lid slid off the peephole. Keys clinked and the door opened. A policeman stepped inside and stood with his thumbs hooked in his belt right behind the buckle. His nose was so red that it seemed to have sucked the blood from the rest of his chalk-white face. A second policeman hovered in the doorway. The keys hanging from a large ring in his hand swung like a pendulum. The one with the red nose began inspecting the cell, ignoring me, as if I was not present. Judging by the number of silver stripes and silver stars on his epaulettes, he must have been of higher rank than the other. His eyes moved from one wall to the next, from the concrete floor up to the ceiling. They lingered longer on the window high up in the wall, as though he was counting the vertical bars. He removed his baton, marched forward, tapped each bar several times and listened as if tuning an instrument. When finished, he swung his baton behind his back, spun around on one heel and barked, "Get up!" With a sweeping motion of his arm, he drew the baton from behind his back and slammed it hard into the palm of his left hand. "Move! Look alive!"

I stood up from the cot.

"Stand there!" he raised the baton and pointed it at the corner. "Face the wall." From the corner of my eyes I saw the second policeman get down on his knees to check the space under the cot.

"Hands up on the wall! Spread your legs!" He frisked me, starting up under my armpits, all the way down to my ankles, then up and down again, poking his fingers hard into my flesh. "Hands behind your back!" He clicked a pair of handcuffs onto my wrists, locked them, grabbed my arm and led me out of the cell.

With a tight grip around my elbows, they marched me along a corridor with bare concrete walls. In the dim glow of low-wattage bulbs housed in wire baskets, which blocked most of the light and gave the corridor on the cellblock side a cave-like appearance, we walked past a dozen cell doors—a series of narrow, grey metal panels with a peephole in each—to a heavy steel gate. The policeman with the red nose turned me against the wall. His mate unlocked the gate and swung it open. Once on the other side, I was pushed face against the wall again and the gate was locked. It seemed that each move was done according to some rule book, a Pavlovian protocol devised to drill prisoners into trained animals.

The corridor on this side of the steel gate was different: here, the walls were papered, and the gleam of bright, glaring fluorescent lights reflected on their patterned texture. The doors were large, padded, and well spaced. When we passed the last one, the men twisted my arms and turned me against the wall. "Look straight ahead." I tried to read the sign beside the door, but I couldn't.

I heard the door open. Felt the squeeze of a hand around my arm and was pushed inside a room. With regulation respect on their faces, the policemen clicked their heels to salute the man who stood behind a desk and in front of a tall swivel chair. One removed the handcuffs, the other pointed to a spot on the floor. "Stand right there." They clicked their heels again, saluted, and left, closing the door behind them.

We turn again. The wipers stop and leave shimmering traces of salt on the windshield. In the distance, the water tower is a giant wineglass, and the vertical beams of the midday sun dance around its belly. We pass my old school and turn onto Kiser Street, which, instead of molten slush, is covered with bumps of frozen snow and ice. The car starts to shake and slides to the curb. Alexandra switches into low gear. "They don't salt the side streets," she explains. I nod in acknowledgement, then reach for the visor, squinting against the sun's glare. In the narrow gap between my eyelids, Mother's place is a dollhouse dipped in liquid sugar.

"I'll go and get my suitcase," I say as she pulls into the driveway. I walk through the fresh snow and hurry to the gate. The key turns with a creak. The side door is unlocked and inside, right under the coat rack and to the right of it, are my suitcase and my small briefcase. I grab them. Then, glancing at the photographs on the wall, I lower the suitcase back onto the floor and walk down to the basement. I turn on the light and look for the shoebox I found a few days ago, when I was sifting through the house for old photos and mementos. It is where I left it. I open it, take a handful of my letters addressed to Mother, and stuff them into my briefcase. I run up the stairs, pick up my suitcase, and head for the car.

"You have everything with you?" Alexandra asks.

"I do," I say and put the suitcase on the back seat.

"Passport and tickets?" I nod. "Let me see." She looks at my ticket, then at the clock on the instrument panel. "We have plenty of time, Dad."

The man behind the desk was dressed in civilian clothes. The enormous belly protruding from above his belt looked like some grotesque, runaway tumour. I stood before him, arms hanging like ropes, wrists burning at the imprints of handcuffs just removed, and fingers pulsing at their tips. His hands—with short, fat, sausage-like fingers—were perched on his hips. His face was flat, a grim mask with no characteristic or distinctive features. The kind one might see a hundred times and still fail to recognize on the next occasion. Except for the eyes. There was something in them that I found disturbing, but I couldn't put my finger on it. Eyes are said to be the window to the soul; his were pale grey, like aspic gone bad. Then I knew—there was nothing in those eyes from which I could draw my usual conclusions about the person behind them. Nothing that would suggest traits of personality, nothing to give some clue to his character. They could have been the eyes of a dead fish, had an occasional metallic glint not revealed a history of stored malice. After a long, motionless gaze, they began to move with small, nervous twitches, appraising and reappraising.

"Why did you do it?" he asked with the sharp, atavistic reflex of a grand inquisitor determined to investigate and to right anything and everything that might appear to be out of order. He leaned forward and picked up his cigarette from the edge of an ashtray sitting between a black Olympia typewriter and a tape recorder. He drew on it and blew smoke into the air. He blinked a few times into the thin cloud in front of his face, then put the cigarette back on the ashtray. He leaned heavily on the desk and observed me with the half-closed eyes of a predator watching his prey.

I stood and stared wordlessly into the blue vapours rising from the openings of his face. Like a poker player considering his hand, I took a quick inventory of my reasons and pondered which ones I should place on the table. Then I decided not to play. I turned my head away from his gaze, in the direction of the wall on my left. I almost smiled when I noticed the new socialist coat of arms created after the revolution of 1956 mounted high, right under the ceiling. Underneath was a portrait of Lenin, with one of Brezhnev on one side and one of Kadar, Moscow's Hungarian puppet, on the other. At eye level, arranged in strict geometrical order, were half a dozen framed awards and recognitions praising the vigilance, the diligence, and the revolutionary alertness of Major Magyar Jozsef, the man I was facing.

He blew long, swirling clouds of blue smoke into the air and watched me watch the wall. "Take one," he said. Out of the corner of my eye I saw him pushing a packet of cigarettes in my direction. I turned my head but didn't make eye contact.

"I don't smoke," I said, glancing at the calendar on his desk. It was Monday, May 20, 1968. "In nine days, I will be twenty one," I thought.

He clawed back the packet and put his hand back on his hip. His shirt was tight against his enormous stomach, its buttons stretching the buttonholes into slits, and the outline of his undershirt was visible. His fat neck went up to the ears sitting flat against his skull. Having taken that in, I turned my attention back to the wall on my left.

Except for the awards and recognitions, the arrangement was almost the same as the one that had decorated the facade of the Party Centre, where, under the socialist heraldry and right above the entrance a large picture of Lenin was lit by half a dozen spot lights. On one side, about a foot or so under Lenin's familiar, goat-like image, Brezhnev glared into the dark night with eyes set deep under the vault of dark, Mephistophelian brows. Compared to the stern fixity of purpose etched into their faces, Kadar's washed-out countenance reminded me more of a tired, old lapdog than that of a leader. Red flags, red brocade, and red drapery were arranged all around them.

It was close to midnight. The spotlights directed up at the portraits left the street level almost dark. Once the drapery that cascaded down either side to the steps leading to the entrance had soaked up the last drop of gasoline, I lit a match. The flames went up with a whump. I felt the heat on the back of my hand and could smell my hair singeing.

We are back at the corner of Attila and Kossuth Streets. My prophet is gone. His pigeons are perched above the church door. With not much else to see, I close my eyes and see myself at that juncture, holding the burning match before the final act. The act I had rehearsed a hundred times in my mind and the one that would change everything. From where and how did I arrive at that juncture?

If I had had one miraculous, reflective moment after emptying the can of gasoline, had come to my senses (which had long abandoned me) and checked myself, like a pilot checking the gauges of the instrument panel before takeoff, if I had said, "Wait, this is crazy," and walked away, my life would have been very different. Or not.

Or if Mother, glancing out the kitchen window that afternoon, had seen me draining the gasoline from my stepfather's motorcycle, had asked me what I was doing, and if I had confessed (which was highly unlikely) that I was about to set fire to the Party Centre, and she had somehow managed to talk me out of it (which is even more unlikely), would the future have turned out to be different? Maybe, but not much. I was too much a slave to my pattern of perverse, juvenile impulses; the more bizarre and the more impossible an idea was, the more satisfaction I got from pursuing it.

All happened as foreseen, scripted in my head and agreed upon a hundred times. I took a step back from the drapery. But not for a sober second thought—it was the run-up for the leap. I touched the burning match to the red rag and ran. When I looked back, the flames were climbing, engulfing Lenin, Brezhnev, and Kadar. Like a sinister, hostile omen, distant but distinct, the five points of the giant red star mounted on the roof above shone with implacable disapproval.

Alexandra stops at a gas station. The attendant, a young man dressed in a jumpsuit and a filthy, padded jacket dances to the car. His head is bobbing like a metronome. He removes one earplug, which now hangs by his jaw, and contemplates us with a complete lack of dedication to his job. Alexandra lowers the window.

"Hey," he says rubbing his hands in front of his chest. He has a large, silver ring in one side of his nose.

"Fill 'er up, please," Alexandra says. "Super."

"Super," he repeats and blows a funnel of vapours onto his hands. The smell of brandy fills the car. He reinstalls the earplug and walks out of my vision. I hear some clanking noise and then, on the roof of the car, thumping to the rhythm of some unknown music. Alexandra leans back and smiles with dreamy detachment, as if observing such contempt for work amuses rather than annoys her.

Wrapped in a large, black coat held together with a string under the collar, an old man stands by the pump next to us. From under a hat covered by a thin mantle of snow, his shaggy, grey mane falls onto his shoulders. The legs of his trousers are mashed into a pair of worn-out rubber boots. With each gust of wind he shivers and bends deeper into it. He has the scarlet nose and cheeks of a drinker, and his eyes are moving with intent— as if searching for someone to address. He turns and the sleeves of his coat flap around, empty. "A double amputee," I think and reach into my pocket. I notice that he is holding something under his coat, perhaps an animal.

We make eye contact. He hobbles alongside the car, his boots shuffling in the slush, pulls what turns out to be a scratchy violin from inside his coat, and plays a sentimental tune. He stabs the bow into the folds of his coat and draws the violin in after it, takes his hat off, holds it up to the car window, and stands motionless, as if gripped by the damp chill in the air.

By the time the firemen arrived, all that was left of the decorations were ashes on the sidewalk and smoke on the wall. The Workers' Guard recognized that there was not enough time to make the mess disappear and to return the facade to its ornate, celebratory self. The best they could do was to hide it under large sheets of screen and construction paper. At an emergency session called by the party bosses and the police, it was decided that the annual obligatory procession of the faithful had to be rerouted.

It would start, as usual, at Marx Square, close to the railway station. But the police motorcade leading the human surf, instead of taking the usual route to Party Centre, would ride to the north side of Kossuth Square to deliver the marchers to their herders. Calls went out to select cadres who were summoned to a briefing. They were told of the sabotage and were advised of the details of the improvised plan.

The next morning, perched on the fence of the House of Culture, I caught sight of the first divisions of workers, peasants, and soldiers that appeared behind the squadron of motorcycle police riding in their parade uniforms. Not far behind them, with faked exuberance on their faces, four young men carried a decorative, rectangular contraption that read

LONG LIVE APRIL 4TH, THE FESTIVE DAY OF OUR LIBERATION

A division of metal workers followed, hauling a float that displayed shovels, spades, pickaxes and other small tools made of steel. With his gnarled hands wrapped around a tall wooden pole, the one in the lead held a giant banner. In stark contrast to the tired, bent, overworked "vanguard of the proletariat," it showed the idealized, homoerotic rendition of a young, muscular, naked male raising a hammer above an anvil.

On the next float, more colourful than the one filled with hardware and hauled by two horses rather than humans, there were sheaves of wheat piled high in a stack, surrounded by baskets of corn and apples, and bags filled with what must have been potatoes, lentils, and beans to demonstrate the abundance of produce that streamed from collective farms to cities and towns. On the banner above, there was a young woman brandishing a sickle and apparently overwhelmed by such joy that she looked to be on the verge of her first orgasm.

I slid off the fence. With the morning paper in one hand and a camera under my jacket, I walked along the sidewalk together with the onlookers following the march, which seemed to be going well, despite the hastily revised plan. I was surprised and at the same time annoyed by the efficiency of the party apparatus in reorganizing rather than cancelling the event. I walked to the Lutheran Church, sat down on a bench, and watched.

For a while, except for the change in the traditional route, everything seemed to be going as usual. A choir of young pioneers began to sing under a cloud of red balloons swaying in the breeze:

April 4th, our cherished, festive day
You brought us a beautiful life.
Our song sings the joy of our heart
Because the people were liberated today.

More divisions arrived and, inevitably, mistakes were made on this unfamiliar, chartless side of the square. Over the course of seventeen years of making the same left and right turns and occupying the same spots on one half of the square rather than the other, both the herd and their herders had formed some hard-to-reverse Pavlovian habits along certain pathways. The improvised route rendered all past experience useless. Despite the nighttime briefing, confusion reigned in the minds of the cadres, resulting in chaos. Those giving orders shouted, "Right," but their arms still swung out to the habitual spot on the left. Those obeying directions may have heard "Move back" while, against their will, they were being pressed forward.

A safe distance from the calamity of the crime scene, standing on a makeshift structure of raw, new pine, the local leaders gravely received the salutes of the first divisions of marchers waving flags, posters and banners. Occasionally, as though waking up and remembering that the day was to be festive, their unparted lips distributed a few glued-on, professional smiles. Dressed in black leather jackets, wearing sunglasses to hide the alert glitter of their eyes, plainclothes police moved nervously among the vast mesh of bodies. The crowd of onlookers standing at the curb was saturated by uniformed police.

Loud voices of command resounded throughout the square. With desperate gestures, the organizers tried to move a stray flock or two to their newly assigned places. Those in the first lines of the subsequent divisions began to teeter. Despite the efforts of the captains, one group moved into a place allotted to another. A group of students collided with the public employees. There was jerking and swaying among the crowd, now skittish with not knowing. They craved and at the same time resented direction. Like waves trapped between cliffs, they sloshed about directionless.

"Hey, not there, here! Move back! Move forward!" the captains yelled, loud and all at the same time, at the surging multitude packing the square—or rather, one half of it—with heaving bodies pressed together. The bosses on the podium stood stiffly, as if their feet were fused onto the platform.

With the confused, timid movements of puppets whose strings have abruptly became slack but not cut or completely severed, the marchers sensed that the guiding hand controlling the strings had become uncertain, nervous. They fell out of step, stumbled and bounced into one another. One tumult sorted out created another. Once the captain of each column representing workers, peasants, teachers and students finished herding their restless charges in front of the leaders and the convulsions slowly ceased, instead of the usual expressions of eternal gratitude for being liberated by the Red Army and the obligatory revolutionary exhortations and promises, the masses received dry statistics of production numbers, delivered in a cold, administrative tongue. This went on until the mood created was more funereal than festive. The waving of banners and flags became hesitant and timid, and then completely stopped. The crowd endured the boredom of the speeches with undisguised lack of attention. It was an eerie, Kafkaesque scene, as the weariness of the somnambulant mass slowly gave birth to apprehension and suspense. People began seeking for clues, searching for answers. Some nervously fingered the tuners of their transistor radios for news of promise, of hope, or of doom. Some, glancing sideways, whispered or murmured apocalyptic words into the ears of their neighbours. Others stood craning their necks, seeking for signs that would unravel the secret behind the pervasive tension, the show of force, and those screens covering the facade of the Party Centre looming behind the linden trees.

The band began to play the "Song of Liberation."

> March forward on the road and never look back.
> Your past is a painful, gloomy thousand years.
> Now finally the sun shines on your head.
> Be happy and gay and sing this song with us:
>
> The song is about April 4th.
> It is about Liberation that we sing about.
> With steeled throats we shout into the wind
> The heroic names of our brave liberators.
>
> Guns blasted and the war machines rumbled,
> The earth was bleeding and there was thunder in the sky.
> As the victorious Red Army finally wiped away
> The tears of many centuries flowing from our eyes.

It managed to elicit only a faint, half-hearted response from the crowd.

When the band stopped playing, an officer from the local army unit together with a Workers' Guard, both dressed in parade uniforms, walked to the Russian Monument carrying an enormous wreath between them. They laid it on the base of the monument, saluted, and stood at attention while the loudspeakers blasted the usual slogans:

"Long Live the Soviet Union!"

"Long Live the Heroic Red Army!"

"Long Live Socialism!"

"Long Live the Five-Year Plan!"

A few hands gave a hesitant clap or two during the pause between each brave announcement—most had their minds elsewhere.

Except for the party leaders standing grimly on the improvised podium, the armed Workers' Guard surrounding them, and the police out in full force, the herd-mass was ignorant of the reason behind the mysterious, last-minute changes. They sensed that something had happened, but did not know what. The rulers knew that a monstrous act had been committed, but were clueless about the identity of the perpetrators and what their deed might herald. The mutual distrust between the crowd and its bosses, protected by an unusual display of force, was palpable and grew with each minute.

I sat on the bench in front of the Lutheran church, pretending to read the newspaper in my lap. Underneath the paper was a camera that I had pulled out from behind the broken window of the *Ofotert*—the state store for optical equipment. I was the only one in possession of the full knowledge of what had happened. I observed with satisfaction that the fire of celebratory spirit had been extinguished by the one I had set the night before. I wanted to document everything with pictures. With equal disdain, I watched the party cadres standing frozen on the podium and the great mass in front of them. In the absence of the police and the cordon of armed guards, a mere shout, a call for rising up would have awakened the crowd from its stupor, would have stirred it into a stampede; the mob would have stormed the podium to throw off and trample its self-appointed leaders before whom they had just finished abasing themselves. "The circus is in town," I said to myself and began humming Bob Dylan's "Desolation Row."

After the announcement of the last slogan, the crowd began to disperse. Banners and flags were lowered. Some were just dropped and left lying on the pavement. The four young men hauling the rectangular contraption off the square looked more like pallbearers than heralds of the happy news inscribed in bold red letters. Between two cordons of Workers' Guards, the local party bosses descended from the podium and were escorted to their black Volgas.

With his sausage fingers, Major Magyar slowly removed the cigarette from his mouth. Like an actor in an old black-and-white movie, he made an awkward attempt at performing the movement with a relaxed, elegant movement.

"Listened to Radio Free Europe too much?" he suggested, faking a soft, almost teacherly voice. The fight between the forced smile and the grim mask was eating into his face, and when neither of them could claim victory, his countenance went flat. "You have quite a history," he said and cast his eyes in the direction of the fat file beside the typewriter. "Sit," he spat the word into the air and darted a fat finger—that had evidently never done a day's real work—in the direction of the chair in front of his desk.

"Fuck you, I'm not your dog," I thought and ignored the order.

I tried to come up with a plausible answer. Yes, I did listen to Radio Free Europe. The government tried its best to jam "the mouth of the imperialists." However, the news, commentaries, and the sounds of music came through the ether even if a few words and tunes faded and became lost in the cosmos. I also read all the banned books I could lay my hands on. *Doctor Zhivago, Brave New World, Animal Farm,* and *1984*. But my motives were inexplicably more complex than mere reaction to Western propaganda and blacklisted books. There was no explaining why I hated everything he stood for and was paid to protect.

"We know everything about you," he said and pulled a tape recording from the drawer of his desk. "We have another one," he added. From the same drawer, he removed a flat box with BASF written on it. He gave me a meaningful look and tapped the box with his finger.

"Do you want to explain," he asked, "what made you denigrate, mock, and slander the president of your local town council? We have your entire tirade recorded. This is the transcript," he said and threw a bunch of stapled typewritten pages on the desk.

I recognized the tape. I had kept it on my bookshelf. It was a musical chronicle of my life as a rebel. In a symbolic manner, it started with "It's My Life" by the Animals: the chords G - Dm - G – Dm, followed by the big, dark voice of Eric Burdon announcing, "It's a hard world to get a break in." If the police endured that prelude, they could listen to the full account of my life as a rebel. From the day in 1956 when, at age nine, I threw my inkpot at the Russian monument, through opening the tear gas canister at the November 7 celebrations at age sixteen, to the day when I burned the decorations at the local Party Centre. Among my future schemes, so insane that common sense should have suggested that none of it would ever take place (but I had no access to that commodity at the time, and for a long time thereafter), they might have found the details of my escape plan from behind the Iron Curtain, introduced by "We Gotta Get Out Of This Place."

But I did not know about the existence of the "other" tape and did not have a clue how it related to my alleged "denigration, mocking, and slandering of the president of the town council." Major Magyar let me stare at the flat box with the BASF logo and the transcript for a moment before opening the box and putting the tape on the tape player next to the typewriter. With another meaningful look, he pressed the play button. After some initial whizzes and crackles, a voice speaking in dry, administrative language launched into drivel about the achievements of socialism. As soon as I heard my own voice, I knew what Major Magyar was talking about. I let my gaze wander to the window and remembered the summer of 1966 when the Australian water polo team had toured Hungary.

The Hungarian Water Polo Association chose my hometown team of the Szentesi Kinizsi to host the Aussies. After the match, there was a dinner party at the local town hall. I was acting as a sort of interpreter between the Hungarians and the Australians and was asked to translate the toast at the dinner.

I could handle it all the way up until the president of the town council got into the obligatory propaganda, claiming that the Hungarians, together with the brotherly Russians, had become the world's best in water polo as a natural consequence of the "progressive policies" of their respective governments. By "progress," he of course meant that events were to unfold to his particular liking rather than according to the wishes of the people. What he meant by "brotherly" I didn't know, because the relationship between the two teams was anything but fraternal. Without thinking that my translation might be secretly recorded, I turned to the Aussies and asked them, in English, if they remembered the famous match between the Russians and the Hungarians at the Melbourne Olympics where, according to the *Herald Sun*, there had been more blood in the pool than water. The older members of the team nodded and smiled.

Major Magyar hit the stop button. He picked up the transcript. "What made you say this?"

He waited then pressed the play button again. "This idiot wants to convince us that when it comes to water polo, Russians and Hungarians behave like eternal friends. For those of you who don't know the history behind this match, I tell you that in November, just days before the Olympics started, Russian tanks rolled into Hungary, defeated the freedom fighters, and installed a puppet government. By the time the Russian and the Hungarian team entered the swimming pool in Melbourne, thousands of Hungarians had been killed and hundreds of thousands had fled the country rather than spend the rest of their lives under Russian boots. The behemoth Red Army might have won the battle, but the Hungarian water polo team, in the most spectacular, and at the same time most violent, match ever played, beat the Russian team 4 to 0. It was the sweetest revenge. The fighting above and under the water was so intense that the Aussie spectators cheering for the Hungarians became unruly and jumped the barriers. The riot squad was called in to maintain order. After receiving their gold medals and weeping for their smouldering, ruined country, the entire Hungarian team defected. Incidentally, one of their members, Ervin Zádor, emigrated to the United States, where he later became the swim coach of a talented teenager by the name of Mark Spitz."

When nothing but a few faint crackles came from the magnetophone, Major Magyar pressed the rewind button.

"As you see," he said—and the cigarette in the corner of his mouth flicked up and down like the tail of a skittish bird—"we know everything".

"Then what else do you want to know?" I asked and, without wanting to, smiled as I recalled the April 4th celebrations that had turned into a funeral march, and the replay of my account of the Hungarian win over the Russians in Melbourne.

He must have believed I was taunting him. Dull fury crept over his face, his eyelids began to twitch. Rage swarmed through him like wasps trapped in a hot jar. He blew an angry sortie of smoke into the air and clenched his jaw. He stepped closer to the desk and stubbed out his cigarette with care bordering on the theatrical. His inert corpulence leaning in my direction was as gross as the hot blast of smoky breath he blew into my face. Without warning, the hand that a moment before had been busy twisting the cigarette became a fist that struck me right in the mouth. I felt the crack of teeth and the salty taste of blood. Enraged, I completely forgot about my situation. I seized the typewriter and threw it at him with everything I had. The Major fell back against the swivel chair and dropped to the floor. The typewriter bounced off his chest and lay beside him, on its side and with a few jammed bars sticking out of its belly. The carriage release was bent.

The streak of black ribbon undulating on the floor ended in a spool beside the baseboard.

I heard the door fly open behind me. The force of the baton landing on the side of my head threw a flock of brightly coloured birds into a sudden flight through my brain. More blows followed, falling as thick as hail. I tried to cover my head with my hands. I felt angry ridges rising under my scalp. In my effort to fend off the blows, I twisted sideways. The policemen and I got into a mute, demented dance. My ears began to buzz and all I saw was yellow and red. Everything happened so fast it felt like bad dream. I gave up when I felt the floor tilt as if shaken by an earthquake. I took a few faltering steps and fell like a crippled marionette.

When I woke up, I found myself on the floor of the corridor. Two uniforms floated into my cone of vision. One of the policemen looming above me was dragging me by the arm; the other was push-kicking me into my cell. "What is this?" I asked myself dumbly, blinking my eyes. "What is this that is being done to me? How did I come to fall into their hands?" The reply came in the form of drumming inside my assaulted head, and then the sound of the steel bolt sliding into its place. My mind went blank.

We are driving at the edge of town. The travellers waiting at the bus stop stand motionless on the sidewalk. Hopping around them, sparrows scavenge for leftovers, while on the outer branches of leafless trees, a few crows sit heavily between clumps of snow.

Someone once said that life is not what we live but what we remember. That, like paintings, one memory is not consequent to another, each remembrance lives by and for itself, as if it didn't matter what happened before or what comes after. My first memory of Mother is not to be found in photographs. It is engraved in my brain as sharp as if it happened yesterday.

Old Small Dog disappears in a hole in the large haystack that stands beside the barn. Mother is standing on the verandah, folding clothes into a basket. I crawl after Old Small Dog. When my eyes get used to the dark, I can see half a dozen puppies tumbling all over her. I snuggle beside the fuzzy little bodies. Old Small Dog must be thinking that I'm one of her litter; she turns to me and licks my face. I laugh. When I have enough of her tongue, I make my way out of the den and stand up in the dazzling sunshine. I shield my eyes from the light piercing my eyes.

I open my lids into slits and peer through the vertical slices between my fingers. There is the barn on the right. Star, the chestnut colt stands beside the well. I cast my eyes to the left and see Mother in the open space between the farmhouse and the small orchard. She is adjusting a bright, white sheet on the clothesline. She appears to be turning into a bird. The wind blows her hair and those great white wings flap up and down. I am scared that Mother will disappear on those gleaming wings that keep rising and bulging with each gust of wind. I stand in front of the haystack frightened. I remove my hands from before my eyes and quickly blink off what Old Small Dog's tongue has left on my face. "Mommy, Mommy!" I cry and run to her in the grass. Mother lets the sheet go and turns around. She steps in my direction and opens her arms. I fall forward and let my heart nestle in her embrace, sobbing.

The beet-nosed policeman jammed a pair of handcuffs around my wrists. After his mate gave him a knowing nod, he pulled the cuffs tighter. The other watched and maintained a placid grin. The pain in my wrist had become a moan in my throat that wanted to come out. I blocked it right there so that it would not travel to my mouth for their amusement.

I remembered Tulok and Bika, the two classroom bullies cornering Hartman in the school yard. They were big boys with hands that could break Hartman's as easy as they could kill a bird by wringing its neck. They twisted his arm and marched him behind the shrubs. With hands pinned behind his back, he pleaded for mercy and offered them his snack, his ballpoint pen, his new belt, whatever they would take. The more he offered, the more they grinned. They must have enjoyed the pleading, the abasement, more than the physical act of inflicting pain.

When the policeman was satisfied with the tightness of the handcuffs, he frisked me—his five fingers on each hand felt like ten as they moved around my body probing every part from my arms to my ankles. For a moment, when his head was at waist level, I played with the idea of ramming my knee into his chin. My muscles twitched, but the thought of blows raining on my head kept my leg still. "I must get out of this mess in one piece."

With a hard grip on my arms, they dragged me to the steel gate. At the end of the hallway, the padded door of Major Magyar's office was already open. They yanked me in. Once inside, they pushed and pulled me about a few times before they were pleased with my placement in front of the Major.

He was sitting with his elbows propped on the desk, eyes disinterested. Except for the slow flutter of his lashes, his face was deadpan. A cigarette was hanging from the corner of his mouth. I noticed that the Olympia typewriter had been replaced with a new Olivetti. There were two sheets of paper fed into it with a carbon between them. The window behind him and above the steel filing cabinet was wide open. I could hear the noise of traffic filtering up from the street. The small patch of sky visible to me was bright blue. The bars in the window cast long shadows onto the floor, creating the impression that they were painted on the carpet. Here and there, the shadow of a bird skidded across them.

"Guess we should leave the handcuffs on?" the beet-nosed policeman asked, unsure, as though he had just searched through his rule book and failed to find the proper instructions. He stood at attention, waiting for approval. The Major let the question float with the smoke that rose from his nose and from the corner of his mouth. Then he half-swivelled the chair and stubbed out the cigarette in the ashtray. He rolled the platen knob of the new Olivetti back and forth a few times, released the carriage lever, adjusted the three papers, then examined his fingernails.

"Sit him on the chair," he said without looking up. That must have taken care of the issue of the handcuffs.

"Yes, Comrade Major." The beet-nosed policeman saluted blank faced, as if he wanted to assure the Major that he understood nothing beyond his duty. He stepped back and made a production of double-checking and tightening the handcuffs behind my back. The other pulled a chair from beside the wall. They pushed me down hard, then saluted the Major, who sat with his eyes absently peering at the keyboard. I heard the door close. There was silence. Against the faint sound of street traffic in the background, I could hear the Major's lengthy exhalations blowing smoke that lingered above the keyboard before drifting in the direction of the window. To distract myself from my situation, I began counting the number of shadows that the birds cutting across the sky were casting on the floor.

I heard the crank of the platen knob and glanced at Magyar. He adjusted and readjusted the blank sheets of paper with the carbon between them with such concentration, as though fitting them precisely one above the other was his sole interest. I was about to turn my eyes back to continue counting the gliding shadows of birds when he suddenly awoke, as if realizing it was his life and not the cigarette smoke that was drifting away.

"Why did you do it?" He asked the same question with no emotion, as if nothing special had happened the last time we had seen each other, and as if my mouth was not swollen, and as if my head was not covered with a white bandage, and as if his previous failure to make me talk had never happened. He placed his cigarette on the ashtray. "I want your motives; the reason behind your actions." His eyelids began to twitch when, instead of answering his question, I let him *fantasize* about my motives. I watched his hands so that I could duck before one of them made a fist and landed in my face.

"Why don't you make a brave and voluntary confession?" he suggested. "How the errors of your ways were shaped by Western propaganda. By Radio Free Europe and Voice of America." He regarded me intently; I gazed past him. I was not avoiding his eyes, merely looking somewhere behind him, as if he were transparent.

We drive onto the road leading to the highway and cross the bridge over the Tisza. I peer through the window and watch the snow-covered river disappear behind us. I turn my head and survey the fields, sparkling white in the midday sun. I feel as though something precious were about to forsake me. I know it is neither the river of my childhood, now in the distance, nor the fields where I grew up. The idea that Mother may soon be gone strikes me with full force. The recognition that I am about to be left in a world without her leaves me bereft. I feel like telling my daughter to stop the car, turn around, and drive back to the hospital.

Years fall away and time becomes unreal. I find myself in the most elemental feeling of childhood. An old photograph is drawn across my mind's eye. It is another day on the farm. I am almost three and I am riding my tricycle, showing Mother how well I am doing. My brother, Andrew, is standing in a crib made of wood, holding on to the bars. He has just learned how to stand but cannot stay upright without holding on to the crib. He is crying, for some reason I still can't fathom.

"You were born in 1947," Major Magyar exclaimed and made a stiff gesture of disbelief. "The year the Party formed the government and created a new social order. Unlike those *former people*, you arrived unburdened by the past," he declared, as though he was talking to an audience. "But by 1966, you had become a complete *social stranger*. I want to know"—he wagged his finger at me and shot a thin, sadistic gleam from the jelly of his eyes—"what made you become a *socially alien element*."

I almost corrected him but decided not to—although there was plenty that I could have said. In the last free election in 1945, the Communist Party had received only seventeen percent of the popular vote, even though their members were trucked from one polling station to another by the occupying Russians to vote over and over again. That with a lot of pressure from Moscow, and by deceiving the other parties about their intentions, they forced themselves into government and took over the Ministry of Interior, with their leader becoming Deputy Premier. By 1947, they managed to subdue and eliminate their rivals. They replaced, purged, blackmailed, or intimidated the judges and prosecutors. They commanded the regular police and established what they called ÁVO or Agency for the Protection of the State. The ÁVO was the equivalent of the Nazi Gestapo. It was in charge of tracking down, arresting, torturing, and sending into internment camps the perceived "enemies of the working class" until, slice by slice, all opposition was reduced to zero. People lived in fear of being arrested, tortured, and interned, with many sentenced to long prison terms or to death by hanging. The goal was to separate people from their families, communities, surroundings, properties, and, finally, from themselves, in order to turn them into push-button robots they called the "socialist type of man." The ÁVO's goal was to make the entire population prostrate in fear before those in power.

It started with the members of the various political parties and continued with those who had no political affiliations, but owned property and had the respect of their communities. Their crime was that with courage, foresight, industry, and care they had worked hard for many generations. For them, the communist takeover meant not only the loss of everything they had when the cadres moved into their homes and took over their lands and businesses, but persecution as well.

The workers, who initially thought that they would get a better deal from their new masters in the "collectivized" factories and farms, realized that they had to work harder and *sacrifice* more for the *ideals of communism*. Among the sacrifices, the first was to give up the right to organize and to strike, which became illegal and was called sabotage. It was explained that once the land and factories were owned by the people, any work action would be against the collective interest. By the early fifties, the separation of the communist bosses from the plebes had become complete. They did not let one single exhortation from the *Communist Manifesto* interfere with the speed at which they removed freedoms—such as freedom of speech, freedom of the press, freedom of religion, which had been gained through the centuries—accumulated fortunes for themselves by appropriating other people's properties, moved into luxury villas, shopped in exclusive stores and were chauffeured around in curtained limousines. They also had their own private hospitals and resorts. Witnessing the perversion of his dreams of a society of equals, one could hear the earth rumble under Karl Marx's monument in London's Highgate Cemetery, followed by a painful moan. Plugging his ears to the consoling voice of Freud, explaining that dreams can be fulfilled in the strangest ways, he desperately cried out, "Bury me deeper, please!"

The Orwellian script of *Animal Farm* was played out in full detail. Soon after the revolt of the animals against their master, the drunken and irresponsible farmer, the pigs attained absolute power. They established a brutal dictatorship by ruse and deception, and by instilling utter terror in the animals with their attack dogs. They declared themselves somewhat more equal than the rest of the animals and moved from the pigsty to the bedrooms of the farmhouse. They got fabulously fat and acquired every evil human trait the animals detested. They began to carry whips, wear clothes, and drink alcohol. They increased the very exploitation that had triggered the revolt. Boxer, the horse and the rest of hard-working beasts of burden were reduced to skin and bones as they laboured for the "common good." When they could work no more, the pigs sold them to the slaughterhouse.

By 1953, the "purge" or cleansing became so pervasive and permanent that anyone at any time could be declared an enemy of the working class. From the farmer who was reluctant to join the local kolkhoz to the barber or blacksmith who were not enthusiastic about working in their respective cooperatives. To be labelled and persecuted as an enemy of the working class had become an all-encompassing threat directed at everyone. No one was safe, not the priest, the teacher, the doctor, or the mother of small children. One could be denounced as an enemy for the most absurd and ridiculous reason. Not even membership in the Communist Party provided immunity from prosecution. In order to maintain a proper level of loyalty among themselves and to ensure constant alertness against the "deviant, loose, cosmopolitan, opportunistic, factionalist, revisionist, Titoist elements" or "enemy sympathizers" among their ranks, they made sure that the purge included regular cleansing of the vanguard itself. The terror that kept the entire society in fear from top to bottom paralyzed both the oppressors and the oppressed.

I contemplated the smoke rising from his cigarette, then the ash growing longer and longer. He knocked it off into the ashtray.

I wanted to tell him I knew well that in order to rise to the rank of a major with the Political Police, he must have proved himself a thousand times in front of his bosses in the good old days of the ÁVO, when anyone could be arrested and detained without due process. Many were tortured to death and ended up in unmarked graves. Unfortunately for him, those days were over. If he wanted to rise further and retire as a colonel, he would have to display great cunning to elicit a confession that would suit the purpose of his political masters. He couldn't rely on beatings alone, which still survived as an old reflex. He could not kill me at his whim.

At the same time, our previous encounter gave me no illusions about my situation before this pillar of the Political Police. His capacity to think was limited to servicing the power he represented. Outside of that dominion, he was unable to form a single opinion. If I did not trust his clutch of history, I had an even deeper distrust of his ability to see the past and the present from any other perspective than that of those obsessed with power. He was one of the last faithful soldiers of the regime. He could march through life led by dogmas and inspired by slogans with such fanatical devotion as though Marx and Lenin themselves were perched invisibly, one on each of his shoulders, piping the relevant quotations from the *Communist Manifesto* into his ears, removing all processes of thought from his mind, and banishing all potential uncertainties from his heart. I nodded to acknowledge the year of my birth and kept to myself my opinion about the way his party had "formed the government."

"We gave you free education," he said with a tone of reproach in his voice. "From kindergarten to university. We offered you every opportunity to become a useful, productive member of our socialist society. What was it that had made you turn against us? Radio Free Europe? Propaganda? The *Beetliss*? The *Aaneemals*? Bob Deelan? The *Rolling Stonz*?" He slammed his fist on the desk with each sentence fragment as he tried to assemble the complete catalogue of all the threats to his beloved regime. "Talk!" he yelled in a thunderous voice, pouring out his bitter, illiterate paranoia together with the sweat that bubbled up from the skin of his forehead. He rose from his swivel chair with such momentum that it rolled all the way back to the wall. Across his face swept a tumult of emotions, none of which found its expression in language for a few moments. Again, I prepared to duck. But there was no need for that. He sighed and gave me an annoyed, defeated look. "You're not talking," he said, frowning at me as if I were a stubborn nail sticking up from a smoothly planed plank. A nail that when pounded with a hammer, instead of sinking, double-bends and derides his skills.

"There is no point in talking. Write whatever you like," I said and nodded in the direction of the new Olivetti with two sheets of blank pages hanging from its carriage. "I do not care one way or the other. I can't tell you anything profound or consequential."

"There is no point," I said to myself and remembered Mayer, adjunct professor at the department of Marxism-Leninism at university, elaborating on the theory of "scientific socialism." As soon as the words struck my ear, the ideas rang not only false but blatantly absurd. Some innate, primary understanding, residing as deep as the marrow in my bones, informed me, without any need for articulated evidence, that what he was saying was sheer propaganda rather than the truth. I watched the man go through the ritual of churning out words joined together into a caricature of reason, and the same understanding told me that he himself had no faith whatsoever in what he was proposing, even if he took it for his job to convince me of its verity. He was carping lies masquerading as truth: lies without which the regime could not maintain itself, lies he had to propagate if he wished to keep his job and slink through his life. Naturally, he had no other wish. I rolled my eyes and shook my head.

He must have noticed it, because during the "discussion" that followed, after graciously accepting the docile attentiveness of the students, Professor Mayer challenged me to give a counter-argument. I shook my head and remained silent. "But, I noticed you had something to say." There was irritation in his voice.

"I can't see anything in what you just said," I said, in a manner of admission, "that would merit an argument."

"That's what you think?" he asked with a sarcastic air. I nodded.

Major Magyar observed me, as if he was waiting for some further explanation. Then he slowly knit his eyebrows together as though an idea had been ignited in his head by what I had just said. Thought wrinkles appeared on his forehead.

"That's right," he said, and with a great display of effort he reached back for his swivel chair and dumped his large body onto it. "Unable to say anything profound or consequential. *Anything profound or consequential.*" He repeated the words, shaking his head. "Perhaps," he said, as if he was having a moment of sudden enlightenment, "listening to the *Beetliss* and all that 'yeah-yeah-yeah-yeah' went onto your brain." He nodded with glee that immediately turned into serious sadness. I was dazzled by his theatrics.

He reached into his chest pocket and, instead of the handkerchief I thought he would pull out to wipe the sweat off his face, extracted a large wallet. He opened it and tossed it onto the desk. "My son, Marton," he said with filmed-over eyes and a voice that diminished into a mutter—hardly more than a whisper, as if he was talking about the last surviving descendent of his bloodline. I craned my neck to have a look. He adjusted the wallet. "Nice boy," I said, and I meant it. At the same time, I thought he had mistakenly showed me a picture of his grandson. When our eyes met, he averted his face as if he was suffering from some shameful secret.

There is hardly any traffic on the highway. Alexandra drives in the fast lane, passing an occasional car or a truck. In the eternal, featureless sameness of the land, with a farmhouse here and there amidst the snow-covered fields, we seem to be suspended in motion, going nowhere. Shifting dark clouds with furls at their edges move up the sky from the west, like galloping black stallions with white manes and slowly cover the sun. The brilliance of the snow-glazed fields turns into milky white, then grey. We run into drifting snow. Like tiny, white moths around a light, small, hurrying flakes begin to swirl around the windshield and the headlights. I peer at the odometer.

"We are halfway to the airport," Alexandra says.

"My grandparents' old farm must be somewhere there," I say and turn my head in the direction of a tiny, delicate line appearing and disappearing—the spire of a village church. "We lived there for a few years."

"How old were you?"

"Could be five when we left the farm. Hardly more than a pair of eyes and a set of ears."

I try to see beyond the spire of that village church. It was on that farm where, from the real and visceral, the first ideas were born behind that pair of eyes and between that set of ears. Ideas that went beyond "Let's go to the village and have ice cream" or "Let's walk down to the creek," but were less speculative than such questions popping up in my head as "Where did the world come from?" (answered by "Someone must have made it") or

"Why are there stars and a moon in the night sky rather than nothing at all?" My very first idea, thwarted by a look on Father's face, was probably the seed from which similar, rebellious ideas were born.

<hr />

"This picture was taken when he was ten," the Major said, each word uttered with such pain as if he was plucking thorns from his skin. The clockwork of authority inside him seemed to have run down; his shrill voice descended into a lamenting tone. Then he did something that was uncharacteristic of a major of the Political Police. He cried. I thought he had lost his son to some disease or to some accident. "There must be a soul," I thought, "hiding somewhere in a small, dark corner of his enormous corpulence." Even if I suspected that it was part of the usual policeman theatrics of switching from unfriendly to friendly, I felt sorry for the man. I wanted to say something, but he pushed his palm forward, ordering me to hold still. His eyes were shiny, swimming in visionary spirit.

"Now," he said with a voice bordering on the hysterical, as if an invisible hand had rewound him, "he has long, shaggy hair like the *Beetliss*"—he made a sound of disgust—"a goddamn beard like yours, and wants to play the fucking guitar." This revelation or confession of his despair over his son's straying from the path he had planned for him exploded in such an outburst that for a moment, I was afraid he would pull a pistol from the drawer and shoot me.

In the silence that followed, he removed his wallet from the desk, folded it, and put it back into his chest pocket. He inhaled deeply and, in an effort to recover from his lapse, fastened his gaze on me. "If the likes of you," he said, in a voice that turned dark and threatening with the resentment of having been driven into showing weakness, "are allowed to spread their disease, he will end up being a useless bum or worse." He pointed his finger in the direction of my chest and broke into a hammering diatribe of irascible fury.

I shook my head and regarded him with pity. The old warhorse had either never been at play in the fields of childhood or had long forgotten not only the contents but also the fresh, innocent flavours of his long-gone youth. Unable to dream, only to scheme, stripped of any feeling for truth and love. For him to listen to how I experienced this world would have been a mere nuisance, a form of sabotage that might undermine the walls he had built against the subversive ideas and fantasies that were now taking root in his son. My interrogator had arrived at the sad realization that the years he had invested in admonishing his son to turn him into an obedient, one-dimensional man might have been all for nought. Marton did not want to be a miserable person treading carefully along the party's line of conformity. He did not want to be a good boy and was unwilling to talk in third person anymore. Major Magyar decided to lay the blame for his son's rebellion at my door.

"But I will make sure you will be removed like a cancerous tumour." He pronounced "removed" with relish. He must have found its taste delicious. "By the way," he informed me almost musing, "your beard and hair will be cut after we are finished." He picked up his cigarette and nursed it between his fingers for a while. He drew on it hard and let the smoke slip from his mouth. He mashed the half-burnt cigarette on the ashtray.

I heard the door behind me open. It was followed by hardly audible footsteps. Out of the corner of my eye, I saw the silhouette of someone in civilian clothes. There was a pistol holstered on his belt. When he moved fully inside my cone of vision, I must have creased my brow, as if trying to remember something vital, because he stopped, turned to me and said, "Yes, it's me, Michael." I recognized Foldvary Laszlo, two years my senior, a student of the history of literature who had lived on the same floor in the dormitory.

"Lieutenant," said Major Magyar "he is all yours."

In the sixties, the Beatles were perceived to be a greater threat to the ideologues of communist bureaucracies than the ICBMs of the US military. They could counter the latter with their own, but were clueless and frustrated in their awkward efforts to stop Sergeant Pepper, whose Lonely Hearts Club Band marched across all borders straight into the hearts of their children. Kids did not want to be disciplined, levelled down, and made uniform anymore.

In their fear that the slightest deviation from the party line would open the door to disruption and chaos, the establishments in both East and West regarded John Lennon with horror: he was the devil whose music and words would lure their youth off the beaten path of power and greed. No kid was inspired by the boring harangues of Brezhnev or the paranoid screeching of Nixon. We all listened to the Animals, to the Rolling Stones, and to the Beatles, and we all wanted to be Eric Burdon, Mick Jagger, Ringo Starr, and George Harrison. Just when the apparatchiks of the regime thought that all human beings under their rule had surrendered their personal dreams, Bob Dylan came along and turned the youth—the future nuts and bolts of their regime—into rolling stones.

It is early afternoon when we arrive at Ferihegy Airport. Alexandra parks the car close to the terminal. The clouds are breaking up, shaping and reshaping each moment. I take my carry-on, and we walk through the open glass door. Inside, people seem to be moving in every direction. But soon, not unlike an anthill, beneath the tumult there is some unspoken understanding, a discipline of sort as people follow directions and begin obeying signs and start walking with purpose. We look for Czech Airlines and line up for check-in.

"I will get back in a few hours," says Alexandra. "I will drive straight to the hospital." Her voice is soft, consoling.

"Thank you."

"I will stay with Grandma for the day."

"It is good of you."

The man ahead of us pulls his massive suitcase to the check-in counter. He looks around with concern, as if he had jumped the queue and wanted to see if anyone noticed. Then he glances at me nervously, hesitantly. When our eyes meet, he turns and hands his passport and ticket to the woman behind the counter. He considers his suitcase with a helpless grimace, then makes an attempt at lifting it onto the scale.

Alexandra touches my elbow. "Dad," she says and nods in the direction of the man, expecting me to do something about the suitcase. I roll my eyes and am about to tell her that a man, bigger and a lot more brutish than I am, should be able to lift his own luggage when I notice that his hands are shaking. He tries to hide it by squeezing his elbows tight against his sides. Feeling bad about my initial thought, and at the same time relieved that I haven't said anything embarrassing, I step to the suitcase.

"I'm OK," he says, with the resigned expression of someone convinced that there is no compassion left in the hearts of men and firmly refusing to participate in any pretence aimed at proving that mercy can still be found. He wipes the sheen of sweat from his forehead and puts an all-out effort into lifting the suitcase. He fails an inch short of the scale. When he lets it go, I grab it.

"Thank you," he murmurs in the manner of one admitting defeat.

Alexandra walks with me to security. There we hug, and I kiss her cheek. We part but keep eye contact until I reach an opaque glass wall, where I stop for a moment and wave. I join the travellers moving to the gates.

It is late autumn. The trees streaming noisily in the wind have suddenly become silent. A few yellow leaves still sailing in the evening air drop, one by one, onto the scorched, grassless ground. The sun is still hanging onto the edge of the sky. Somewhere between the farmhouse and the flatbed truck loaded with furniture, Mother, Father, and I stand as still as the evening around us. Andrew is asleep in his crib, sucking on his thumb.

For the last couple of weeks, our life on the farm has not been as it usually is. The changes started when a gang of angry men came daily in army jeeps and shouted at Grandfather. First, they just called him names like damn kulak, which I didn't understand but knew was bad. (Later, I will learn that "kulak," a term adopted from the bolshevik devil's dictionary of permanent class struggle, is a special label, applied to all independent farmers who own land, a few cows, and horses and resist the drive toward large-scale, state-controlled, factory-like operations. Lenin called them bloodsuckers, vampires, and plunderers of the people, who fatten on famine.) Then they pushed him around. Father and Grandfather argued a lot. Each time they did, Mother took us into the bedroom and closed the door to keep all those harsh words out. Things were spinning out of control and I felt helpless because I knew I could do nothing about it, nor could anyone else.

Grandfather and Grandmother left a few days ago with all their belongings piled on the same flatbed truck that is now sitting in the farmyard with our furniture on it. They chose to abandon the farm rather than yield to pressure and join the kolkhoz, the communist version of the farmers' collective. Uncle Dios gave my grandparents shelter for a day or two, only to join the many who were herded into the internment camps set up for kulaks and other "enemies of the working class." Grandfather and Grandmother came back to say goodbye to us, because we will be leaving soon too, although not to an internment camp.

The three of us watched my grandparents walk down the Goose Trail that gently winds its way among undulating and delicately rounded hills. They walked in step with each other, and the rays of the dying sun shimmered around their heads as they passed the last piece of cleared land. A wedge of geese drifted down the sky in the direction of the creek and landed behind the cattails with fading honks.

Grandmother and Grandfather reached the creek, their silhouettes indistinct against the background, like dancers on stage in a nameless ballet, and disappeared into the dark now falling like a curtain. Frowning into the twilight, Father's profile hardened. He raised his arms and dug his fists into his eyes. "It's all right," said Mother, putting her hand on his back. Father shrugged it off and clenched his fists.

"It's not all right," he murmured, turning to stare at the vacant barn as if it was somehow unaccountable.

Mother's hand returned to Father's back. "We will find a way," she said.

This is how our wanderings start. There will be countless stops, and at each brief station on our long journey, Father will become more and more disheartened and sullen. Mother will try to keep us quiet with tales and stories, and keep our spirits up with songs. For Mother, each song is a path to freedom. Freedom from poverty, freedom from angst and worry. With songs, she is able to summon courage in the face of hardship. Whenever our endless trek depletes her reserves, she will sing. Whenever we turn to her in despair, she will have a story to tell.

But tonight is just the first night of our odyssey. It is a magical evening—at least, it seems so to me. After a long drive from the farm, we pull up to a beautiful building, like a glass castle under the cold sickle of the moon. A bright red star glows above its entrance. After listening to Mother's fairy tales, crammed in the cab of the truck, I think I must be in dreamland. My sadness over leaving the farm is gone in an instant. It feels strange that Mother and Father fail to share my enthusiasm. "It is wonderland," I sigh and glance over at Mother. "Are we going to live here?"

"It's a nightmare," Father grunts. "I used to work for the owner, a nice man, and now I must go hat in hand to a bunch of red-ass commies who turned it into a kolkhoz. They can't tell a cow from a donkey or a tractor from a plough. They will ruin everything." I have no clue what a kolkhoz or a red-ass commie is, but from the way Father is talking I know we are not into something good. I have an idea, but I need more information.

"Why did Grandpa and Grandma" I ask, "and we" I add, "have to leave?" I have a sense that it is because of those angry men who have run us off the farm, but I want to hear Mother or Father corroborate it and provide me with the details. After a moment of silence, I resume my questioning. "Did those men take the farm?" Mother nods. "They took what was ours?" Mother nods again. My suspicion has been confirmed. Gripped with the indisputable logic of my idea, the words burst out of me unbound. "Why don't we go back and set fire to the farmhouse, to the barn and the haystacks, and let them have nothing?" Father shuts me up with a look.

I vaguely recall a brief visit to Auntie Agnes, whose land had already been "collectivized": Father's and Mother's inquiries with old farmhands about her fate had been abruptly interrupted by the arrival of the same sort of angry men who had run my grandparents off their land.

The judges of the Appeal Court found that the lower court had erred in its finding that, when I poured kerosene onto the red flag, red brocade, and drapery decorating the Party Centre, my criminal act had been directed against the Soviet Union. They came to this conclusion right after the Prague Spring and the movement to "give socialism a human face" had been stamped out by the armies of the Warsaw Pact, led by Moscow.

In 1956, the Russians had taken it upon themselves to crush the Hungarian Revolution. In 1968, they wanted to show the world that Prague had incurred the wrath of the entire socialist family. In order to give the appearance of a united front against any deviation from the line drawn by the Kremlin, an *ukaz*, or edict, was sent to the puppets in East Berlin, Warsaw, Budapest, and Sofia, demanding that they join the invasion of Czechoslovakia. Together, they smashed the nascent liberalization in the bud. But their victory was empty. They could not even claim that it was a good fight against the "enemies of the working class." Instead of throwing Molotov cocktails, like their Hungarian neighbours in 1956, the Czechs, always less sanguine in temperament, merely spat on the windshields of the armoured vehicles until the wipers could move no more.

In the spirit of the effort to portray a family of socialist nations led by a wise elder rather than a single bully, the appellate judges wanted to deflect my arrow aimed at the Russians. They argued that the red flag, and generally the colour red as a symbol, represented the *international revolutionary working class* rather than the only the Soviet Union. Therefore, burning it was an attack against the entire international workers' movement—a much more serious crime than an attack on Russia—and therefore deserved harsher punishment.

There are several theories floating around about the origin of the colour red to represent revolutionary violence. Some maintain that it became the symbol of communism during the 1871 Paris Commune, but others trace it back to earlier times—more precisely to 1772, the year preceding the Reign of Terror in France. They claim that the red flag as a symbol of the revolution was born of cruelty beyond the sickest imagination. In August, a crazed mob of thirty thousand *canailles* stormed the Tuileries Palace, attacking the Swiss Guard, who had already surrendered and laid down their arms, and brutally massacring them. They tortured and mutilated the wounded and decapitated the bodies. The demented mob hoisted heads and limbs on pikes to be marched around in Paris, and when they ran out of body parts, they tore the guard uniforms into pieces, soaked them in large pools of blood, and used them as flags.

I observe the travellers at the gate. I cannot fail to notice that the older ones are chatting or reading books, while the younger ones are leaning and sprawling on the benches at awkward angles, as if the strain of waiting were unbearable. Their eyes are closed or stare into nothingness. The ones with earplugs are tossing their heads back and forth, as though they were in the grip of some mysterious mental disorder.

It's strange how my perceptions have changed. When I was in my teens, I regarded the old as no more than crushed bugs still moving in twitches and spasms on stiff, shifting legs. I found the hesitant movements of their groping hands ridiculous. I viewed their translucent skin, exposing blue veins, with disgust. Above all, I was convinced that their brains had stopped working, as evidenced by the eerie sounds of moans, groans, squeaks, harsh aspirations, and painful breaths coming from their mouths and expiring before their meanings could be understood. I agreed with Hecuba, who called the elderly "hornets": buzzing around in one place, but going nowhere in particular.

Now, I look at old age as the remnants of a hard life one has managed to defend against being completely devoured by others. I like to see old people playing and listening to music, drawing and painting, reading and writing and travelling. They can finally afford to do things that they couldn't in their younger years.

I catch sight of my suitcase man. His eyes are closed, his head is tilted sideways, and his chin almost touches his chest. I take an empty seat beside him, check my boarding pass, reach for my wallet, and pull out the picture of my mother. Her dreamy expression, which I so admire, is one of someone longing for something better.

It is late spring, and I am about five. The first spring after our arrival at what has turned out to be the final station of our wanderings. Mother has already cleaned, repaired, and painted the rickety house that Father has rented and which stands, conveniently for him, right across from the local tavern.

The sun rising above the neighbour's roof lights up the red tiles on the ridge, which glow like a long line of embers in the sapphire blue sky. It has rained all night, and the smell of moist earth hangs in the air. After a few minutes on the swing hanging from a low branch of the walnut tree, I go to the verandah to play with our cat, Cica. I tie an odd sock to a string and draw it along the floor. When she pounces, I pull hard on the string, but her timing is usually better; her claws rip into the tissue of the sock and almost tear it off the string.

Mother is tending her tulips. She has a roll of twine in her apron pocket, a pair of scissors in one hand, and a bunch of stakes in the other. The rain has beaten down her plants; some are leaning sideways and some lie flattened on the ground. She straightens the stems and ties each to a stake.

Cica is tired of chasing the odd sock, which by now looks like a shredded rag. She yawns, ambles to the sunny steps of the verandah, and curls into a ball. I am about to ask Mother if I can go and see the kids in the park when I hear her calling, "Come fast! Look what I found."

Thinking that she has perhaps happened on an old toy, a lost ball, a building block or a marble, or has found some other hidden treasure when driving one of the stakes into the ground, I drop the string and run. Mother is holding a small, feathery thing in her hand. She places it gently in my palm. "Hold it. Be careful. I will be back with the ladder."

I stand in the garden and watch that wet little ball pulsing wildly in my cupped palms as if it were all heart. Its fluffy feathers are stuck to its pink skin, its eyes are almost as big as its head, and its beak is yellow around the edges. I hold the soft, vibrating thing and wait for Mother.

She comes back with the ladder. Cica comes too, with intent, her ears laid flat to her skull, her tail flailing, but Mother shoos her away. She stands the ladder against the lowest branch of the cherry tree, adjusts its footing on the ground, then takes the baby bird from me and places it in her apron pocket. She steps up the ladder. "Come," she says.

The mother bird keeps flitting anxiously from one branch to another with weeping, disconsolate calls. "Don't worry, don't be afraid," says Mother.

"I am not worried and I am not afraid," I think as I carefully climb up, only to realize—when she adds, "Your baby will be fine"—that she is not talking to me.

Once I am beside her, she shows me the nest above her head. She takes the bird from her pocket and places it in my palm. She steps up onto the next branch. Asks me to pass the frightened little creature back to her and places it in the nest.

The closer to the end of her life she is, the younger Mother appears in my mind. She is lying in bed with morphine dripping into her vein, but I think of her as a young woman admiring snowdrops and saving a young bird. Perhaps, as illness is taking her away from me, I am trying to pull her in the opposite direction.

I had been sitting on the bench in the back of the armoured truck for hours before it suddenly stopped. The chain locked to my handcuffs at one end and to a ring anchored in the floor prevented me from flying forward. There was the heavy rumble of metal rolling on metal, and the truck started to move again. When it came to a halt and the engine was cut, I knew we were inside the infamous Gyűjtő prison.

To the clatter of keys, the door swung open and an old, uniformed guard stood in front of me, his rotund face beaming with friendliness and his enormous stomach thrust forward from his chest like a shelf. He welcomed me as if I were not a prisoner but a guest at his inn. "How old are you?" he asked.

"Twenty-one."

"We need new blood," he said, grinning, "or we will be forced into early retirement. Ten years ago, we had thousands of politicals. Now we have no more than a couple of hundred. Most of them old fucks. This way." He swung his baton in the direction of a steel door.

Walking behind me and whistling a tune from Lehar's *Merry Widow*, he took me along a series of corridors and through a series of doors. The farther we went, the spookier the place became. I thought of the hundreds of freedom fighters executed in this prison after the tanks had crushed the revolution; I thought of the thousands crammed inside these walls to serve long sentences for opposing the Russians and their henchmen. Despite the happy melody filling the corridors, my heart sank. My escort opened the door at the end of the final corridor and saluted a guard sitting behind a desk under Lenin's goateed visage. He sucked on a cigarette without acknowledging our presence. My friendly man waited for a moment, then slid a file onto the middle of the desk and left, still whistling the same tune.

I stood and watched the guard peering at a bunch of files from above his glasses. Before I could make much out of his face, he swept the stack of papers to the right with one hand and pushed his glasses up the ridge of his nose with the other. He tilted his head up in my direction and frowned, as if trying to recognize a distant relative in me. "Prissson isss exactly the sssame asss the military, jussst totally different," he declared, pronouncing each "c" and "s" with a long hiss and leaving me to make what I wanted of his assertion.

Had I not been educated in dialectical materialism, I would have recoiled at the blatant and simultaneously ridiculous contradiction of the statement. (But to this day, whenever something is too complicated to describe, I use this bizarre comparison. When my friend and fellow book club member Joseph wanted to know what kale looked like, and I was at a loss as to how to describe the plant, I told him it was exactly the same as lettuce, just totally different. When he shook his head in bewilderment, I told him the story of the prison guard. Since then, for Joseph and me, some things are exactly the same and at the same time totally different.)

"Ssstep clossser." I did. At first, I thought of his lisping as an affectation. Or an inability to hold the cigarette with his jagged teeth between his lips and speak at the same time like a normal person. But then he removed the cigarette from his mouth, knocked the ash into the ashtray, and hissed, "More clossser."

I stepped forward and stood a few inches from the desk. He opened a file and pondered the first page, a cigarette clamped between his teeth. The grave lines split his face into its anatomic planes: the aquiline nose that stuck out of his face like an axe-blade, the slightly curved lips, the shiny cheekbones and jaws cut sharp. When he finished digesting my file, he jiggled the cigarette around his mouth, seemingly deep in thought, and then absentmindedly snuffed it out in the ashtray. He looked up and studied me with curious melancholy, as though he doubted that the person he was reading about and I were the same.

"Your contact?" he finally asked, with smoke billowing from his mouth.

I stared at him.

"You deaf?" he asked and stabbed his forefinger in the direction of his ear.

"You mean my contact with the outside?" I asked.

"You not deaf! You jussst ssslow in the head," he guffawed.

"My mother," I said.

"Name!" I gave him Mother's married name. "Her maiden name!"

"Her maiden name?"

He rolled his eyes in exasperation. "Yesss," he said with a long hiss that bared his jagged, orange-coloured teeth.

"Ilona Deutsch."

He wrinkled his brow, uncomprehending. "Ssspell," he said.

"I-l-o-n-a D-e-u-t-s-c-h," I said, pausing between each hideously scrawled letter and watching the furrow in his brow going deeper and darker with each painful movement of his pen.

"You said D-u-t-c-h?" he asked, when he was finished with "Ilona" and repeated each letter in a solemn manner as they were something to be memorized.

"Ilona D-e-u-t-s-c-h,"

"Sssay it more ssslow."

"I–l–o–n–a D–e–u–t–s–c–h."

His pen, held tight between his nicotine-stained fingers, moved heavily with laborious, tractor-like slowness, sometimes going through the paper. He paused after the completion of each letter, looking askance, as if he was doing homework under supervision.

When he was finished, brows still wrinkled in concentration, he scrutinized his illiterate calligraphy. Not finding disconcerting fault with it, he picked up the blotter and rolled it over the liquid shine of his scrawl. His mouth moved slightly. I was just about to reassure him that he had got it right when he gave me a cunning look.

"You German?" he asked abruptly, as if something had been revealed to him by that enigmatic formation of letters.

"Nope," I said. I was about to give him a brief lesson in my family's history and how the name Deutsch was acquired when he glanced at me with bemused contempt.

"The lassst German I booked," he said with import, "hanged hissself." He let the picture of the German prisoner hanging in his cell sink into my head. "Make sure," he grimaced "that you are invisible or"—he raised his index finger to the level of his neck and made a slashing movement whose meaning was obvious—"itt fogsss kifingss," Hungarian for "You too will die here," but with such ridiculously bad grammar that I thought he was joking. He waited for a moment to see if he had managed to convey the idea that prison was survivable if I lay low, and that my life would either be brief or a sorry mess if not. I nodded.

He asked for Mother's address, closed the file and pushed it to the edge of the desk. "You can receive and sssend four lettersss a year, twenty linesss each. You can have two sssupervisssed visssitsss a year, twenty minutesss each. There shall be no politicsss, not a word about prissson conditionsss in the outgoing lettersss. Your contact shall not write about politicsss. I will inform your mother about thisss." Each word passed like a long serpent out of the circle of his mouth.

I notice that I still have Mother's picture in my hand. I remember the first letter I received. I see her beautiful handwriting.

Just as her love helped me endure Father, Stepfather, the bullies, and the police, and encouraged me after my neck surgery when I thought I would spend the rest of my life in a wheelchair, her words contained in those twenty lines allowed four times a year became my lifeline for the next six years of my life. It was not only the wisdom she tried to impart, but the way she presented her thoughts—with a total lack of melodrama and lamentation—that helped me to survive prison with an unbroken spirit.

In her subtle way, she let me know that I came from a long line of survivors who kept going despite incredible cruelty and hardship. Some perished. They did not seek or provoke what fate had in store for them. Those who lived through terrible times carried on with their lives without holding a grudge against the world or those who had harmed them, and without feeling sorry for themselves. Had I the slightest inclination for self-pity in this watered-down version of the ÁVO, Gestapo, and Kapo systems—with no serious torture or threat of death—Mother's first letter would have nipped it right there.

The suitcase man wakes up and gazes around, blinking. When our eyes meet, he nods, pulls a laptop from his carry-on; he opens it and presses the start button. His eyes are fixed on the icons that come alive on the screen one after the other.

"I should get my notebook," I say to myself "or my memories will disappear as fast as they pop up." I open my carry-on, take out my notebook and consider my knotted scribbles on the pearly shimmer of the fine paper and think of my dear Beryl. She always buys me the nicest notebooks, so that I can fill them with my jumbles of words.

With slanting rays, the sun is going down fast, a red ball falling out of the sky. We climb down from the big walnut tree, Andrew and I. Mother stands by the summer stove on the verandah keeping our dinner warm. The smell of lentil soup and casserole wafts in the evening air, and the candles stand on the table, waiting to be lit.

It is getting dark fast. I am about to climb back up the walnut tree to see where the sun has gone when Mother comes from the verandah. "Grab the basket," she says. "Bring kindling from the shed." She wants to keep us busy. Idle, bored, and hungry, we would otherwise whine and ask silly questions about dinner. It is not the first time Father has been late. All three of us know well where he is and why we have to wait, but Mother doesn't want to talk about it. She doesn't want us to think about it. "Hurry up, guys," she says. Her voice is tired. She turns the light on, and the moths soon begin to flip-flop around the bulb. Andrew and I pick up the basket. We go to the shed, feel our way in the darkness inside, and find the cut wood stacked against the far wall.

Mother opens the summer stove, stirs the dying embers with the poker, and places a few sticks of kindling on the cinders. They ignite and start to crackle. We watch the flames twisting and rising, and when they became steady, she puts a larger log on the fire, stirs the soup and moves the casserole to the side. Soon, the air is thick with smoke and cooking smells.

"Tell us a story," Andrew whines.

Mother puts the lid back onto the pot. "Let's go and sit on the steps," she says.

We sit on the steps of the verandah. The air grows cooler and we cozy up to Mother. The moon lights up the leaves on the trees, and when they move in the breeze in front of the neighbour's salt-white roof, it is a ghostly sight. We press ourselves against Mother and watch the stars blazing in the sky.

"I've told you many stories," Mother says. "It's your turn."

"Mine?" asks Andrew.

"I'll tell one," I jump in. "I walked home from school and stopped to play in the park. I saw a sad-faced puppy sitting on the grass. It had golden hair and eyes like two chestnuts. It had long, long ears ..."

"You just made it up ..." Andrew cuts me off, and if Mother were not there between us, I would kick him hard.

I place my notebook on the small table next to my seat and let my mind wander back to what Matheos, my cellmate and one of the resident prison historians, said when I mentioned the old guard with the curious, hissing voice. He explained to me that the man had an accent, not a speech impediment. That he was Greek and had been either exiled or self-exiled after the defeat of the communist guerrillas.

"Soon after World War II," he elaborated, "hopes for peacefully managing the ideological differences between democracies and Moscow were dashed. This was mainly due to Stalin's eternal fear and intolerance of internal dissent and to his paranoia about the intentions of the West. It is true that he was badly betrayed by his first Western ally, Hitler, with whom Stalin had plotted to attack and divide Poland. To his utter disbelief, Adolf—his imagined buddy—stabbed him in the back."

"As for the Western powers, after a series of communist takeovers and Moscow's role in the Greek Civil War, they had no reason to trust Stalin either. Churchill, never short of poetic terms when they were needed, announced that an 'Iron Curtain' had been pulled down between the countries ruled by Moscow and the free world. With this, the Cold War began."

Matheos explained to me that the fighters of the Greek Communist Party, part of the resistance that ranged from Royal Loyalists on the right to Trotskyists on the far left, turned to "red terror" to take over or eradicate the other Greek resistance groups. Those who declined to join them were systematically murdered. Their indiscriminate violence cost the communists the popular support they would have needed to conquer Greece without Russian help. Their political defeat was followed by a military one when the nationalist Greek army, supported by Britain and the United States, became stronger.

The retaliation was terrible. Right-wing gangs killed not only communists, but also villagers who had been forced to provide food and shelter to them. In all, three thousand communists were executed, many imprisoned and an even larger number were exiled and self-exiled. Entire families ended up in refugee camps in various communist states. Unskilled in anything but fighting, the men became prison guards in Hungary. They were famous for their cruelty and brutality. With no loyalty to anyone but the ÁVO and driven by a mad sense of revenge, they beat and tortured political prisoners. But with the years and in the less harsh regime of goulash communism, where the old slogan "Those who do not stand with us stand against us" was replaced with the new "Those who do not stand against us stand with us," they mellowed.

"As if we didn't have enough crap of our own," Matheos reminded me, "we imported more."

The suitcase man is playing chess against himself or against an opponent programmed in his laptop. For a moment, I'm back in my grandparents' home in Zenta. I walk by Mother, sitting at the concert grand piano that, to my childish mind, was a fierce crocodile rising from the floor with its jaws open. She is playing Chopin. I watch her profile and her hands moving back and forth. Then I move on and look for Grandfather in the library. He is reading the newspaper. He glances up at me, lowers the paper, and smiles. "Want to consider a game of chess?" he asks.

"If you pass the test, you will work in the Transsslation Officcce," he said. Whatever you read and transsslate isss, and will be, a ssstate sssecret. If you reveal to anyone what you are or were doing there, you will be punished. Undersssstood?"

"Yes," I answered, wondering what sort of "state secrets" I would be reading and translating.

※

In her first letter, Mother encouraged me to be curious about, and not afraid of, prison life. She suggested that, instead of fear and despair, I should regard it with amazement and wonder. "You will find many interesting people and lives," she wrote. "Characters of all kinds—in uniform and in prison garb."

In a profound maternal affirmation of life, instead of lamentation over my imprisonment, Mother may have considered my incarceration a visit to the underworld, a sort of death from which I would return to life somewhat wiser. While other mothers might have cried, she recommended books. I held her letter in my hand as if it were a sacrament that held the promise of a better world which, one day, I would be able to return to and have a place in.

※

I open my briefcase and search for my first letter among the ones I took from Mother's remembrance box.

March 20, 1969

Dear Mother,

Thank you for your letter. You must have been waiting for my reply. The time has arrived. It is spring and the swallows have arrived—I can hear their calls when they fly by my open window.

I'm glad you are not worried about me, but rather encourage me to make the best of my time here, which I will do. I will be able to read good books. The people I meet are eccentric, to say the least—I guess one does not end up in prison for having a normal and or banal character. There are journalists, priests, and lawyers. All in all, I learned more in a few months than I did in an entire semester at university.

Thank you for recommending Moravia. I grabbed The Woman of Rome *right away. Great novel. I liked his collection of short stories as well.*

I also read a translation of Hemingway's Old Man and the Sea. *The best short story I have ever read. I can hardly wait to read it in English.*

My work is interesting, but I can't write about it.

I'm sorry I disappointed you and I'm sorry for all the aggravation I caused. While you lived in the belief that my only concern was to do well at university, I did things that took me to prison. I can't, and even if I could, I would not want to explain what made me do that. I do not want to excuse or accuse myself. You may understand when, one day, I will be able to talk freely about it. I hope that one day I will make you proud. Everything that is good in me comes from you. I'm grateful for it and will do my best to prove that your efforts were not wasted.

It will be three months before we can exchange another twenty lines. Give Judith a big hug and say hello to my friends.

Love You,

Mityu

I entered the mystical world of the notorious prison with naive curiosity and excitement. I could hardly wait to meet kindred spirits: veterans of the Revolution of 1956, intellectuals sentenced for spreading subversive ideas, spies, priests standing up for religious freedom, soldiers refusing to take part in the armed intervention that crushed the Prague Spring. With them, I thought I might be able to start something big, or at least be part of it. But it was not going to be like that at all.

With a few notable exceptions, instead of brave heroes eager to fight the regime, I met tired old men who happened to be at the wrong place at the wrong time. Most were a disheartening spectacle—anything but revolutionary material. As if all the cruelty they had seen and performed had left them with the taste of ashes in their mouths, most prison guards, like the "Greek," were withered, desiccated, and burnt-out remnants of their old sadistic selves. Their dedication to the regime had long lost its militant aggressiveness, and the hole in it yawned wider and wider until there was not much left of their zeal. With their youthful stores of hatred and cruelty dimmed, depleted, and spent, the futility of oppressing prisoners was apparent to them. They went about their job with casual negligence.

The younger guards, however, were a tougher lot. Most of them were country bumpkins fresh from their mandatory years in the army. They found bullying inmates more fun than going back to harvesting potatoes and stacking hay in the kolkhoz. Freshly indoctrinated into the spirit of vigilance, they took advantage of every opportunity to make life hard for counter-revolutionaries, traitors, and spies. One huge bulk of a man wrapped with skin more like a hide was brimming with sadistic malice. The prisoners called him "Apeman" because of his sloped forehead and anthropoid anatomy, which made him broader in the nape than in the skull. He hated without any need for justification—he could have been in the service of either the Gestapo or the ÁVO.

I learned fast and soon acquired a fair understanding of prison lingo. Among the first was "schmasser," which stood for prison guard. "Hippish" meant frisking combined with a complete search of the prison cell. The "besugo," or whisperer, was an informant.

An old schmasser came, a frail, stunted man with a face shrivelled like a dried-up apricot. He exchanged a few words with the Greek. He then took me over, walking with slow, dreamy steps to what was called the Left Wing. One of the huge complex shaped like a double star. At the stairway, he stopped and lit his cigarette before leading me to the second floor. After fiddling with his keys for the longest time, he unlocked a door, and gestured me to step inside a cell occupied by three men— my future colleagues, if I passed the test.

"Quite a relaxed chap," I commented, once the door had been bolted shut.

"Oh, Cuccos," replied an older man with silver hair. He looked like a retired professor and, as I would later find out, his cellmates called Uncle Andy. "A bit more relaxed," he said "and he would be dead. But what got you here?"

"Set fire to a communist party centre," I said, slightly exaggerating the fact that I managed to burn only the decorations on its facade.

"What?"

"Well," I explained, "I soaked the red brocade and the red flag with gasoline. The building itself suffered no damage other than a smoky facade and a few charred window frames. My friend set fire to the podium. We did it the night before the April 4th celebrations, and they had to reroute the march and erect a new podium."

"How did they catch you?"

"Not sure, and it wasn't right away. I still don't know how they found out about it, but I guess they opened my letters."

"Letters?

"To my brother. But how about you?"

Uncle Andy had cloudy, tired, old man's eyes set deep in his face eroded by captivity and by age. In a voice bordering on a whisper, he told me that he had been a pharmacist. That he had been sentenced for fifteen years for spying for Uruguay.

My jaw dropped and I shook my head. "Uruguay?"

He told me that a friend of his, who had emigrated to Uruguay after the communist takeover, had returned for a visit some ten years later. They were sipping coffee in the open terrace of a restaurant in Siofok, overlooking Lake Balaton when a formation of fighter planes appeared in the sky and roared over the lake.

"My friend asked me about the planes flying above us. I told him they were Russian MIG fighters stationed at a nearby base. The waiter overheard us and called the police. When I asked for the check, he came with two detectives, and I was arrested on charges of spying. The waiter was the witness for the prosecution. That is how I found out that every waiter, every hotel employee, is automatically a police informant."

I was eager to find out what threat my other cellmates could have represented to the "working class" and asked one of them, a hollow-faced man with curly grey hair, to tell me his story. He was probably in his mid-sixties, and he was making noises with his mouth as though conversing with himself.

Matheovits Ferenc—everyone called him Matheos—had been a judge in the *ancien régime*. After the war he had become a representative in the party of Christian Democrats. At one of the staged trials of 1949, the communists sentenced him to twelve years. He was released during the Revolution of 1956 and found a job as a construction labourer. In 1964, he was sentenced again for ten years on charges of conspiracy against the communist government. This is how he described his arrest:

"With a few old friends," he said (and murmured a few words to himself), "we were drinking wine in my back yard. We were laughing and joking and ended up forming an imaginary government: I was going to be the Prime Minister, one friend the Minister of Foreign Affairs, another the Minister of Justice." He stopped talking and began pacing back and forth in the cell, muttering and grunting. I thought he might be preparing to say something significant, but as the strange noises continued, I began to think I might be experiencing some auditory hallucination—hearing the grunts of a hog coming out of a human.

"My neighbour on the other side of the fence overheard our drunken fantasies. He called the police. We never even noticed that half a dozen gumshoes had arrived from the Political Police and were eavesdropping on us. We were charged with conspiracy to overturn the rule of the working class. Because the conspiracy happened in my back yard," he laughed—it was the mad laugh of someone who finds the story of his own life so ridiculously absurd that the only way to tell it is to make it a comedy out of it—"they made me the head conspirator, and I was sentenced for ten years in prison. My neighbour testified against me and told the court that my friends and I met regularly. That we were planning to ask the Western powers to intervene and to install us as the government. I tell you," he said, glancing at the other two, "one can't say a word in this country without an informant reporting it."

He resumed his pacing. Although Matheos seemed to be a bit loony, he became one of those few prison friends whom I knew I could trust. An incorrigible sceptic, questioning the truth of any proposition, he—a Christian democrat—both doubted the existence of God and rejected the atheists' claim of the nonexistence of God. His favourite philosopher was Wittgenstein, who maintained that "any one [fact] can either be the case, or not be the case, and everything else remains the same."

And so, on my first day in the Gyűjtő, I found out about the all-pervasive network of informants the Political Police relied on to smother dissent. My first reaction was to hate and despise those, who behind a smokescreen of charm and friendliness, spied on and betrayed their fellow prisoners. I imagined a time when, exposed and uncovered, they would be brought before the court of infamy to be punished. "I hope," I told Uncle Andy "that one day we can put them right here, in this very same prison."

Matheos laughed. "It is full of them already," he said. I failed to understand how anyone could live with himself, knowing well that he was being rewarded for betraying others.

The third prisoner in the cell had, up to that point, not said a word, only observed us with a calm and benign expression, without judgment. Like an obscure figure from another life, he stood motionless by his bunk. Some faint, wordless instinct, a vague, fleeting intelligence that was gone before it could have been grasped, told me that, unlike the other two, he was not there by accident. That he had been put there to watch over me, to guide me through what was going to be my life for many years to come.

Tabody, for that was his name, was a tall, powerful man, formerly a hussar captain, with a chest like a wall. He had waited quietly until Matheos and Uncle Andy finished regaling me with their stories, and he now told me that the first time the communists had charged him with treason was in 1947. After his release in 1956, he had started his theological studies, working as a labourer by day. Now he was imprisoned on charges of "spying for the Vatican" and abusing the generosity of the government, who graciously let the Church continue religious education within prescribed limits, by going outside of the official channels.

Tabody had quite a reputation among both schmassers and inmates. Matheos told me that one Christmas he was celebrating a mass in his cell when two rogue guards opened the door and taunted him with profanities. He was not amused. Made the sign of the cross with one hand, picked up a chair with the other, and in a rage, chased the frightened schmassers all the way to the stairwell.

"Just think of the poor souls," he said after I had ended a second rant about informants, and then proceeded to explain just how the Political Police recruited them. "Most of them are imprisoned on trumped up charges. They are thrown into a cell where they pine for the freedom they lost and their families they miss. They feel being sucked down into an abyss by some vicious force, plunging down faster with each day with images of their wives and children left without a breadwinner, waving goodbye to them. When they are ripe for the picking, they are taken to the political officer."

Tabody must have noticed that I was not impressed with his argument. He stepped closer. "You might not give a damn," he said. "Don't forget that you are young, no wife, no kids to be missed. What is unendurable and the grinding of teeth for others, for you it is an adventure. You should also remember something else," he said with a wink. "You did something which, one way or the other, is punishable everywhere. You were the one who kicked their red asses first."

I shot him a quizzical glance.

"What I want to say is that you are not here by some terrible mistake or by some accident like most of the prisoners, whose only crime was that they happened to be the wrong person in the wrong place at the wrong time."

"I know, I'm not," I acknowledged. "I could have been jailed at sixteen." I proudly regaled them with my tales of sabotage: that, as a kid in 1956, I had stolen ball bearings from the Russians repairing their tanks; at age ten, thrown my Russian textbook into the stove at school; and, at age sixteen, opened a tear gas canister on the anniversary of the Bolshevik Revolution.

"That's exactly what I mean," he said. "But there are only a few prisoners who feel the way you do: that they are here for a reason. Most of them are imprisoned as a result of make-work projects for the Political Police. They feel shipwrecked and washed up on the shores of a very lonely and very unfriendly place."

"It doesn't give them a licence to spy on others."

"Let me introduce our Translation Office," said Tabody, indicating the others with a sweep of his hand. "Matheos," he tilted his head "is *kosher*. Uncle Andy too. So is Akos. Geresdy, our boss, is the official eyes and ears of the Political Police. Which means he is harmless. Mahorka is an amateur. Földes is a bright and interesting chap; a journalist convicted for sending a letter to the UN about human rights violations in Hungary. A perfectly honest man. However, watch out for Gabi. He is curious, intelligent, and friendly. A true professional. He saved his life by betraying three of his friends, who were sent to the gallows. All four of them were charged with spying. He did not become a *besugo* for an easier lot in prison. He became one to save his life and dedicated that life to the profession."

I gazed at him, waiting for more.

"He is a smart, uninhibited con man, who gains your trust, then betrays you without remorse," Tabody explained. "He has long acknowledged to himself that what he does is morally indefensible, has come terms with it, and doesn't waste his time wrestling with matters of conscience."

"With all due respect," I said, and turned my head in the direction of Matheos and Uncle Andy, "how do you know who is a spy and who's not? How do you know that I am not one?"

"After eighteen years in prison," Tabody smiled "I do not have to *know*. What I mean is that I do not need any evidence, any definite proof. I just have to look at someone, take in the way he talks, watch the way his eyes move, the almost imperceptible transformations of his face, listen to the tone of his voice, and either a bell rings in my heart to tell me that he is *kosher* or an alarm goes off in my head like a Geiger counter."

I glance at the laptop to see how my neighbour is doing in his battle with himself or some artificial intelligence. I count the value of his assets: one queen, one rook, one bishop, and half a dozen scattered pawns on his side. Looks like he is losing against his adversary with a concentration of advanced pawns and an extra bishop. I stand up and walk to the window. My plane is sitting on the tarmac. The propellers mounted on its wings are spinning. It must be the same craft that took me from Prague to Budapest two weeks ago. Looks like the duct tape covering the edges of the small areas of repair on its body is holding well. Through an opening in the clouds, a gleam of sunlight lights up the grey panels. In the angle of the rays, the rows of rivets, like mica strewn on the wings, begin to glitter.

"If I had not met Tabody," I wonder, "what kind of a person would I be today? How could I have resisted the relentless, corrosive creep of suspicion and hatred?" I remember Mother's words about the human soul, which, she maintained, is a very large, and at the same time, very empty vessel that wants to be full. That it is up to us what we fill it with: love, compassion, and understanding; or envy; or hatred. Or a big lump of indifference.

Tabody was right. Gabi would gauge, sound, and weigh me with the skill and devotion of someone who traded more than a few years and some favours in a Mephistophelean pact with the Political Police. He would set his traps and try to lure me into them. Like an animal torn between hunger and caution, I often fell into them. Or he would observe me with the patience of a classical portraitist, assemble my psychological profile, brush stroke by brush stroke, carefully assess the strength and weaknesses of my personality, and provide his masters, the political officers, with a blueprint of what he understood to be my character. They then would know which tools to use to take apart the bolts and nuts that held me together and break me down into manageable pieces from which they could reconstruct me into a malleable *type*, one that could be programmed and reprogrammed according to their will.

I played the game of mutual deception with Gabi, and we fought it out to the last moment. His personality was complex and variegated, and he possessed the ability to simulate someone he was not: a friend, a curious and caring friend. He could worm himself into your mind, into your soul, and before you noticed, he had already gained insight to your thoughts. He would start a conversation about a book and steer it with such finesse and elegance that I would often not discover that he had lured me into the net of politics until it was too late. It was this ability that separated him from the amateurish simple-mindedness of Geresdy and other dilettante informants.

I pretended I was ignorant of his ties to the Political Police and of his calculation and basic assumption that the regime would outlast generations of rebels like me. He, in turn, pretended to be an agent of the CIA recruiting young Hungarians for the immediate, inevitable, and violent showdown with the communist regime which I was hoping for.

But none of us could predict the events written on the celestial wheel called history. My brainless expectations of a violent uprising against the regime proved to be just as wrong as Gabi's cold computations of the forces shaping the future. Communism collapsed under its own weight without a revolution, without a single gunshot, and without a drop of blood spilled. Gabi, who had bet on the survival of the regime well into the next century and based his contract as an informant and agent provocateur on this probability, was utterly shocked and disappointed when the unexpected chain of events left him without a job. Worse than finding himself suddenly unemployed, he was also exposed. He received the worst of all punishments for his years of deceit, duplicity, and betrayal. In an irreversible recognition of his situation from which there was no escape by explanation, he stood naked and smelling amidst the cackle of voices and derisive scrutiny, a subject of symbolic expulsion or public stoning. Or—as one of our fellow prisoners, Földes, commented—history caught Gabi with his pants down. He stared bewildered in the blinding light of exposure like the drunk who steps behind the idling streetcar to relieve himself in the dark and realizes that the streetcar has left the station only when the lights fall on him. Had he been able to see into the future, would he have chosen a different path? Maybe. Maybe not.

Half asleep, I feel the ascent of fever from my chest to my head. I am hot and cold at the same time, shivering one moment and sweating the next. The light makes its way through my eyelids. I gaze out the frost-patterned window at the snow-laden branches and lick the parched corners of my lips.

Mother comes with a glass of lemonade and puts it on the night table. Lifting my head, she makes her tender, maternal inquiries and goes back to the kitchen, from where she returns with a small, dark bottle and a large spoon. She shakes the bottle and unplugs it. Pours some cherry-coloured liquid into the spoon and holds it in front of me.

"Open your mouth," she says. I swallow the bitter-tasting potion. "Now drink some lemonade and wash down that bad taste." The lemonade feels fresh and soothing to my tongue but harsh to my throat.

She goes back to the kitchen, comes back with a small plate, and slips a slice of apple between my lips. "The chicken soup is ready in a minute."

"Thank you Mommy," I say, giddy with fever.

I hear the clanging of the lid and the sound of the ladle against the side of the pot. The kitchen clock announces midday with a cheerful chime. Outside the window a woodpecker hangs upside down on a twig.

Mother comes back with a cup of hot soup and a napkin. She puts the napkin under my chin and holds the rim of the cup in front of my mouth. "I can hold it," I say, but my hands are shaking. Mother moves the cup to my lips and gently tilts it. I close my eyes and sip the warm soup.

Still feverish, I am soaked. Mother comes with a dry pillow and puts it under my head. She sprays a little lavender on it. I abandon my lump, inert body to her hands, which peel off my wet pyjamas. She places one cold, wet towel on my chest and a smaller one on my head.

"I will do the dishes," she says "and will be back with the guitar. I will sing you a song."

The boarding call sounds. I close my notebook, grab my carry-on and briefcase, and walk to the window. In the distance, above the treetops, a flock of starlings—mere specks that grow into a swirling black cloud—is performing synchronized stunts in the air. I gaze at the tempest of birds and watch as they whirl down in the direction of the large, snow-covered field beyond the tarmac. They disappear, and I join the long queue of travellers. Staring at stillness behind the window, I try to bend my mind back to my memories, back to that first day in the Gyűjtő.

"I bear no hatred or grudge against them," Tabody said. Matheos stopped his grunting. Uncle Andy and I looked at Tabody expectantly, readying ourselves for a sermon on forgiveness. "When you know only your side of the story, you know only one half of the truth."

"Imagine that after a few weeks of skidding down into the slough of despond, you are taken to the political officer. Dressed like a real gentleman, he offers you a seat on the sofa of his plush office. His secretary wants to know if you want coffee or tea. He offers you the choice between a Camel and a Marlboro. As if you were old friends, he asks about your family, mentioning your wife and your children by their names. He is well prepared. He has studied your file, memorized every significant and insignificant detail of your life. The schmassers and his informants have given him everything he needs to assess your vulnerability, the strength of your resolve.

"'How's the wife, how are the kids doing in school, what are their prospects?' He is full of compassion, full of empathy, acting out twenty-five years of practice in prison psychology. Because he wants to give you some time for the things he says to sink in, he sends you away without going much further. You stew in your own juice for a few weeks. One day, a schmasser gives you a letter from your wife, specially authorized for good behaviour. You read it a hundred times and know every word of it by heart. Then your family arrives for a visit. You are told that it is a special one, outside the regular brief event when sad faces appear for twenty minutes on either side of the wire mesh. When he thinks you are ripe for the picking and eager to play the game, he sends for you, and it will be you who offers yourself for sale."

"Remember," said Tabody, "you always betray yourself first. After that, all other betrayals come easy. From the moment you agree to that deal, you report everything you see and hear and promise to continue doing it long after you are out of prison. In turn, you get released a few years early, get your old job back and, of course, while you're still in prison, your family can visit you more often, right there, in his office."

"It is as simple as this." He stood up, a tall man, big as an oak. He fixed me with his eyes, as if he wanted to sear into my brain what he was about to say with insisting, implacable logic. "On the one hand, you put a few years of your life, your health, your family, and the future of your children into one pan of the scale. Into the other goes your integrity. You might appreciate the latter, but the law of gravity will take care of the matter. Your integrity will be a feather in the scale against the weight of your loved ones."

Even if one knew that the eyes and ears of the Political Police were everywhere, the discovery of the most unlikely spies was a shock. After the fall of communism, Joseph, a good friend of mine with whom I had spent time in prison, went to see the archives of the state security. Besides receiving confirmation of what we already knew, he was astounded to see the names of some fellow prisoners whom we had thought of as friends and above being in the employ of the Political Police.

Not long after Joseph called me with this information, I read *Revised Edition* by Péter Esterházy, the famous Hungarian author and scion of one of the oldest and noblest families in Hungary. He knew he was being watched and suspected that the police knew more about him than they could possibly gather by simply following him and opening his letters. After the fall of communism, he applied for a permit to read his file in the archives of the Political Police for reports possibly written about him. Once the visit was authorized, he went to find out which one of his "friends," "fellow writers," or "fans" had made paid contributions to his file.

The man in charge of the archives, a retired political officer, advised Peter not to dig up the past. "I suggest you leave those reports alone. They do not matter anymore. Not knowing about them may be bliss," he said. "You might discover ghosts that will haunt you forever," he warned him. "Get on with your life and don't stumble on what's behind you."

But the words of caution from someone who might have been the one who kept the records of his life made the author even more curious. Now, more than ever, he wanted to know the secrets of his own biography. He insisted on reading his entire file. When he opened the first one and looked at the first page, the ghost the old cop had warned him about flew right into his face. Wide-eyed, head spinning, he recognized the beautiful handwriting of his revered father, Count Matthias Esterházy.

My guess is that the count made a Faustian deal with the ÁVO: besides spying on others, he agreed to report on his own son, perhaps to protect him. This was the price he paid so that the future author could go to university—which otherwise would have been impossible for the offspring of a "class enemy."

The plane has already pierced the tumultuous lower layers of the clouds and now flies high above them. Down below, they seem endlessly bright and endlessly calm, covering the earth like a silver shroud, glowing in the angle of the light thrown by the sun.

Dead leaves in the air, memories float in my mind. I try to catch a few so that they do not sink into the dark mud of oblivion. Most slip through the net and fall. Perhaps it is the way it should be. If I could save them all, my head would be nothing but a huge archive of remembrances.

It is noon. Mother is in the middle of her annual spring cleaning. Through the open door and windows, fresh scents flow in from the garden. They slowly push out the smell of vinegar that she mixes into the water when she scrubs the floors. "Germs do not like vinegar," she explains when Andrew and I, always underfoot and impeding her work, begin to whine about the sharp, acidy smell. "We don't like it either," I say. "Are we germs?" Mother rolls her eyes, but keeps to herself whatever she thinks of us and simply goes about her work.

Rugs, blankets, pillows, eiderdowns, bed covers, and draperies are piled up everywhere: on the railing of the verandah, on chairs and tables. They hang on branches to be aired by the breeze and sanitized by the hot rays of the sun.

Mother is already banging away on the large rug hanging on the clothesline. She has a song for everything. "Dirt, dust, go away, we want to keep our house clean," she sings, and the work is going better with each improvised song. The wind lifts the cloud of dust above the yard. When the puffs cease and the rug seems to have shed its load, she drops the wicker beater onto the grass. "Come on, guys," she says, waving at us. We roll up the rug and drag it back to the house.

The work is almost done. There is only one more rug left to be beaten. Mother goes to check on our lunch, which is cooking in pots and pans on the summer stove.

A sudden gust of wind bulges out the bedcover on the clothesline. It billows wildly and almost takes flight. The next gust brings cherry blossoms from the neighbour's yard in a blinding white cloud that swirls above the garden and falls on the grass like rosy snow. The dandelions glow among the blossoms as though they were so many little suns. Low-flying clouds, dark as if charred, roll in above the roof and block the sun.

The rain comes down suddenly and hard. Andrew and I stand stunned, with water streaming down our faces. "Hurry up and get the pillows first!" Mother wakes us from our stupor. She dashes from the verandah to the clothesline. Andrew and I start running back and forth between the house, and Mother almost falls over us as she rushes inside hugging an eiderdown.

The rain becomes a true deluge. Large drops spatter on the roof and bounce up from the walkway. Vertical streaks of water fall from overflowing gutters. Sparrows seek shelter under the eaves, and bees and butterflies come inside through the open windows.

The downpour stops as fast as it started. The sun shines as though the shower had never happened. Big, heavy drops of water hang on the leaves of the cherry tree. Mother laughs and throws me a towel "I'll wipe the clothesline, you dry the chairs. Then you move back the pillows and I dust the rug. Let's finish this job."

"What if it starts raining? I ask.

"We will start running," she laughs.

"It does not make any sense," I protest.

"You know the old saying?" she asks.

I grimace. I am hungry and more interested in having lunch than in cleaning and listening to stupid sayings.

"The lazy are always ready with an excuse," Mother says.

As Mother had foreseen, my life in prison would be more of an experience than punishment; from the very first day, I found my time behind bars exciting. For quite a while, I looked on prison life with the pure wonderment and curiosity of a child. When I stepped into the Translation Office, I knew that I had entered a place where I was going to learn more than in my entire life in classrooms.

Those prisoners who had a decent knowledge of English, German, or French, were assigned to translate foreign books and articles obtained by spies and agents, gleaned by embassy staff, and sent to Hungary. Besides Uncle Andy, Matheos, and Tabody, there were another half dozen political prisoners in the spacious and well-lit office. The place seemed like heaven: with large desks, typewriters, dictionaries, and textbooks, it looked like a library or the editorial department of a publishing house. No schmassers supervised us while we worked. We saw them only when we were escorted from our cells, when they brought us lunch, and when, at the end of the day, one or two of them came to return us back to our cages.

Our boss in the Translation Office was a fellow prisoner, Geresdy, a journalist convicted for twelve years on charges of spying for Radio Free Europe. He was a short, balding man with a spatter of scabs on his skull. His ears stuck out sideways as if they wanted to escape in opposite directions. Thick glasses sat on his constantly leaking nose, giving his eyes the appearance of a fish in an aquarium. Matheos, who otherwise had no interest in *besugos* except to avoid them, confirmed what Tabody had said: that Geresdy was a *besugo*, but a harmless one. "We all know who he is," said Matheos. "He too knows that we know. End of story."

On my first day in the Translation Office, Geresdy greeted me, getting up from his desk and offering his hand. "Welcome," he said, revealing overlapping, rodent-like front teeth. "Do you know that we translate confidential material here?" he asked, wringing his hands. I nodded. "You know, you are not supposed to talk about it or write about it to your contact and must keep quiet about it even after your release." I nodded again. "You know"—I was becoming a little impatient with his incessant "you knows"—"how privileged we are to work here."

"I guess."

"What languages do you know?" he asked.

"I can read and write English and some French."

"Have you ever translated from English?"

"Mostly the mandatory classics, ending with Blake, Keats, Shelley, and Byron."

A mulish perplexity crept onto his face, betraying a lack of familiarity with English romanticism. "We will see," he said. He signalled with his hand for me to follow him, turned around, stepped to the desk next to his and introduced me to Peter Földes, a stocky, middle-aged man with thinning red hair and glowing eyes. His mouth was framed with a web of wrinkles that gave him a curious, impish look. There was a book with a French title on his desk, together with the latest edition of Larousse.

Later, I would learn more about him. He had been imprisoned for sending a report to the UN of the long list of human rights violations in Hungary. A well-read man with a malleable mind, he could switch between any political credo without apparent agonies of conscience. With a total lack of reflection, he could extol the virtues of communism or socialism in one breath and advocate multiparty democracy in the next. He could profess to being a Hungarian patriot, a cosmopolitan, and an avid Zionist, all without being bothered by the contradiction inherent in those declarations.

He could tell the most implausible tales, poker-faced as his stories spiralled, directionless, until it was impossible to tell who was the victim and who was the aggressor, who was right and who was wrong. Most of the time, a narrative would be left unfinished in favour of another as he darted from one subject to another.

After the Greek's description of prison being same as the military, but totally different, I saw no problem with that. What mattered to me was that, besides being a translator, Peter also worked in the prison library. He was a most promiscuous reader and had an excellent literary taste. His mind, like a pelican, dove into a sea of books and came up offering one title after the other. After Mother and Matyas, my English teacher, Peter became the next best source of books for me. I had always been obsessed with reading, devouring books like mental nourishment with such appetite and such haste that I sometimes came down with "food poisoning." In prison, thanks to Peter, reading became bliss. I took books into my mind as Catholics take the sacrament.

"Well," Földes said, as we were introduced. He got up from his desk and offered his hand. He gazed at me with open curiosity, an expression that he retained for years and years thereafter, all the way to his last day in prison, when he shook my hand and looked at me as if he was seeing me for the first time. "What brought you here?" he asked.

"You guys can talk about that later," Geresdy cut in, still wringing his hands.

From Földes, we moved on to meet Gabor Nemeth, or Gabi, the spy and *besugo*. From my cellmates' description of him, I had imagined him as having a monstrous appearance, only to meet a tall, handsome, and friendly man. He peered at me as if he was wondering how much I had heard about him, and what I thought of him if I had heard everything. After our introduction, Gabi asked me about my education and chatted with me about authors, artists, and composers. With some humour, he informed me that before the state had "adopted" him for fifteen years, he had been a lawyer. He was self-assured, polite, witty, and articulate, and so charming that I began to doubt that he could harm anyone. Although Geresdy showed signs of impatience, he didn't interrupt Gabi. Only when Gabi said "Good luck," indicating that our conversation was over, did he turn to Cserbakoi who was spending time for "counter-revolutionary activities." Cserba—bushy brows, large dark eyes, and prominent nose—greeted me with the exuberance of a shipwrecked sailor stuck on a deserted island.

The next one was Varga or, as the prisoners called him—referring to his liking for a lethal Russian tobacco—Mahorka. He seemed to be a strange fellow. He slowly pushed his Mussolini jaws forward and, without the slightest effort to show interest, glanced up from the large Mercedes Shop Manual he was translating, observing me with the passive, unreceptive eyes of a recluse leaning out of his hideout for a brief peak at the outside world. Baring his large, grey front teeth, he said, "Hi" in a voice that lacked infliction and timbre—like a fly buzzing on the window—and struck no chord in me. His greeting completed, he returned his attention to his work. As it turned out, it was not personal. He showed no interest in anyone, nor did he ever offer assistance to a fellow prisoner needing help in translating a difficult text or fixing a broken typewriter. He thought of himself alone, because he knew nothing but himself. I found out from Tabody that, unlike Gabi, who performed a superb act to disguise himself, or Geresdy, who wanted us to believe that being an informant was part of his role, but not of his character, Mahorka never felt it was necessary to show anything but his true self: wicked, despicable, and nasty, and possessed of a distinct lack of vanity, which allowed him to crack vulgar, unfunny jokes or to report on a fellow prisoner, untroubled by any feelings of remorse.

The only person close to my age was Akos Kalmar, a young, stocky, mustachioed pilot who had wanted to defect with a MIG 21 fighter. He was the most restless person I ever met; with arms and legs constantly in nervous motion, he seemed to have the temperament of someone who could flip at any moment. Despite the mistrust darting from his eyes and the aura of nervous energy around him, I hoped we would become friends.

From Matheos I knew that Akos had been caught and arrested by the military police on his way to his plane on an airforce base. Just about the same time, his wife was taken off the train to Yugoslavia. They had not known that their telephone calls were being intercepted and that the security services knew everything about their plans.

"I heard you are a pilot. I'm Michael." He assessed me with eyes vibrating in their sockets.

"Heard from whom?" The vehemence with which he asked the question shocked me, and I stood wordless for a moment.

"From one of my cellmates," I said and tilted my head in the direction where Matheos sat. He shot a glance at Matheos and me and twisted his moustache.

"Ok, then," he said sharply and with the tension of a person sitting on a bomb with the fuse lit.

Geresdy led me to a desk beside a large window. "This will be your place," he said, with that incessant hand-wringing of his. "*If* you pass the test," he added.

I stepped to the open window. The sun was halfway up the sky. It had been a long time since I had enjoyed, undisturbed, the tickle of its rays on my skin. I inhaled the fresh breeze and gazed at a small patch of grass, a tiny oasis that stood out from the bleak, grey prison yard, and rested my eyes from the bright light. I turned around and leaned against the iron bars. The warmth of the sun increased and felt like a large, firm hand on my back. It was a strange feeling: the sun and the wind behind me, reaching to me through the bars, and me facing a room full of prisoners, a room where I would spend many years of my life. I heard the chords in my mind and hummed *Et maintenant, que vais-je faire, de tout ce temps que sera ma vie. De tous ces gens qui m'indifferent* ... I kept humming, and when I stopped, I turned my face back to the sun. With my eyes closed and my hands wrapped around the bars, I had almost slipped into a fugue state when I heard the sounds of approaching steps.

"Come."

It was Geresdy. We walked to his desk, which was in the far corner of his office, which overlooked the entire room. He lifted a large book from the top of a pile, hardcover with a green jacket, and handed it to me with an air of import. I had not seen a book since my arrest. When I read the title, I could not believe my luck: in my hands, I held a brand new copy of Solzhenitsyn's *The First Circle*. I held it as if it was the only book ever written, containing all that could ever be said.

I had heard a lot about Solzhenitsyn, the Russian author sentenced to serve time in a labour camp for his political views. I learned from the broadcasts of Radio Free Europe that the manuscript of both *The First Circle* and *The Gulag Archipelago* had been banned in the Soviet Union. What I did not know was what had happened to those manuscripts, how they had been gotten out of Russia, and how *The First Circle* had been published. What I did know was that I would have cheerfully gone to prison only to be able to read this book. I was excited and at the same time scared. "If I pass the test," I thought, staring down at the book in my hand, "I have a chance to survive prison working in the Translation Office and without the lobotomy that comes of spending years in the *Schusterei*, where prisoners take apart old army boots."

"Let's see," Geresdy said. He took back the book and opened the large volume somewhere near the end. His small, mouse-like face shrank smaller as he scrunched it, scanning the lines, and his eyes, small buttons behind the thick glasses, shifted back and forth. When they stopped moving, he put his finger on a paragraph in the middle of the page. "Start from here," he said, handing me the book with a sceptical smirk. His misaligned pupils seemed dilated behind the thick glasses.

I stared at the page, and for a moment, my entire English vocabulary deserted me. My lips were stiff with stage fright. My lips formed the words, but no voice came out. I thought of my English teacher Matyas, who in my high school years had taught me a lot more than just grammar. He loaned me books. He encouraged me to read modern authors in addition to the classics. He gave me a copy of *The Loneliness of the Long Distance*

Runner. A year later, *On the Road* and *One Flew over the Cuckoo's Nest*. I thought of Professor Matzko at university, who spoke about the music, the melody of the language. I took a deep inhale, read the first sentence, flipped it in my head, and let the words come out in Hungarian. The sound of the words and the meaning they carried lifted my spirit higher.

"*Unfortunately for the people and fortunately for their oppressors, human beings, as long as they are alive, always have something that can be taken away from them. Even those imprisoned for life and deprived of freedom, of the sky, of their families and properties forever, can be thrown in a damp punishment cell where they are starved and beaten ...*" I stopped for a moment and cleared my throat to remove the tremor of excitement from my voice. I also wanted to get rid of my fear that I would not be able to improvise the correct translation of what I was reading. But my excitement overcame my despair.

"*They suffer these extra torments just as painfully as their original loss of liberty.*" A nervous quickness pitched my voice high. I wanted to control it, but I could not. "*In order to avoid adding such extra sufferings, most prisoners obediently submit themselves to the humiliating and demoralizing prison regime which slowly kills their soul ...*"

Tabody, Matheos, and Uncle Andy had left their desks. The three of them walked to where Geresdy and I stood in the corner. They stopped a few steps short of his desk and regarded me encouragingly, which made me nervous again.

"OK," said Geresdy. "Continue from here."

"*But some will find peace in their hearts.*" I continued, but then had to stop because I could not see for the thin film of tears that covered my eyes. I blinked a few times. I read the sentence and tried to find the words that would make a perfect translation of it, but all of them were lacking in one way or the other. Then the nervousness disappeared, and the right words came to me with sudden energy. They arranged themselves in my head, each animating the next. I raised my voice, as if I wanted to be heard not only by Geresdy, Földes, Tabody, Akos, and Matheos, but by the entire prison.

"*Some possess the fearlessness of those who have lost everything. The fearlessness that is not easy to come by, but once gained would stay forever with them until they die.*"

Overcome by emotion but no longer steeped in worry about how Geresdy would rate my translation, I fell under the spell of what Solzhenitsyn said about fearlessness. I stood for a while and didn't quite know if what I had just said was a statement of supreme reassurance or one of ultimate terror.

I looked around, feeling dizzy, as if I had been holding my breath for minutes. I felt I had lost consciousness and was dreaming everything, with the floor dropping away from my feet. If my translation were to be rejected, I would spend years in the *Schusterei*, the cobbler shop, tearing apart old army boots. Tabody stood with a smiling, half-solemn expression, intoxicated by the beauty of the words, Földes beamed as if he was tasting their meanings, and Akos stared at me as though he took solace from what I had read. Even Matheos stopped his perpetual grunting. Except for Mahorka, who sat on his chair as if tied to it, the entire Translation Office stood to hear the verdict. Tabody tapped me on the shoulder.

"Awesome, kid!" he said.

"Way too flowery, too emotional," Geresdy said. His utterances were accompanied with frequent shoulder-shrugging, as if he doubted what he had said, wringing his hands, as usual.

"Better than the English version," Gabi commented, and in my gratitude I completely forgot Tabody's warning about the man.

"Perhaps better than the Russian original," Földes declared with such enthusiasm that Geresdy raised his hands in surrender.

"Your quota will be ten pages a day," he announced. "I need one original and two carbon copies. By the way," he said, "your job is not to create some poetry but to supply a simple replica of the original."

I walked to my desk and stood by the window clutching Solzhenitsyn. I closed my eyes, face turned to the fresh air, and didn't care if the quota was ten, twenty, or thirty pages. I turned around, placed the book on the desk and fed three sheets of paper with carbon in between them into the typewriter. I began to type:

THE FIRST CIRCLE

Alexandr Solzhenitsyn

I gaze at the endless sky above the cotton-white sheet of clouds below and reach for my briefcase. I open it and pull out another one of the letters I wrote from prison to Mother.

June 20, 1969

Dear Mother,

Thank you for everything. I hope my letter finds you in good health. No reason for you to worry—I feel great. I could spend my entire life here; reading good books, meeting interesting people and exercising (I can do fifty hand-clap push ups). I look at my time in prison as some initiation without which my life would have been that of banality, my mind limited and my character stagnant. It is a rite of passage—entering the cave to see the light better. Except for all the trouble I caused for you, I do not regret anything. I'm not saying this to console you.

Thank you for recommending Three Men in a Boat. *The funniest novel I ever read. Jerome K. Jerome's ability to find humour in everything is incredible. It's not the kind of humour that makes one laugh out loud. I just kept shaking my head each time he described a goofy move, an awkward situation, or a strange encounter with a simple object. They have only one copy of Oscar Wilde's* The Picture of

Dorian Gray *in the library. I'm on the waiting list and will read it when it is available.*

I'm about to finish Plato's Republic. *What a disappointment. The ordered life of an anthill where poetry is banned and dry reason and manly endurance rules. No individual aspirations, no choice, no dilemma, no personalities—a clockwork called state with humans as cogs and wheels that move as prescribed and predicted. The state is the ruler of life, protecting us from ourselves. Obeying its commands is our only freedom.*

Love You,

Mityu

How symbolic, how fitting that the first book I was to translate was about the first circle of hell! A walled green garden, where, according to Dante, the philosophers of Greece and other non-Christians were held. They were born before Christ and thus were denied access to heaven, but enjoyed a privileged life in this small garden right in the heart of hell. In the Soviet Gulag system, it was a special prison, where intellectuals, scientists, and engineers worked on various tasks given to them by the security agencies. If they did a good job, they could stay in this privileged circle of hell. If they failed or refused, they were transported to Siberia's deadly camps. Incredibly, during my wanderings, I ended up in not only the same circle of hell, but translating a book written about it.

Each day, after my quota of ten pages was done, collected, and taken to those in the Ministry of Interior, who wanted to know what Solzhenitsyn had written about the hell created by their masters in the Kremlin, I returned to my desk and devoured the book.

The story is basically this: Innokenty Volodin, a rogue Russian diplomat disillusioned with Stalin and his system of terror, made an anonymous call to a doctor who had discovered a special, very much needed medication. Within the framework of an existing scientific exchange agreement between France and the Soviet Union, the doctor was about to send some samples to Paris. The authorities, in fact, wanted him to give the medication to his French colleagues, because they planned to fabricate a big political case from his "selling" Russian discoveries to foreigners. In that anonymous phone call, Innokenty warned the doctor not to send the samples.

The doctor heeded the mysterious warning and did not send the samples to his colleagues in the West. He was arrested anyway, and a case was fabricated against him. But the Stalinist Political Police wanted to know who was behind the call they had intercepted. They recorded the voices of every employee at the Ministry of Foreign Affairs and ordered a brilliant mathematician and a group of imprisoned scientists and technicians kept in this first circle of hell to find out the identity of the caller. They were to analyze the spectrographs of the intercepted conversation and compare it to the voices of a dozen possible suspects, knowing full well that if they refused to do so, their fate would be sealed: they would be removed from this green garden and sent to the Gulags of Siberia for hard labour. Despite the certainty of suffering and the prospect of death, their conscience would not allow them to do the job and reveal the identity of the enigmatic caller.

The First Circle made me realize that, even if the crimes of Rákosi— Stalin's Hungarian puppet— and those of the ÁVO were terrible, they paled in comparison with the frenzy of wholesale murder and torture under Stalin. It was as if the entire society had been caught in the vortex of some drug-induced insanity. The pages took me through a labyrinth of terror, where millions vanished as cruelty piled on cruelty in the entire Soviet Union. Stalin and his henchmen were served sturgeon, lobster, and caviar on silver plates and ate thrushes' breasts with truffles even as they ordered the arrest, torture, and murder of their victims. It was as though Solzhenitsyn took my hand to guide me through scenes of torture chambers, ritual murders, half-frozen corpses, gallows, and rotting coffins all the way to Satan's Ball, where the brew of a new society was being prepared in a huge cauldron. Nobody was safe, not even the head of the feared security apparatus. When Yagoda, Stalin's man in charge of maintaining the purity of communist dogma, was arrested and executed, the inventory of the items in his possession included hundreds of ivory carvings, rare wines, silk shirts, and pornographic material. When his successor, Zhdanov, met the same fate a few years later, the list of items was about the same.

"What kind of people were they?" I asked myself as Solzhenitsyn guided me through the show trials, in which the powerful leaders of the fearless Communist Party, who had almost managed to turn the entire world on its head and terrify it, now marched forth like doleful, obedient goats and bleated out everything they were ordered to, cringingly abased themselves and their convictions, and confessed to crimes they could not possibly have committed.

But the cleansing and cauterizing of the Party was just the beginning. Soon, millions of ordinary citizens were called upon to "unmask" their compatriots. People saw spies, saboteurs, wreckers, agitators, reactionaries, Trotskyists, Titoists, and Zionists everywhere. Those who, for some reason, did not fit any of these categories but still were deemed to deserve punishment could always be labelled as enemies of the working class. When the terror generated by Stalin and his henchmen reached its zenith in an all-encompassing witch hunt, denunciations became so widespread that neighbour reported on neighbour, and fathers betrayed sons. And all the while, through its powerful propaganda apparatus, for the credulous outside world, the Soviet Union managed to project the image of a peaceful, harmonious paradise of equality and progress.

It projected that image so well that many in the West (Stalin endearingly called them "useful idiots") regarded Moscow as the socialist Mecca, even after the events of 1956 and 1968 and the publication of *The First Circle*. They must truly have been idiots or utterly insincere. With the depressing example of Russia and its satellites, who in his right mind would have wanted to see France, Britain, or Italy transformed into Hungary, Romania, and Albania? To live under the dictatorship of a police state, where show trials were served up as entertainment for the masses? Submit to censorship? March to the drum beat of propaganda, wearing drab clothes all in the same colour—that's what they wanted?

Like circus animals, we were herded behind the fence around the peninsula of a large room. Once we had encircled the caged area and each one of us was standing with a schmasser beside him, the door connecting the peninsula to the visitors' area was opened and, led by a schmasser, people began to flood the room, each searching for a face behind the iron mesh.

I saw Mother looking for me with searching eyes. I waved and she ran to me. She stood gazing at me and gave me the smile of smiles. "Thank you for coming," I said, watching the schmassers out of the corner of my eye. "Don't worry, I'm fine. I'm translating Solzhenitsyn," I whispered when I saw both schmassers step back and lean back against the wall. They would not have recognized the name anyway. Mother opened her eyes wide. I winked.

"How's prison?" she asked.

"It's heaven!" I exclaimed in a half-muted voice. "It's a book club. In comparison, university was boring." Mother must have thought that I had lost my sanity and reverted to my childhood hallucinations after less than a year in captivity. She seemed at loss for words. "I can spend years translating books," I explained.

"How's your neck?"

"It's perfectly fine."

We have arrived in Prague. The plane lands and taxis to the gate in dense fog. I can see no farther than the tip of its wing. As I glance down at the notebook on my lap, I remember how I started writing a journal of my life in prison. In English, I wrote down what had happened each day on a piece of paper divided into squares, much like the pages of my elementary school arithmetic notebook. Because it was against the rules, I applied a simple encryption in case they were found: vertical lines starting from the bottom of the page and for each letter of each word I used the one prior to it in the alphabet. I placed each piece under the rubber mat under my typewriter. In a few months, the small lump under the rubber mat had become a small hill. When Gabi and Geresdy weren't looking, I put a batch in my shirt and moved it to the washroom where I found a new hiding place for my diary in the gap between the wall and the toilet tank.

It is late summer. We are walking along the path to the river, Mother, my brother, and I. Mother has left her bicycle locked to the last hydro post at the edge of town. She is carrying a basket in one hand and leading Andrew with the other. After the rain, the air is as clear as a diamond. The sun's rays have come down from the sky and lifted the moisture from the path. Grasshoppers catapult in the air, butterflies are doing aerial stunts above them, and the wings of dragonflies are throwing small sparks in my eyes. I stop to kick off my sandals, and the ground feels soft under my feet. I catch up with Mother and toss my sandals into her basket.

To the left of us, there's a cornfield with long, sturdy stalks and golden leaves. We walk by a part that has already been harvested. The land has been laid bare, some of it waterlogged after the rain. A stork stands motionless in the middle of a puddle in the waterlogged field. Swallows cut through the bright blue void above. On the right, there's a large meadow of wildflowers and grass along the path, and in the distance, the church spire.

Mother stops and puts the basket on the ground. She stretches her back, then lifts Andrew from the path, which has become a narrow tunnel between the wall of corn on one side and the high grass on the other. Andrew blinks a few times; his eyes open wider and wider to take in all the sights from his higher perch. They finally stop at the trees behind the bend and he keeps staring stupidly in that direction.

Right ahead of us, about halfway to the river, there's a copse of a few dozen trees, mostly willow and poplar behind the bend. That's where we've always stopped for a picnic. "I'm hungry," Andrew whimpers. "Just a few minutes," Mother says and slides him back down to the path.

Soon after Mother's visit, I found out that prison was anything but heaven. When I went back to my cell from seeing her, Tabody was gone. Matheos told me that he had been transferred to the cell next door while I was talking to Mother.

"Why?" I asked.

"Who knows? We will find it out from Cuccos," he said.

That night I also found out that my neck was not so fine. I noticed a small swelling in the back of my neck, right where I had broken two vertebrae, diving into shallow water two years before my arrest. My fourth and fifth vertebrae were fused with a wire, and Major Magyar's men must have hit that spot when they roughed me up after the typewriter incident.

A week or so after I told Mother how much I loved my life behind bars, right after lunch, a schmasser came to the Translation Office and called for Akos. When I asked Tabody about it, he told me that Akos had been taken to Krizsik, the political officer. "Krizsik has more power here than the Commander himself," he explained. "He can grant early release for those who cooperate and make life hell for those who defy him."

Akos was away for more than three hours. Tabody was worried; I could see that from the way he glanced up at the door each time there was the slightest noise on the outside. It was almost time to be escorted back to our cells. Matheos and Földes were confabulating at the bookshelf. Gabi was sorting out the carbon copies of his daily quota. Uncle Andy stood at the window beside his desk, held one bar with each hand and pushed his face up against the sun, eyes closed. I was about to pull the last page out of the typewriter when the schmasser opened the door and let Akos stumble in. He was white as a sheet. Sweat was dripping from his nose and his chin. He went straight to his desk and sank down on his chair, speechless. With his head propped up on his hands, he stared at the keyboard of his typewriter with an incredulous look—as if in his absence the letters on the keys had morphed from the Hungarian alphabet into strange hieroglyphs. I got up from my desk and walked over to him. "Are you all right?" Akos left me standing without noticing my presence. "You OK?" I asked again. He shook his head.

"Fucking Krizsik," he said. His eyes were wild, almost feverish. He shuddered as if pain were running through him. He squeezed his tormented head with his hands and began to sob. I put my palm on his back to quiet the shuddering shake of his shoulders. "Fucking Krizsik." He shook my hand off his back. "Leave me alone," he pleaded.

"What happened?" I insisted.

"That filthy bastard," he muttered. "Leave me alone, just leave me alone," he kept repeating with hoarse sobs.

I stood clueless. Didn't know if I should stay or walk away. I felt relieved when Matheos and Földes arrived and I could withdraw to my desk. With helpless, pantomime hand motions and talking loudly and simultaneously, they desperately tried to engage him. I saw Tabody rising from his chair. Four or five long, quiet strides and he stood above the three with radiant dignity, then silenced Matheos and Földes with a gesture. He put his hand on Akos's shoulder. I heard the quiet resonance of his voice, but could not understand what he said.

That night we woke up to loud bangs — a cell door being kicked then hammered with a fist. There was a mad, insane laugh. We heard the sound of boots, the muffled noises and heavy, smothered breathing of someone being overpowered and restrained against his will. The sounds became distant and there was silence. Akos did not show up next morning in the Translation Office. When we asked Geresdy, he informed us that he had been moved to the *dilihaz*, the local asylum.

One Sunday afternoon about a month later, as I sat perched on my bunk bed by the window of my cell, I peered down into the yard. I saw six or seven slump-shouldered prisoners plodding their way from the *dilihaz* to the hospital in loose single file. Their heads, shaved in convict style waggled with each step. With arms hanging slack, they moved with the halting, hesitant motions of mechanical toys with weak batteries and fading remote signals.

I recognized Akos among them. The shine was gone from his eyes, as if a veil had been pulled over his face. What had once been a piercing gaze from intense, amber eyes had become a vacant stare from a ruined face. The erect, military posture of a young fighter pilot had slumped to a stoop, and his brisk gait had become a shuffle. His slack, drooping jaws made grinding movements; he was drooling and talking to himself. The sun reflected on the saliva dribbling in strands from the two corners of his mouth. Like that of a robot, incapable of any other motion, an arm, a remnant of what it had been, kept batting away what he must have imagined were insects buzzing around his head.

"Look! It's Akos!"

Matheos, grunting and eyelids twitching, was pacing back and forth in the cell like a captured beast. He had been droning on for hours, and my call failed to draw him out of his strange monologue.

"It's Akos!" I yelled.

"What?" he asked.

"Come and look! They destroyed him." He climbed up onto my bunk. Wordless, we watched Akos and company stagger across the prison yard like crippled soldiers returning from the front. "There is no justice!" I banged my fist on the windowsill.

"Justice," Matheos muttered, "is a rare commodity. Forget about it." He cleared his throat a few times as though he wanted to get rid of the grit left behind by all that grunting. "We have such a poor idea of justice and such slight capacity to live according to its concept that we are predestined to live by the rule of power. In the West," he said with a roll of his eyes, "politicians talk about progress and opportunities, the efficiency of their governments and civil liberties. Sometimes about equality, compassion, and fairness. When all we need is justice that precedes and encompasses it all."

The next day in the Translation Office, I told Tabody that I had seen Akos walking among the mental patients. We stood by "my," window, and he listened to me, showing no emotion. Then he looked up as though scanning the sky for something, folded one hand into the other, and, with eyes closed and face upturned, began to pray. I felt like joining him, but didn't know how. I stood and watched his mouth move and his hands squeezing the blood to the fingertips.

"Only God can help him," he said when he opened his eyes. He parted his big hussar hands and laid them on the windowsill. I didn't know what to say. He then explained that when the old-fashioned cruelty of beatings and physical torture of prisoners stopped, it was replaced with a more insidious way of controlling the stubbornly rebellious: instead of violence to the body that left visible scars, they destroyed the mind.

Tabody explained that those who constantly challenged the system were taken over to the *dilihaz*, where they were silently broken. After their brains were fried with electric shocks, they were kept in an obedient, soulless state with antipsychotic drugs. He revealed to me that everyone, including him, dreaded the thought of high voltage racing through the brain. That even if he managed to endure beatings, starvation, and freezing cold under the ÁVO regime, he feared being pumped full of drugs and becoming a zombie with no human will to resist.

He told me that after a previous confrontation with Krizsik, Akos had spent twenty days in the dark cell. That was his punishment for throwing a chair at Krizsik when he wanted Akos sign up as an informant and get out of prison a few years earlier. He had suggested that the longer Akos stayed in prison, the longer his wife would be able to be unfaithful to him.

"I noticed," said Tabody, "that after the dark cell, Akos became obsessed with Krizsik. To the point that he saw the political officer looming everywhere and blamed him for every evil aspect of prison life besides the ones he was truly responsible for. He was convinced that Krizsik was not only a sadistic ex-ÁVO torturer (which might have been true) but had also been a member of the Arrow Cross in his youth and apprenticed in killing Jews. He vowed to kill him once he was out of prison. I warned him that if he failed to control himself, the next step would be the *dilihaz*. That after a few treatments and pills, not one cell in his brain would be left the way it had been. I begged him to ignore Krizsik. I told him to evade, fend off, dodge, and ignore every perverse provocation, every implied or direct threat. Tune out and disengage—pretend to be deaf." Tabody looked at me as if he was not only repeating his advice to Akos but also imploring me to listen. "I do not know exactly what happened," he sighed. "You saw how it ended."

He must have been less than convinced that I had grasped what he said about Akos and Krizsik in all its gravity. He laid his hand on my shoulder and shook me. "I tell you about a friend," he said. "He kept writing appeals to prove his innocence. Writing an appeal is an intolerable imposition in itself, a declaration of war on their 'justice system,'" he explained. "When year after year his appeals were ignored, he started declaring his innocence loudly everywhere. When we were out in the yard on our afternoon march, he would suddenly jump out of line, cup his hands around his mouth to make a funnel, and announce that he had been convicted on a trumped-up charge. The schmassers jumped him and took him to a solitary cell. When he was let out, I told him to stop stating the obvious. That in case he didn't know, we were all just as innocent, but whining about it would not help. He didn't listen. When a bunch of suits from the Ministry of Justice came to check prison conditions, he ran up to them and told them that he had been convicted for nothing and that all his appeals had been ignored. That was the final straw. He was taken to the *dilihaz* with no appeal against the stream of electrons and drug injections, which ensured that his mouth opened only for food and not to express thoughts."

"Here," he said "we walk a fine line. On one side there is the abyss of insanity, on the other, fathomless corruption. One misstep and you are in free fall—and it is anything but 'free.' Once you've lost your footing, you have no say and no control. Either side takes you right down to the bottom."

The plane slowly moves ahead on the snow-covered tarmac. I think of all those who had spent many years behind those walls before me, some released long before my time, some long dead, but all still alive in the ocean of prison gossip, if not as persons then as reputations.

After I saw what had become of Akos and considered what Tabody had said, I was not looking forward to my first encounter with Krizsik. I knew myself and was not quite certain that I would be able to ignore, dodge, and evade everything the political officer had in his arsenal. At the same time, I knew well that if I failed to be smart, if I let him poke down deep into me to plant the poison of his words into every nerve of mine, Big Nurse would win the final round. There would be no flying free or AWOL, no stopping along the Columbia River while hitchhiking to Canada. Ken Kesey's script was appealing on the outside, and so were all those roads of Kerouac. But the levity of inspiration they had given me when I was free and dreaming about all kinds of wild adventures, had to be changed into grave and serious consideration. Prison was a very different realm—from which no roads went anywhere.

The swelling on my neck kept growing. It became hot and pulsed at night when I lay in bed. In a month, it grew to the size of a golf ball. One day in the Translation Office, I asked Tabody to take a look at it. He already knew about my diving accident and the surgery.

"Kid," he said, after peering at my neck for a minute, "you have no choice." I gave him a questioning glance. "I would not see Doctor Mengele for common ailments," Tabody said, "but this looks serious."

The year is 1953. I am six and Mother is thirty-one. "Half my age," I mutter and close my notebook.

I see her standing at the kitchen table. I am having buttered toast with warm milk. I eat without much gusto—my mind is elsewhere. This is going to be my first day in school. My books, two notebooks—one with lines and one with grids—and my pencil holder are already in my brand new school bag. The scents of freshly sharpened pencil and new leather cancel out the fragrance of the toast. My head is swimming in an ocean of excitement and fear. Kindergarten days are over; I am going to be a big boy.

I have seen the school a few times. It is a two-storey building, but when I looked at it from the top of the walnut tree in the back yard, I sat higher than its roof. I told Mother that I would rather go to school by myself, but Mother said she wanted to go with me for the first time. That I could go alone after that. I argued that the first time was the true adventure and her being with me would take all the fun out of it.

She makes a sandwich and wraps it in wax paper. She opens my school bag and places it in a separate pocket with care. I don't like her fastidiousness. Finally, she says, "Time to leave" in a cheerful voice—as if *she* was the one going to school.

"Finish your milk." I lift the cup half full of warm milk to my lips, and it gives me a big moustache. "Wipe your mouth." I'm annoyed. I lift the edge of the table cloth and wipe the milk off my face. Mother shakes her head, but does not chide me for it.

The route to school winds through crooked, narrow streets. "Remember which way we turn at each corner," Mother says. "Tomorrow, you will go all by yourself." She holds my hand and squeezes it at each landmark.

Here and there, I see a boy and a girl walking on the sidewalk. "I can go by myself now," I say after the third turn. "I know where the school is."

"You will, tomorrow," says Mother.

I see more kids walking in the same direction with school bags on their backs but without mothers. I pull my hand from hers. My mind is scuttling around in small circles of shame and worry with furious impotence.

We are on Petőfi Sándor Street. "Always watch for trucks at the intersection," Mother says and grabs my hand when an old Csepel wheezes by in a cloud of its own black smoke. After the crossing, I yank my hand free, slide both hands into my pockets, and walk either in front of or behind her. When I walk ahead of her, I feel like a dog on a leash. When I'm behind her, she is an obstacle.

"Your shoelace," she says in a cheerful voice, which I hear as anything but cheerful. I notice that the bow has come undone, and the two laces flip between my shoes and the pavement like broken whip ends. I blush and murmur a few bad words she doesn't hear; but I would not mind if she did. I shuffle a few more steps, then crouch down and tie a bow with rebellious diligence. I keep my head down to avoid eye contact with the kids passing us.

When Cuccos came to do his regular check on the Translation Office, I got up from my desk and registered to see the "doctor"—whom we prisoners called Mengele behind his back—who came over once a week from the prison hospital to take care of the health issues of fifty or sixty inmates within less than an hour. The convicts maintained he had started out as a vet, but the animals became nervous in his presence and kicked, bit, and bolted. He then went to Moscow to study medicine and practised what he had learned on prisoners. His brief attempt to treat livestock had a long-lasting effect. He regarded us as animals. Not up there with sheep, cows, and horses, though—our ratings were somewhere below that of insects.

According to prison lore, one inmate went to see him with a bad headache. "How many years you got?" asked Mengele.

"Ten," said the patient, wondering how the number might affect the diagnosis.

"Then your head has a pretty good reason to ache," said Mengele and dismissed the astonished man.

Another complained about dizzy spells. He was told to hold on to something at each episode and sent on his way.

"Even those convinced," Matheos laughed, "that there is a grain of goodness to be found in every human being would be disappointed with him."

I heard the clanging of keys and the hard metallic noise of the lock. The door swung open. Apeman stood with his arms hanging loosely out in front of him, as if he was better off on all fours and was standing erect by accident. "XA 53 84," he grunted and pulled up his belt with one hand. I stood up.

"Come," Apeman grunted, motioning me with his arm. He didn't move like a person, but rather like some prehistoric beast. "You have a doctor's appointment."

The plane stops at the gate amidst a small convoy of approaching trucks. I watch the men go about their work in the cold wind that is swirling the snowflakes around. I close my eyes and think of Chimera, the monstrous, fire-breathing creature of Greek mythology, whose body is composed of several disparate animal body parts. Although the prisoners had given Apeman his nickname because of his gait, his stooped posture, and his arms, which hung down to his knees, he had the neck of a bull, the snout of a hog, and the eyes of weasel.

There was a long line in front of the doctor's office. Inmates were swallowed and then spat out from its orifice. When it was my turn, I entered and stood in front of Mengele, who was sitting behind his desk with his head buried in the long list of names. When he looked up at me, I stepped back as if jolted by an alarm in my blood; he was studying me with complete disdain, as if my mere being were a personal affront, an indecent sight.

"Your name?" he whispered, in a voice with the resonance of a death rattle. His eyes went back to the list and the narrow slit of his mouth remained open, revealing a yellowish tinge like that of slowly healing scar. I gave him my name and prisoner number and watched him check it on the list. He took a file from the top of the heap on his desk, opened it, and frowned into it with caustic scrutiny, his pen poised in the air.

On his desk, on a white piece of cloth there was a glass jar full of cotton balls. Laid out beside it, there was a small forceps, a pair of scissors, something that looked like a dentist's probe, and a scalpel. According to a prison joke, he had used the latter to cut himself out of his mother.

"It's not for nothing that Mengele is called Mengele," I thought, as I quickly took in the man. His stiff and spotless white coat matched the chlorotic pallor of his skin, and his incredibly thin neck shot up from it like stripped wire, atop which sat, like a knot or a strange growth, his bald head. A pair of rectangular glasses was perched on the ridge of his triangular nose, which protruded bleakly above a slit of mouth. Poring over my file, he gave off the impression of an evil alchemist, a brewer of brain-killing potions, who had cold acid rather than blood coursing through his veins. At a sight so repugnant, I felt an unnatural chill, averted my eyes, and rested them on the ceiling. The cold sweat of fear was creeping up from my sides to my armpits. Face to face with him for the first time, I instantly understood all the things I had heard about him.

He rubbed his nose, then twitched it up and down as if to make sure the itch was gone. I found my thoughts wandering to how someone seemingly devoid of warmth would make love. Just as I was concluding that it must be—if he fucked at all—not unlike scratching an annoying itch, he gestured me to step closer, with an electric, oscillating movement of his finger. As I did, I felt as if ice had descended over my head and spread into my chest. I felt I was at the mercy of the demented, inhuman power of a pervert.

"Your problem?" the whisper came out of him stifled, almost soundless.

"A swelling of the scar on the back of my neck."

He adjusted his glasses with studious correctness and looked up, squinting at me for a long time, as if I was something small and very hard to see, an insect perhaps. I stood in his stony stare and, for the first time in my prison life, was scared. When he wrinkled his forehead, it seemed to me that the plates of his skull were shifting forward. His fingers, like spider legs, began to crawl in the direction of the scalpel.

"Turn around," he said, his finger making a small counter-clockwise circle in case I had failed to comprehend his words. I turned. Out of the corner of my eye, I saw his skeletal frame rising from the chair. I stood staring at the white wall while his finger poked my neck like a beak. Pinching the swelling with his thumb and forefinger, he squeezed—and then I felt a sharp stab. I wanted to reach back, grab his hand, and break every bone in it—but wanting is as far I went. I merely clenched my teeth—hard—and when I saw his shadow slinking away, I turned around. He reached for the jar, lifted the lid, and pulled out a cotton ball. I smelled iodine.

I felt tapping on the spot where he had stabbed into the swelling with the scalpel. He repeated it with another, then another, cotton ball and affixed the last one with a band-aid.

"What happened to your neck?" He blinked a few times in rapid succession; his eyelids moved like mechanical shutters in front of the small, grey eyes sitting deep in their sockets. He peered at my file over his glasses, which were in peril of sliding off his nose.

"Had an accident," I said. He touched his pallid, yellow scalp and jotted a note in the file.

"How, where, when?" The words dripped out of his mouth. I had hardly begun talking when he made a gesture of disgust with his hand, as if waving away some bad smell, picked up his pen, and made some notes. Out of the corner of my eye, I saw him closing the file and putting it on top of the heap on his right.

The next day Apeman came to the Translation Office. He stood at the door, swinging a form, and called my name and number.

I gave him a quizzical look.

"Hospital," he grunted. The sting of Mengele's stab was still fresh in my memory.

"That way," he raised his baton in the direction of the gate at the end of the corridor.

"Seems to me," he said, walking behind me and making a pleased, smacking sound with his lips, as if he were savouring some delicacy, "you gonna fucking die here." He announced this with such primal joy, with such gnomish candour, that for a moment I wondered if he had jumped out of his mother seeded with malevolence. "If that hump on your neck is cancer," he mused "and to me"—he paused as if he was in the serious business of diagnosis—"it looks very much like cancer, game's over. Turn left," he barked. We arrived at the entrance to the hospital. He stepped forward, removed the large ring of keys from his belt, fumbled with it for a moment, and unlocked the door.

"Read him his death sentence," said Apeman, greeting the technician—who ignored his attempt at humour. He took me to a small, badly lit room, hung a lead vest around my neck, and made me stand in front of an ancient X-ray machine, which looked as if it were homemade or even perhaps the very prototype with which Wilhelm Röntgen had taken his first picture of the human skeleton.

He placed a chair in front of the machine. "Sit here and face that frame," he said dryly, indicating a rectangular piece of metal. "Don't move." He left the room. I heard a buzzing noise. He came back, made me turn ninety degrees on the chair and repeated the procedure.

"Won't give it a year." Apeman elaborated on his forecast on the way back from the hospital. "And you are going to smell the violets from six feet under. In a numbered grave," he added. "You know," he said, smacking his lips again, "you are the property of the state, alive or dead, till the end of your sentence."

The swelling on my neck became hotter and hotter each day, and the pressure under my skin grew unbearable. I was standing by my desk in the Translation Office when Apeman opened the door and bellowed "Where's that freak?" Everyone, except Geresdy, who jumped, ignored him.

"You, XA 53 84." He pointed his baton at me. "You must be growing a second head," he guffawed, walking behind me on our way to the doctor's office. "If that one has normal brain," he chuckled, "we keep it and cut the old, bad one off. Halt," he said and pointed his baton at the wall. "Stand there." He knocked on the door. Out of the corner of my eye, I saw Mengele's assistant appear.

"XA 53 84, step in."

Mengele was holding a large film up to the light on his desk. He kept craning his unnaturally thin, athrophied neck, moving the film slowly up and down with the fastidious movements of his hand. "The device"—he spoke with metallic finality in his voice—"that secured your fourth and fifth vertebrae is broken." He adjusted his glasses and continued to peer at the image. "The sharp ends," he explained, hardly moving his mouth, as if it was costing him a tremendous effort to speak, "inflamed the tissues." I nodded.

"Were you in a fight?" he asked, peering into my file. The only "fight" I had had was the one when I was beaten by the police as a result of my throwing the typewriter at Major Magyar. Had I not seen Akos drooling and catching imaginary flies, I might have volunteered to mention that incident. I might have also suggested that a few of the blows raining down on my head might have landed on the back of my neck. But I feared that if Mengele found out that I tended to react violently to provocation, he might feel justified to send me to the *dilihaz* for an assessment from which I would never come back.

"The fearlessness that Solzhenitsyn talked about is certainly not easy to come by," I thought. Perhaps the only way to gain it is to become an Akos Kalmar. The thought of me sleepwalking with a group of drooling vegetables fending off nonexistent insects filled me with dread. Each time I looked at Mengele, the same thought unspooled in my head.

"No, I was not." I said, a bit surprised at the speed with which I had learned the art of concealment. At the same time, I was hopeful that the file on his desk didn't have anything about the incident.

"Strange," he whispered. "Those wires do not break by themselves."

"I might have done some exercises," I suggested, "also a few stretches that might have snapped it." Mengele killed the idea with a cold, weary look of disgust.

"The wire has to be removed," he wheezed and made a note beside my name on the list with a precise, motor-like movement of his ballpoint pen, which was as skinny and as translucent as his fingers. "You will be transferred to Tököl."

"When will that be?"

Mengele replied by closing my file. "Your contact will receive a notice of the transfer."

"That is not necessary," I protested.

He twirled the pen between his fingers in a calculated show of impatience. When he looked up at me, the demonic glare of his eyes made me step back. "What's necessary and what's not is not for you to decide." His lips snapped like metal. I was afraid of what I might say, because if I said the wrong thing, I would end up in the *dilihaz* instead of Tököl. I didn't trust myself to speak calmly and explain why I didn't want Mother to know about Tököl. I gave Mengele a wordless nod and followed his assistant to the door.

I had been imprisoned for almost a year. I heard from others that the central prison hospital in Tököl was run by doctors like Mengele. My prospects didn't seem to be great. But that was something I felt I could deal with. What I didn't want was to give Mother another reason to worry. I was twenty-two, and from the day I was out of diapers, I had given her more trouble and anguish than she would have had had she adopted the entire population of a juvenile delinquent centre.

In Prague, it is a short walk from one gate to another. I have an hour until my flight takes off to Toronto. I walk, pulling my carry-on. A dozen ultra-orthodox Jews whirl by with great haste, as though they were competing for a spot on Noah's Ark.

I find a seat and stare out at the cold winter sky behind the panes of glass. I think of Mother and try to remember how her life was unfolding when she was twenty-two. Without completely fading into oblivion, but like birds flying away, my memories of what I have learned about her life shrink into nervous dots. With grinding slowness, my mind moves back to a tragic part of history, with Mother right in the middle of it.

The year was 1944. SS troops moved into Hungary. The leader of the Arrow Cross Party became the new premier. His demented murderers were let loose throughout the country and in the capital. Knowing well that their time was up, Eichmann and his *Judenkommando* were in a frenzy to speed up the deportation of all remaining Jews to concentration camps. During all this, Mother was trekking with Father through the winter snow from Aunt Agnes's place in the country to Budapest. There, she hoped to obtain a *Schutzpass* from Raoul Wallenberg. To avoid the roaming Arrow Cross gangs, Father and Mother travelled at night and rested during the day. Upon their arrival in the capital, Mother was hidden in a cellar while Father searched for food in the streets above. Between the explosions of bombs falling from the sky, he could hear the big guns of the approaching Red Army. Father, a gentile with proper papers to prove his pedigree, saw men, women, and children being dragged out of buildings and led to the riverbank. He saw bodies shot into the Danube. Mother never knew whether, when the door to the cellar opened, it would be Father or her executioners. Nor she did know if the next explosion would bury her under the building.

At twenty-two, Mother was mature beyond her years. My twenty-two years, in contrast, had left me with little to show for them except my juvenile adventures—which were nothing compared to her trials.

I watch the dense, murky clouds and the snowflakes bouncing against the airport window. The plane is sitting on the tarmac like a giant snow goose stretching its wings. I must admit that I do not enjoy remembering my life in prison. Sometimes I want to forget my memories of prison life altogether. I experience more anguish recalling such memories than I experienced at the time they happened. I would rather return to moments of childhood—even if they seem to be trivial and of no consequence whatsoever.

The sun is shining down, but most of its rays are caught by the willows at the water's edge. Dragonflies and butterflies flit among the tree trunks like fairies. In the dense jungle of vegetation along the narrow path that takes us to the pond, bees hum over the blooming wildflowers. With a sound like arrows being released from a bow, grasshoppers snap themselves up from the ground. Not far from the water, we are sitting around the picnic basket, Mother, Andrew, and I. There's a series of small ponds by the river; originally, they were pits from which the earth had been removed and used to build up the levy. They are a bit more than waist deep, and their water, warmer than that of the nearby river, is home to turtles, frogs, and toads. Newts, snails, and salamanders live under logs and stones lying around, and ducks build their nests on tree stumps that stand above the water. The young hatchlings drop right into the pond and move around briskly among ferns and water lilies. When their mother calls, they quickly surround her, floating motionless like a bunch of fluffy flowers anchored in the water. Sometimes she tips up to feed on young shoots of pondweed, with only her tail above the water and her little ones tip up too. Closer to the shore, schools of small fish stream under the lily pads. If we stay quiet, we can see an otter diving to catch fish or crayfish, a muskrat chewing on a twig, or a long-legged heron wading, in search of a catfish to harpoon on its sharp bill.

These ponds are our open-air classrooms, where Mother gives us lessons and explains to us the workings of nature's countless small wonders. "Come," she calls to us from the water's edge when we are finished with our sandwiches. We get up from beside the basket and run to her. The sun shoots through the branches, and the long shafts of its light seem wonderfully pure, primal. The water is clear, and its surface is alive with the trembling reflections of poplar and willow. We marvel at tadpoles swarming in shallows. Mother explains to us that frogs lay eggs and that when tadpoles are hatched they look and swim like fish.

"Later, they grow legs," she says. "From then on they move in the water like true frogs. Watch that one," she says, pointing at one. It is kicking its long legs and gliding faster than the water bugs skating on the surface of the pond. What I thought was going to be a lesson in zoology has turned into something else.

"Watch that frog carefully," she says, touching my shoulder. "That is the way you must kick your legs when I will hold you in the water. It's time for you to learn how to swim. Let's practise on land first." She flexes her legs into a half squat and lunges up in the air. "Like this."

Laughing, Andrew and I start to jump, swinging our arms up in the air.

"Let's do the real thing," Mother says. She takes her shoes off and wades into the pond. "You first," she points at me. I pull off my shirt, use my toes to peel my sandals off, and follow Mother into the water. It is warm and feels soft against my legs. "Come on," she laughs and grabs me under my armpits. "I will hold you by your shorts and you will kick like that frog. Draw your knees to your chest and kick back. Try to grab as much water as you can with your feet. When you kick back with your legs, push your arms forward and feel the glide. Remember the frog."

I try my best to mimic the frog and do what Mother says about grabbing water, but the conversion of the visual, symbolic, and abstract examples into concrete action result in only a pathetic, uncoordinated wiggle of my arms and legs. I am churning the pond like a crippled fish.

"OK, let's do one thing at a time," mother says. "Stretch your arms forward. I will hold your hands, and you kick with your legs."

Mother keeps towing me around in the pond, holding my hands. I am getting better with each kick. When she lets my hands go and holds me by my shorts, I almost feel the glide she is looking for. "Very good," she says, praising me. "Now take a break and look for frogs. See how they swim. Imagine yourself doing the same. Now it's Andrew's turn." She calls to my brother, who is standing by the pond without much enthusiasm.

Contrary to the rumours that painted Tököl as a dark, evil Frankenstein lab where warped doctors sliced open and then sewed up inmates for their sadistic pleasure, the Central Prison Hospital was not much different from a civilian one. Perhaps for older inmates imprisoned for fighting the Russians, the place was still associated with the betrayal and subsequent execution of the revolutionary general, Pál Máleter, who had become Secretary of Defence in the revolutionary government. He was invited by General Mikhail Malinin, commander of the invading Russian forces to negotiate an armistice. When he and his entourage entered the building where the meeting with Malinin was to happen, agents of the KGB immediately arrested them. The KGB later arrested the entire Hungarian revolutionary government, despite an earlier promise that they would treat them as partners in negotiations. Most of them were executed or sent to prison. The fate of Máleter and the memory of freedom fighters who had been murdered or wounded and left to die in the beds and on the floors of Tököl hospital by the likes of Mengele must have been seared into the minds of older prisoners forever.

I stare out the window at the plane on the tarmac and think of Katyn, the fate of Raoul Wallenberg and the millions of nameless victims of persecution, terror, and banishment to the Gulag and remember what Matheos had said when he described the Russian national character. With a hatred of all things Russian, he explained that the Russian state was a direct heir to the cruel and barbaric system imposed by the hordes of Ghenghis Khan. Through centuries under the Mongol yoke, Russian princes, eager to save themselves from being deposed by their Mongol masters, not only freely denounced and slandered one another but were eager to marry into the families of their rulers. In only a few generations, more than fifteen percent of the boyars carried the genes of Ghenghis Khan.

Centuries of bondage bred servility, Matheos continued, and centuries of debasement led to baseness. Generation after generation of experiencing brutality led to the brutalization of the entire society, to the savaging of human relations. The denial of dignity of any sort distorted people's sense of values, and instead of decency and fairness, they admired ferocity, thuggery, and slyness and not only accepted, but appreciated, the unaccountable, tyrannical ways of their masters, which stood in stark contrast to universally accepted human values.

The Byzantine manners of labyrinthine manoeuvring, machinations, devious concealment, and obfuscation that characterized their Eastern Orthodox Church did not help either. Add the oppression of a harsh climate to the oppression by man and almost a century of depraved bolshevik rule, and you have a mentality that is crafty, deceitful, grasping, and devoid of decency on one side, and eager to wallow in every distressing, melancholic thought and ruminate on the negative on the other. Russians still live under the cynical, corruptive force of the worst, loud-mouthed lies that long generations of their leaders have been incapable of rejecting, as they refuse to honour their pledges or to act according to common sense, logic, and reason.

Matheos told me that Theodore Roosevelt, after being awarded the Nobel Prize for his efforts to broker peace between Russia and Japan, sadly remarked that he could not understand why the Russians would insist on lying shamelessly and without any scruples whatsoever when they knew perfectly well that everyone involved in the negotiations knew that they were lying. They adhered to their cynical lies throughout the negotiations, despite the fact that no person of even the slightest intelligence would believe them. He thought of them as utterly insincere and treacherous, with no concept of the truth, no willingness to look facts in the face, and no regard of any sort for others.

In the receiving room, I exchanged my prison garb for a white hospital gown. A nurse led me to a large room and showed me to my bed, one of two dozen arranged in three rows. It was morning. The inmates had just finished eating their breakfast and were chatting in language filthy beyond belief. Swear words hurled back and forth in bouts of profanity.

I heard "*Dik*" and glanced at the elderly man sitting on the bed right beside mine, holding a brick-shaped wooden box. He had sleepy, cunning eyes. "A fucking *gadžo*," he said, using the term that gypsies typically applied to all non-gypsies. He spat on the box, and rubbed it with the corner of the bedsheet without looking at it. His long, root-like feet dangling over the side of the bed were the colour of clay. He put the wooden box on his bed and stood up. "Hungry?" he asked. He reached under his hospital gown with a crabbed hand, pulled out a piece of bread, and pushed it in my face. I shook my head.

"What got you in prison?" I ventured.

"I accepted the money people gave me," he said.

"Huh?"

"Look, gadžo," he said, "I'm an educator. People are greedy. It makes them credulous. They can easily be duped into believing that they can get a lot for a little."

"What do you mean?"

"Like they give me a hundred and get a thousand back. They want something for nothing. I prove them wrong. I give them nothing for something."

"Hm."

"Look at those guys," he said and turned his head in the direction of our roommates. "They are cowards. Thieves and burglars, doing their sneaky stuff behind people's back. Not me. I go face to face and persuade the suckers to hand over their money. But what the fuck's wrong with you, son?" he asked with an indolent and at the same time curious gaze, twisting his long, grey moustache.

"What?"

He rolled his eyes.

"What the fuck's ailing you?"

"There's a wire in my neck." I said. "It has to be removed."

"A wire in the neck?" he asked with open eyed amazement. "Like, stuck in your throat?" Before I could reply, he shook his head and opened his arms in disbelief. At the same time, he glanced at the small group gathering around us in a manner of inviting them to witness our dialogue. "Fucking dumb gadžo!" He raised his hands and shrugged, bewildered. "Can't even swallow a fucking wire."

"Before you do it the next time," he explained, as if he was lecturing an entire audience, "you bend the fucking end that goes down your fucking pie hole at an angle like this," and flexed his finger into the shape of a hook. "That way you can push the fucking wire down and it can't be pulled back. Got it?"

I must have looked as though I had failed to understand, because he straightened his finger and bent it again. "This way!"

(I had no clue what he was talking about until I found out later that most of the patients in the room were gypsies waiting for surgery. In order to gain a brief respite from working in the fields in chain gangs, they would swallow a long piece of wire that had to be surgically removed. It meant a brief stay in pre-op, a longer one in post-op. Their idea of a holiday).

"Tell us, gadžo," he said, taking stock of the small crowd gathering around my bed, "what did they lock you up for?"

I already felt like a boy scout in white shorts standing clueless on board a pirate ship, and I didn't want to appear even more different. "Arson," I said without elaborating. If I could have foreseen his reaction, I would have said something else. The old man wrestled with the word for a moment then his eyes lit up in sudden enlightenment.

"You mean you went around setting fires like a fucking mental? Are you committed?"

"I guess," I said accepting his indisputable logic without an argument. "I'm locked up for six years." He nodded gravely, and the small crowd around us nodded in acknowledgment.

"I tell you, gadžo," he said in a fatherly tone, and put his hand on my shoulder, "you look at it the wrong way. You ain't locked up my boy.

Nobody's locked 'cept the prison door. You are free here, freer than on the outside. Take my advice," he said, shaking me by the shoulders, "don't try to shit higher than your ass." I nodded again without knowing what exactly he meant, but just when I thought that the matter was settled, after a brief, whispered consultation among them that grew louder and louder, one of them, with a surly air and apparently ready for violence, stepped forward.

"You from the *dilihaz*? he asked.

I had tried to find a way to extricate myself from the mess I had created by claiming to be an arsonist. My silence in answer to this was taken by the old man as further proof that I was slow-witted. He pushed the man back. "Leave the gadžo alone." he said. "Can't you see he's nuts?" With that, the issue was decided. They moved over to the other end of the room. One of them started to drum on a pot, another on a chair, and a third clapped two spoons together. The rest slapped their thighs and step-danced on the floorboards. When all the drumming, clapping, and step-dancing joined together, it was as if a freight train had rolled into the room.

One by one they uttered choked, halting, hiccup-like, hypnotic sounds. Some hummed. Their entire bodies convulsed with small, spasmodic movements, shoulders and pelvises thrown back and forth as though in a struggle to unlock the rhythm and melody of a song. I lay on my bed motionless, but inside my skin, my nerves and muscles began to move and my breathing became more rapid. The inarticulate, wild utterings became a chorus of voices, and the shaking and throwing of body parts a dance.

I'm a professional burglar
In and out of jail and road gang
I find no shame in my trade;
Money ain't falling from the sky.
The streets are dark
Everyone's sleeping
Roma tsavo's busy picking
A lock or two in the middle of the night ...

"What do you think?" asked the old man when the room became quiet.

"Think what?" I turned. He handed me the wooden box he was busy polishing. I inspected it and shook my head.

"A coffin," he said. "My coffin, with my dead body in it."

Just when I arrived at the thought that the box I was holding was an expression of his death wish and felt sorry for the man, he reached over and lifted its lid. An enormous penis swung up from between the legs of the body carved into the wood.

"When I die," he laughed, "my cock will have to be killed separately."

They were a merry bunch. Their vulgar talk and rough play passed for affection. Their aggressive curiosity was a sign of friendliness. When they weren't singing their hilarious songs about love, sex, crime, and horses, they held conferences and exchanged ideas on various forms of theft, burglary, and horse trading and listened to the old man lecture on fraud. Unfortunately, before the end of the day, the hospital administration read my file and found out that I was a political from the Translation Office. To stop me from corrupting the morals of those who had strayed somewhat but for whom there was still some hope of reform, I was removed from the company of this carefree gang and found myself alone in a solitary room, humming the last gypsy song I had heard which went something like this:

> *Roma tsavo rests in the shade*
> *Watches a big dumb peasant stacking hay*
> *His horse is not too far way*
> *That horse will be mine before the end of the day.*

The next morning I had a visit from an elderly doctor. He arrived with two young interns in his wake. One was a serious-looking, athletic man with a moustache and crew cut. The other was a girl with a small, upturned nose and a sweet, round face that seemed to me to be spun from pink sugar with a berry for a mouth. I kept opening and closing my eyes as if seeing a mirage. They walked to my bed and pored over my chart. The older doctor studied the X-ray and examined my neck.

"How did it happen?" He asked.

"A diving accident," I said.

"Where did they do the fusion?"

"Central Trauma Hospital."

"Looks like we will have to remove the wire," he said. With a mischievous smile, he turned to the two young doctors.

"Who's going to do it?"

"I'll pass," the man said. "If you don't mind."

The young woman doctor, whose hair shone like the sun but purer—I had not seen a girl for more than a year—was enthusiastic. "I have never done anything like this," she exclaimed in broken Hungarian. "Let me do it." I winced. I didn't know what to say. The fact that I would be her first case was not too encouraging.

"He's yours," the old doctor said. "What the hell," I thought, "a date with such a beauty in the O.R. is worth dying for."

"Natasha is an intern from the Soviet Union," the older doctor explained, peering at me above his lowered glasses with the same impish smile. My first thought was that she had been sent by the KGB, and I imagined her cutting my carotid artery with a scalpel.

"She is good," he said reassuring. "I will be there with her in the OR."

"*Harasho*," I said. "Good." Natasha gave me a smile that melted the hardened crust of prison life off my heart. She clapped her hands like a child. There was a small gap between her front teeth that gave her face a girl-like appearance. Her enthusiasm won the day. "She can't be KGB," I comforted myself.

The old doctor pushed back his glasses and scanned my file. "You work in the Translation Office?" he asked.

"I do."

"Well," he said with a sly smile. "I would say we both are lucky; each in our own way."

"How so?"

"We just received a piece of new anaesthetic equipment from Germany," he said. "The instructions are in German, English, and French. None of us speaks any of those languages. How long would it take for you to give us a translation?"

"A day or two," I said. "It depends ... "

"You better do a good job," he laughed and slapped me on the back. "You will be the first patient to be hooked up to it. You don't want to find out that you used the wrong word. The nurse will bring you the instructions and a typewriter. If you need a dictionary, let her know."

They were at the door and about to leave when he turned back to me. "By the way, what the hell did you do that got you in trouble?" I almost told him he could look into my file if he wanted to know, but realized it was plain, well-intended curiosity.

"My allergy," I replied. "I react badly to the colour red."

"We have no cure for that," he said.

Natasha and the younger doctor came back every day to make sure that they understood everything about the machine. The banter between the three of us lasted all the way until I gave them the last page with full faith in Natasha's ability to remove the wire from my neck and in the correctness of my translation of the manual. Still, when one morning the nurse came with a gurney and wheeled me into the operating room, pictures of my entire life of twenty-one years whirled around in my head in random, rapid flashes, only to fly away, just as the soul leaves the body at the moment of death.

I must have used all the right words in the translation, because I did not feel a thing and did indeed wake up when someone slapped my cheek. I opened my eyes. The white blur in the cone of my vision slowly became a person. Natasha was leaning over my bed. She spoke with intent. She whipped her ponytail up and down and her mouth opened and closed, but I was still too groggy to comprehend what she was trying to say. It took me some time to understand her broken Hungarian: "*Hogy vagy?* How are you?"

"*Harasho*," I mumbled. "*Blagodarnost.* Thank you."

Before my discharge, the old doctor told me that, had it not been for my status as a political, he would have been able to keep me at the central hospital. I could have been some sort of "technical personnel," translating medical journals and typing reports. That they would have made sure I had an easier life than in the Gyűjtő, with its political officers, dark cells, and the *dilihaz* looming over my head like the sword of Damocles.

Still in Prague, I glance out at the plane sitting on its wheels, catching snowflakes with its wings. A truck pulling a train of half a dozen carts appears at the edge of my vision. It winds among the red cones laid out on the tarmac without apparent design or purpose. I wonder what kind of a person I would be today if the old doctor had somehow managed to keep me in the hospital. If I had served my sentence sheltered and protected from all the calamity that was waiting for me upon my return. I open my briefcase and from the dozen envelopes stacked in one of its pockets, I pick another letter.

December 20, 1969

Dear Mother,

Thank you for your letter. I am glad that you and Judith are well. Since my last letter, I have had a small procedure done on my neck. The wire that was used to stabilize my broken vertebrae has become unnecessary, for the vertebrae had fused. It was decided that it should be removed. It all went well. No reason to worry—I am fine.

Thank you for Madame Bovary *and* Middlemarch. *After Madame Bovary, I thought I had read the best novel of its kind—then came George Eliot. I have read quite a few good contemporary books lately. I must say that for a prison, the library is quite good. The one I liked the most was* Herzog *by Saul Bellow. Saul Bellow is an American author who was born and raised in Montreal, Canada. His*

Herzog *blew me away. I liked it so much that I read it late into the night in my cell each time when the moon was up long after the light was turned off. I immediately read his other book,* Henderson the Rain King. *You should read them both. I know you will love them just like I did. I think I will read* Herzog *again; it is so complex and so full of references to people I do not know but should that I do not think I was able to absorb everything at first reading. It would be great to read them in English, although the Hungarian translations are very good, unlike that of* Catcher in the Rye *which, I think, must be a terrible rendition.*

I also read The Centaur *and* Rabbit, Run *by John Updike. Loved them both. Again the translation was great, done by Göncz Árpád, who happened to spend some time in the same section of the same prison—which means that there is hope for me too!*

I just finished The Confessions of Nat Turner, *also translated by Göncz Árpád. Loved it. I know you have less time than I, but if you can find these books, you will certainly enjoy them.*

I am at the twenty lines allotted to me and have to say goodbye. Merry Christmas and Happy New Year.

Love You,

Mityu

It is early spring. The lilacs are already blooming in the garden and their scent wafts through the evening air. The sun has already dipped behind the roof, and after a few final calls, the birds in the trees have fallen silent.

We have just finished dinner, Mother, Father, my brother, and I. From spring to late fall, Mother likes to set the table on the verandah. After dinner, we often stay outside, and when Father is neither drunk nor depressed, Mother fetches her guitar and we sing a few songs. Now he is in a good mood and we are too, because of it.

Father has a beautiful baritone voice. Like with everything else, from the way he ties his shoelaces to how he holds a spoon, Andrew takes after him, and although he is two years younger than me, his voice already has a deeper pitch and a fuller range.

But it is always an effort, a struggle, for Father to sing. He sings as though he had to overcome not only some great resistance in his throat and mouth but the reluctance of his mind as well. He never has this problem when it comes to swear words, which flow out of him like an avalanche. Mother, on the other hand, sings as naturally as a bird, as if she could turn the air she breathed into whatever tune and melody she wanted. She strums a few chords and began to sing.

Spring brings rain and flowers.

She glances encouragingly at Father. Father clears his throat and joined in.

Every bird is looking for a partner.

And when Andrew starts to sing, they are a trio.

Whom should I choose, my Darling?

I have little or no talent for singing and join in only when they are already in unison, hoping that they will drown out the squeaks and croaks in my voice and its tendency to jump an octave instead of a note.

I choose you and you choose me.
Our love will last forever.

Father steps inside, and Mother and Andrew keep singing. When Father comes back, I can smell brandy. We start another song, but his voice, thickened with drink, is off. He leaves again as soon as the second song is over, and this time when he rejoins us, he has trouble pronouncing the words. After his next visit with the demijohn, he fails to return. Mother lays the guitar flat on her lap, and we wait without saying a word. It is dark in the garden, and the house is locked in silence. Mother turns off the verandah light, opens the door, and ushers us inside. As she hurries us through the kitchen into the bedroom, I catch a glimpse of Father, his head limp on the table and his arms sprawled, with one hand holding the demijohn. Nauseous, I lie in bed with my eyes closed. Like a ghost, the picture of Father keeps me awake. It will be a long time before I can fall sleep.

Upon my return from Tököl, to my relief, I found my journal intact behind the toilet tank. *The First Circle* was also still on my desk with the bookmark exactly where I placed it.

It was noon. The clouds were gone and the sun's rays lit up the Translation Office. With their backs to the window, Tabody and Matheos stood side by side, rocking back and forth with their eyes half closed, enjoying the warmth. Földes and I were still having our lunch at my desk. Between spoonfuls of tasteless pea soup, Peter gave me an update on a batch of books that had arrived in the prison library: *Catch-22* by Joseph Heller, *A Clockwork Orange* by Anthony Burgess, and *The French Lieutenant's Woman* by John Fowles. He was right in the middle of his review of *Catch 22* when the door opened. A wiry man with a raptor-like face stepped in. He was wearing a black leather bomber jacket and holding a book in his hand. I looked questioningly at Peter, who had stopped eating and was holding the spoon halfway to his mouth. He watched the black raptor walk to Geresdy.

"ÁVO," he whispered.

"Huh?"

"The Hungarian CIA."

Raptor stood above the little, balding man—a carnivore above his prey. He leaned forward and, with one hand in his pocket and the other lifting and lowering the book with controlled and determined motions, spoke with import. Catching the sunlight sideways, the predatory features of his face became more pronounced. As he spoke, Geresdy kept shrinking, or rather sinking, in himself. I was expecting him to fade away when the raptor tossed the book onto his desk, turned around, and, after a quick survey of the prisoners in the Translation Office, strutted out of the room.

Geresdy held the book as if it weighed a ton. With diffident motions of his hand, he inspected its front and back for a minute and then walked straight to my desk. He stood there, a small heap of misfortune, staring at Peter and me. With one hand he held the book, with the other he wiped his forehead, revealing dark maps of perspiration under his armpits. "How soon can you be finished with Solzhenitsyn?"

"A week or two."

"Make it a week."

"Why?"

"This is urgent," he said and placed the book on my desk. I looked at the cover: *Strangers on a Bridge: The Case of Colonel Abel and Francis Gary Powers* by James B. Donovan. I felt fortunate to be able to read and translate *The First Circle*, but the horrors of Stalinist Russia had left me depressed. I was glad it was going to be over. After the endless stories of incredible cruelty and terror, the details of lives lost in the sea of camps and prisons of the Gulag, any other book was going to be bliss.

Peter picked up the book and leafed through it in a casual manner. Matheos, Tabody, and Gabi came over. The book travelled from hand to hand. "Why me?" I asked.

"Gabi just started another important book," Geresdy explained. Gabi nodded.

"OK," I said without enthusiasm, trying not to reveal how much I looked forward to my new project. I was tired of the endless misery, the torture, the countless tragedies described in *The First Circle*. It made me feel bad that I, someone who had at least done something to provoke the ire of the regime, lived in a more forgiving prison than the thousands of innocents suffering in the Gulag. Unlike them, I knew that one day the prison door would open and I would walk out a free man. In the Gulag, all they could hope for was to survive each day.

The story of Colonel Rudolph Ivanovich Abel, the Soviet master spy, took me from Russia and Siberia to New York City, where the colonel set up his network, was caught, tried, and convicted. He was later exchanged in Berlin for Francis Gary Powers, the American U-2 pilot who was captured May 1, 1960, when his plane was shot down over the Soviet Union.

Initially, I had difficulty translating Donovan. Although he wrote in clear and precise English, the legal terms he used, such as "due process," "burden of proof," "tainted evidence," "good faith," and "leading the witness" got the better of me. Most of these concepts and terms did not exist in the communist justice system. In political cases, such as spying, the job of the court was to convict the defendant on whatever charge the Political Police chose to lay against him and to sentence him to whatever punishment the Political Police demanded. The courts were mere puppets of the political powers.

The dictionary was vague and unhelpful. I needed help from Matheos and Gabi, the two lawyers, to be able to give meaning to "jury selection," "motion to dismiss," "cross examination," and "guilty beyond a reasonable doubt." But instead of receiving a primer course in America's common law, all I got was a long discussion, as even our resident lawyers could only guess at the meanings of most of these legal concepts and could offer little help as to how to translate their equivalents into Hungarian. With Peter's help, we took books from the prison library, such as Harper Lee's novel *To Kill a Mockingbird* and Jerome Lawrence and Robert Edwin Lee's play about the Scopes Monkey Trial, *Inherit the Wind*, to see how others had translated such legal terms. We found them most helpful and so adopted the Hungarian versions of "charge the jury," "presumption of innocence," and "inadmissible evidence" used in these books. By the time I finished translating the court proceedings, I could have passed the bar exam in any country where common law formed the basis of the justice system.

During our many animated discussions, I suspended my aversion to Gabi, the informant, and regarded him as a fellow debater—my guard was down. I talked freely about the sham show trials in communist countries and the total lack of judicial fairness that characterized them. I am certain he conveyed everything to his boss, Krizsik, who, on the basis of Gabi's account, classified me as a hard-minded enemy of the working class.

Soon, the book became the centre of attention, not only for the three of us, but for the entire Translation Office. Sometimes, four or five prisoners would gather around my desk and give me ideas on to how to translate references we Hungarians didn't have a clue about. One such reference was "to the tune of Rudolph the Red-Nosed Reindeer" introducing the words of a song that Jim Donovan (both the author of the book and Colonel Abel's defence lawyer) had composed with his wife and children after regaling them with the day's court proceedings. One evening, after dinner, they gathered around the piano and came up with these lyrics, which I still remember:

Rudolph Ivanovich Abel,
Was a very happy spy,
And whenever spies would gather
They would say, "What a guy!"
Then one dark and stormy night
Came the FBI:
"Rudolph, in our very sight
You did dare to spy tonight!"
Now Rudolph's days are over,
But all other spies agree
Rudolph Ivanonich Abel
Will go down in history.

Once I had managed—with the help of Matheos and Gabi, and with even more help from the Hungarian translations of *To Kill a Mockingbird* and

Inherit the Wind—to find, guess, or invent the correct Hungarian equivalents of the various legal terms, the book was a pleasure to translate. It was a fascinating description of the biggest spy case of the Cold War, the life of a Soviet agent in New York City, with all the cloak-and-dagger trappings of a Hollywood thriller: secret, coded messages left in hollowed-out coins; cash picked up from hiding places such as lampposts in parks; and meetings arranged between members of the spy network who knew each other only by aliases or nicknames.

International attention to the trial (except in communist countries) was similar to the buzz over the match between the world heavyweight champion Sonny Liston (The Big Bear) and Cassius Clay (aka Muhammad Ali). Of course, the Russians denied that they had anything to do with Abel. When I got to the part where Nikita Khrushchev publicly declared in Moscow, "As God is my witness, the Soviet Union has no spies," I read it aloud. The entire Translation Office, including Geresdy, broke out in loud, spontaneous laughter. I decided to risk facing the wrath of the top echelons of the Communist Party and translated it, "As Marx, Lenin, and the KGB are my witnesses, the Soviet Union has no spies." I had an argument ready, in case they wanted me to be punished for such an obvious deviation from the original text: Khrushchev, as leader of the Communist Party and therefore an atheist, should have invoked those whom he considered a power higher than God.

The part describing the secret negotiations concerning the exchange of spies in Berlin confirmed everything I disliked about the Russian character: their awkward insistence on lying in the face of facts; their constant twisting and slipping and sliding and maneuvering as they were doing their utmost to avoid reaching an honest and straightforward deal—all without the slightest sense of shame. In fact, the only sympathetic person among all the Russians in the book was the master spy himself, Colonel Abel.

I want to read my next letter to Mother, then change my mind. As I gaze out at the plane sitting on the tarmac, my mind goes back to the time when I had finished translating Donovan's book and was waiting to be punished for the way I had put words in Khrushchev's mouth; but the punishment never came. Looked like the ones who read it either failed to notice the point I was making or, like Colonel Abel, possessed enough of a sense of humour not to get upset over my sarcasm.

The third book I translated was *Between Two Ages* by Zbigniew Brzezinski, a political scientist, Harvard professor, and future National Security Advisor to President Carter.

On the morning of April 3, 1970—the second anniversary of my burning the party centre—the door of the Translation Office opened and in walked Apeman. With him, his decorations parading across his chest and his shoes polished to such perfection that they mirrored his trousers legs, Lieutenant Colonel Klucso, Commander of the prison, stepped in. His eyes leaped like floodlights from one prisoner to another—from Mahorka to Cserba, from me to Gabi—as if he were gauging whether or not we were sufficiently impressed. When Tabody locked eyes with him, Klucso's gaze slid to Matheos, who kept his on the keyboard of his typewriter. From Klucso's nose, full of craters and bumps, as though invaded by some tumorous disease, came loud, sniffing sounds. Aside from that, the room was completely silent. I thought—and so did everyone else—that Apeman and the prison Commander were coming for Matheos. There had been an incident the previous day.

On that day, when Apeman came to escort us to the Translation Office as usual, the loudspeakers were already blasting party propaganda in praise of Moscow, the Red Army, and the twenty-fifth anniversary of the dawn of the new socialist way of life in Hungary. When we arrived at the centre of the prison, we saw that some guards were hanging red brocade on the wall. "Never happened before," Uncle Andy commented. "Perhaps they want to rub it in for us."

Matheos stopped for a moment. He admired the preparations with arrogant curiosity. He inspected the guards arranging the socialist decor in the large corridor and began to mumble to himself, as was his habit. I was about to nudge him on when his eyes lit up. "I have a better idea," he said, talking to the guards as much as to us. "Hang Klucso in the middle, Krizsik on the right, and Apeman on the left. That would be a sight to remember!"

Apeman must have recognized the names, including his own, but could not put together the full meaning of what Matheos had said. Sloped forehead creased, he slammed his baton hard against the shaft of his boot, and threw a frown at Matheos.

"As a priest," Tabody said, shifting his gaze away from the flags, "I must dissent. Ditto as a political prisoner."

"I consent," snapped Mahorka and broke into a loud laugh.

"This is crazy," Cserbakoi said, shaking his head, and we all began to laugh—as though all the cheerfulness that had been pent up inside us had suddenly found its way out into the air of the prison, liberated. As out laughter reverberated through the corridor, Apeman knit his eyebrows together in puzzlement, then anger. "Shut up you all! Keep moving!" he barked, and we continued on our route.

"That idea was a little extreme," Földes said, once we were in the Translation Office.

"Which idea?" asked Matheos "Decorating the prison?"

"The hangings," Földes said with an impatient roll of his eyes. "You were a judge. Now you advocate lynching, mob style? Joined *la canaille*?"

"Don't lecture me, Peter," Matheos grunted. "My ancestors were members of the nobility when yours were still wandering the globe, peddling rags."

"Let's go back further in history," Földes laughed. "Mine were already cheating the Roman tax collectors in Jerusalem when yours were still just managing to leap from trees onto horses."

Matheos broke out into a laugh. "Fair enough. I should have known better." He slapped Földes on the back.

Except for Mahorka, we all laughed. A slow, but intense malice twisted the muscles of his face. He gave Földes a sideways glance and snarled, showing an upper row of large, bad teeth like a row of upended gravestones. "Smartass *zsido*," he hissed. "Smartass Jew."

Földes took a deep breath. Instead of saying anything, he closed his fingers into a fist, held his breath and turned red. Then, as if the anger that had risen inside him had been defeated before it could become an act he would have regretted, he slowly exhaled the air he was holding and walked to his desk.

Taken aback by his hateful remark, I looked at Mahorka and rolled my eyes. He sized me up and telegraphed with a glint that whatever he thought of Földes, he thought of me as well. I did not want to get into a fight with an informant; I shook my head and walked to my desk.

"What is wrong with Mahorka?" I asked Tabody later in the day.

"Many things are wrong with Mahorka," he said "Why?"

"He called Peter a smartass *zsido* behind his back."

"He is a bloody antisemite," Tabody said. "It is, as with most of his sort, part of a wider, anti-intellectual attitude," he explained, leafing through the dictionary on his desk as if he wanted to find the right words. "His hatred encompasses but goes beyond Jews. He hates everything that he finds too complex to understand. He lacks and despises humour. He is uncurious about everything to the point where to show less interest in ideas about art, science, philosophy, and religion, he would have to be brain dead. He is not comfortable in the company of those who like to question, debate, examine, and investigate. Look at Földes. With his pathological curiosity and argumentativeness, he is the embodiment of everything Mahorka detests."

Now, with Apeman and the Commander standing in the Translation Office, I wondered whether Apeman had understood Matheos's comment about decorating the prison after all. Or if Geresdy and Gabi had reported the brief exchange between Matheos and Földes.

My concern, it turned out, was needless: Klucso's sudden appearance had nothing to do with any of that. A civilian followed the Commander, carrying a briefcase. They both went straight to Geresdy, who jumped from his chair and stood, this time not wringing his hands but holding them clasped, like an old lady in church. The civilian took a book from his briefcase and put it on Geresdy's desk. Among other words such as "important," I overheard him say "urgent." Geresdy glanced over at me a few times as he talked, fiddling with a button on his shirt. I had a feeling that whatever the book lying on his desk was, I was going to be the one to translate it. I was already finished with *Strangers on a Bridge* and was translating a current issue of *Foreign Affairs*.

After Klucso and the civilian had left, Geresdy picked up the book and walked over to my desk. "Forget about *Foreign Affairs*," he said. He pulled the three pages from my typewriter in an unusual display of determination that he otherwise lacked. "This is urgent! When I say 'urgent,' I mean *urgent.*" He gazed at me from behind his thick glasses with an air of import. I almost laughed, because he was a small man with the head of a mouse and the most timid expression. "I mean fucking urgent. The gentleman with Klucso," he explained in all seriousness, "was from the Central Committee. He wants to know what's in this book as soon as possible. At the end of each day I have to collect the translated pages, and I want to see as many of them as you can churn out of your typewriter.

Night is falling in Prague. A veil of snow is hanging from the sky, and snowflakes cling to the hull of the plane. The fluorescent lights of the lampposts start flickering, casting blue circles on the snow gathering on the tarmac. I think of the events that catapulted my life into unseen directions.

How I managed to navigate in certain moments and in certain situations—none of them I could see coming—is a mystery.

"Let's go to the market!" says Mother with unfettered excitement. Her cheerful voice fills the entire yard. She has a flair for the improvised, for the spontaneous, and never does anything half-hearted. She launches us into doing whatever comes to her mind with such enthusiasm that we are instantly drawn into the vortex of her energy. When she says, "Let's clean," it means that the furniture will be moved, floors swept and mopped, windows buffed to a shine, and door knobs polished. In an unsmiling world of apathy and lethargy, she can make the most mundane chores fun, an exciting enterprise.

Like squirrels, we tumble down from the walnut tree where we've been perched and drop from its lower branches. She hangs her shopping baskets on her bicycle, Andrew opens the gate, and we are on our way. Mother never has a list. "What do we need?" she asks and immediately answers herself: "Potatoes, onions, cucumbers, beans, and lentils. We also need some cheese and butter. On the way home, we will stop at the baker. If we have money left, you each can have a roll with fresh butter."

It is summer. We walk briskly along the sidewalk under linden trees. We stop for a moment to watch a stork, nested on the chimney of the abandoned warehouse on the corner of Kossuth and Klauzal Streets, feeding its young. Above them, swallows dart back and forth. The closer we get to the marketplace, which is only a few blocks away from the railway station, the more people we see carrying bags and baskets of fresh food, some walking with live fowls slung over their shoulders. Carts are parked by the curb, tethered to trees. I gaze into the soft, brown eyes of the horses and sometimes touch their sides, which gently shudder under my hand. Soon, I can see rows of large wicker baskets filled with potatoes, onions, watermelons, and corn cobs. These rows have become shorter each year as more and more small farmers have been forced into kolkhozes. The market will keep shrinking until it completely disappears by the late fifties, eventually to be replaced by drab, Stalinist structures, warehousing the new, "socialist type" of men and be renamed "Karl Marx Bloc." By that time, most staples will be sold in state-run stores, where long lines of people, clutching government-issued food tickets, will wait for hours to be served. Risking jail, the brave ones will still sell and buy fowl, eggs, and meat on the black market.

But for now, there is still a market. Mother leads us to the far end. Sullen and dejected, their heads covered with dark scarves, old women from the nearby farms stand behind rickety tables, offering cheese, butter, curd, and sour cream in mournful voices—more like sad wailing than cheerful invitations to purchase. Mother goes straight to the stand of someone she knows.

"Aniko," she says with a smile. Her voice lights up the faces around her, and curiosity breaks up the gloom and indifference. In a few minutes, the vendors are all smiles as they join in the talk about everything from the harvest to the weather, and from children to grandchildren. Aniko talks with such speed and enthusiasm that the words fall out of her mouth as though someone had opened a dictionary, shaken it, and let the words tumble and assemble themselves into sentences as they fell. When she finally runs out of breath, I ask Mother if we can walk over to the next row, where small livestock are sold, while she makes her purchases. Mother doesn't like to go to that part of the market, for she disapproves of the way the poor animals are handled, but she lets us admire the lambs, kids, piglets, and rabbits.

"All right, now it's time for the bakery," she says and pulls her shopping bag from one of the baskets on her bicycle.

There is only one independent baker left in the entire town. He has managed to resist the pressure, the threats from the cadres of the Communist Party, and has refused to join those bakers at the so-called bread factory who now produce the bland, formless loaves that the people call "toothcrackers." His wife, Ildiko, takes care of the customers in the store. She always gives us kids small, warm *pogácsa*, *kifli*, or *zsemle*. The baker himself, a big, ruddy-faced man, works the ovens. We see him only when he hauls out large trays of freshly baked bread, buns, rolls, and croissants and places them on the shelves. His eyes twinkle with good humour, and his beard, moustache, and eyebrows are covered with fine flour, as if he had just stepped inside from a snowstorm.

To get to the bakery, we take a small detour among dilapidated bungalows and crumbling sheds back to Kossuth Street. From the end of the laneway, we can see smoke rising from the bakery. Firemen and police surround the building. A small crowd of onlookers is watching the goings-on. Old women whisper behind cupped hands. Some policemen are busy erecting a barrier; others are pushing back the curious. One of them notices us, swings around, and raises his hand with such a savage movement that he stumbles and almost falls.

"Turn back!" he barks after righting himself. His face is burning like a furnace.

"What happened?" Mother asks.

"None of your business! Turn back!" he yells furiously, his lips trembling with anger. Behind him, the crowd is being dispersed by policemen swinging batons.

Mother stands and shakes her head with wordless disdain. The policeman raises his baton. My heart sinks. I pull on Mother's skirt and scream "No!" at the uniform towering above.

That is my first encounter with the police. How could I imagine that, years later, these encounters would become a pattern?

"Let's get out of here," Mother says. She turns her bicycle around and leads us back along the laneway.

It will be years before we find out that the bakery was set on fire by agents of the ÁVO. The owner was charged with arson and sent to prison.

When I think of the book thrown onto my desk for translation, I can't remember it in all its details, because it was more the grasp it gave me on how our world was going to evolve: Brzezinski foresaw the effects that technology and globalism would have on societies, the development of transnational elites, the outsourcing of jobs, and the personal obsolescence of individual workers. He talked about an age when the entire world would become a huge machine. He laid down American strategy for all the changes he saw coming for the rest of the century and beyond. Reading its pages, the communist leaders must have been less enthralled by the shining rainbow of the great socialist enterprise—a rainbow with Moscow at its foot, arching all the way to Havana.

Between Two Ages was a great read, and I felt very lucky to have been able to translate it. It still remains one of the best books ever written on global matters, and it is still relevant on every issue it addresses. Besides influencing my thinking, it also had an effect on my life in prison: the fact that I was translating it set the scene for my first contact with the person who ruled over the Gyűjtő.

From inside the terminal at Prague, I survey the tarmac—the plane is still catching snowflakes, but the lights have stopped flickering—and fall to contemplating. My entire life has been so weird that if I were to put it into a novel, readers would have to suspend disbelief well beyond what they might be used to. I think about the strange combination of necessity and chance, the collisions with the powerful, which finally sent me to prison, where—of all places!—I was one of the very few with access to books not only unavailable but also unknown to most. Had it not been for Brzezinski writing this book, the embassy staff in Washington sending it to a particular member of the Central Committee, and Geresdy putting it on my desk rather than giving it to Gabi, for all my despising of them I might have been tricked into being an informant, or in my desperate fight against that terrible role, might have been turned into a zombie. None of which happened.

Books. I think of what Ralph Waldo Emerson once said in praise of them: "How thankful we ought to be for these inestimable blessings, for this numberless host of friends, who never weary, betray or forsake us."

June 20, 1969

Dear Mother,

Thank you for your letter. So glad that you and Judith are fine. I enjoy every day here, my life in prison could not be better.

I read two books. One of them had such an effect on me that I am afraid that anything I read hereafter will be lightweight in comparison.

It was recommended by a fellow prisoner who said that if I am serious about literature, I must read The Sound and the Fury *by William Faulkner. After the first few dozen pages I almost gave up on the book—or on my ability to persist. I am glad I didn't. Although reading never got easier, it gave me such a picture of the time, of that particular, dead-end society and of the family, like a Van Gogh self-portrait. I had to concentrate so hard on each sentence and on each paragraph that I became often overwhelmed—had to close my eyes and rest my mind feeling as though the author had hoisted me on his pen to make me feel the sufferings of his characters. When I finished the book, all things seemed light. It was beyond doubt my hardest reading ever, but I would be less without having read it. I was to read* Absalom, Absalom *right after but did not feel up to it—*The Sound and the Fury *put me through the wringer, then hung me out to dry.*

I read The Caine Mutiny *by Herman Wouk instead. Very interesting, entertaining, and well-written book. Certainly not a lightweight. You would love it. Thank you for* The Red and the Black. *I will get to it as soon as I can.*

Love You,

Mityu

Mother, a few days before she went into hiding from the Nazis.

A few years later with my brother, Andrew, and I, on the farm.

Growing up with Andrew.

Karl Marx

Lenin

Brezhnev

Kadar Janos, who betrayed the Revolution of 1956 and was installed by the Kremlin.

The local communist party center was located in the left section of this block.

Long live the Party, Long live the Hungarian people building their socialist society.

The annual, obligatory march of schoolchildren and workers carrying signs extolling the virtues of socialism.

Ervin Zador, Captain of the Hungarian Olympic Water Polo Team in Melbourne.
In 1956 after the infamous match with the Russians.
He emigrated to the USA and became the swim coach of Mark Spitz.

The Gyujto Prison in Budapest.

Justice Matheos.
Judge and member of Parliament.

The statue of Tabody erected
after the fall of communism.

Addendum to the search warrant executed by the Political Department of the Police Headquarters listing the items seized. Among them: 4 letters, 33 postcards written in English, a spool of magnetophone tape, a Solingen hunting knife, a ring with monogram *FM* and high school certificate.

My first letter from the circa twenty letters I was allowed to write. I tried to write with small letters to be able to cram as much as possible into the 20 line limit.

Certificate with the seal of the prison and the signature of commander Klucso stating that I worked as an English and French language translator from May 5, 1967 until May 17, 1974.

A few weeks after I began translating Brzezinski, I was standing at the open window of the Translation Office, hands on the ledge, head pushed against the bars. It was spring, and the fresh air coming from the prison yard tickled the skin of my arms and neck. The stunted tree growing out of the side of the maintenance crew's tool shed was green, and a dove was building a nest in the fork of its branches. I had closed my eyes and was listening to the wind and the faint chattering of birds when I felt someone touch my shoulder.

"Taking a break?"

"Meditating," I said without turning my head.

"I pray at my cell window," Tabody said.

"Same thing," I replied, smiling. I turned and sat on the window ledge.

"Exactly the same, only totally different," said Tabody with a laugh, and I laughed with him.

"It looksss to me," I said with a chuckle, "that the Greek hasss been giving the sssame lesssonsss on the sssamenesss of opposssitesss for quite a while."

"OK," said Tabody, "what do you do when you mediate?"

"Well," I said, "let me see. As little as possible. I try to be alone with myself. My thoughts and feelings are directed inwards. I try to remove myself, isolate myself from complexities. I try to arrive to a point where I have no thoughts at all, and I'm at peace with myself and with the world."

"Peace," said Tabody. "I'm at peace when I pray, and that is where the sameness ends. For what I do when I pray is devotional. My self, my ego, my persona become utterly unimportant. Prayer has little to do with the self; in fact, I completely abandon it. Instead of removing myself or isolating myself, what you are doing when you mediate, I try to be alone with God. When I seek the presence of God, the burden of my entire existence disappears. When I speak with God," he said, pressing the fingertips of his big hands onto the windowsill, as if he was about to play the piano, and staring gravely up into the bright spring sky behind the bars. "I place my anguish, my worries, my despair, my entire life in His hand. It gives me an inner calm, a form of grace where there is no waste of energy or hesitation or regret. Where my mind is neither behind nor running ahead, but stays in the moment. Without God and without my faith in God, I would be nothing more than a smart, naked ape who happens to talk."

I was about ask him if he considered me a "naked ape" when he raised his hand.

"I tell you about a friend of mine," he said.

"I was in Kistarcsa, in the internment camp. It was originally set up by the Nazis to lock up Jews and other undesirables. After their defeat, the ÁVO used it for their own, very similar purposes. I met a Jesuit monk. For him, going to prison was a sort of duty, a pilgrimage he made, not out of fatalism but according to his faith. He withstood mental and physical torture like no other. He combined his Christian faith with Buddhism. He maintained that our last thoughts and feelings would determine the quality of our thoughts and feelings in our next lives. Life is short, and the time of death is uncertain. It comes upon us like a thief in the night. We must make sure that every moment of it is lived calmly and mindfully in order to avoid repugnant feelings, such as hatred, rancour, revenge, and envy sticking to us at our exit ... "

That was the moment when Apeman opened the door and called out my name and number. I slowly raised my hand and waited for him to say what he wanted, but no verbal reply was forthcoming. One hand still on the door, he merely gestured with the other, summoning me with a few rapid, impatient movements of his forefinger while the baton dangling from his wrist swung back and forth like a pendulum. Not wanting to run like a dog called to heel, I slipped off the ledge without hurry, sauntered to my desk, closed my dictionary with considerable ceremony, and began tidying up the clutter.

"What is it?" I asked, without looking up from the typewritten pages I had begun sorting.

"You will see," he growled, tapping his boot with the baton. "Get moving!"

"Krizsik, the operative," Tabody said with a smile. "It will be exactly the same as meditation and exactly the same as prayer. Just totally different."

I walked over to Apeman. "Idiot," I said to myself as I passed his bulk. As if I had shouted it out loud, he contorted his face in a sneer and whipped his head in my direction.

"Don't be a smartass! Roll your damn sleeves down and look proper," he said, his jaws set tight with scorn. I stopped and languidly rolled down first one sleeve, then the other. I was led out of the multi-level star-shaped structure with its iron stairs, iron landings and iron catwalks to a steel gate guarded by a schmasser, who exchanged a wicked glance with Apeman. The schmasser opened the gate, and slammed it behind us.

Apeman led me into an adjacent building. "Stop!" he yelled as we approached a staircase. "Up there." On the second floor, we passed two or three office doors. Apeman ordered me to stop and stand by the last one. He knocked on the door, opened it wide, and sternly gestured me to step inside.

I entered an office that could have been that of a bookkeeper: several, large, metal filing cabinets lined one wall, and cardboard boxes were piled one on top of the other. Krizsik sat behind a desk, fiddling with a pen.

"Prisoner XA 53 84," Apeman reported with a salute. He made a stiff about-face and walked out. Krizsik continued twiddling his pen, mute, as if he needed a period of quiet to prepare his words. His face was freshly shaven, exposing the large pores that gave me impression of a sponge, ready to suck up and digest everything, and his grey hair, neatly arranged to cover the bald spot in the middle, was shining with grease. He looked like a vain, prickly man.

It is July, and the small park across from our house is lush green. I stand by the ditch half covered with weeds and watch the march of tiny creatures that have just metamorphosed from tadpoles into frogs. No larger than the bumblebees hovering above the dandelions, they slowly make their way into the grass.

With their feet on the seat, Tulok and his lieutenant, Bika, are perched on a bench like two ravens. They pass a cigarette between them and puff big clouds of smoke into the air. They do not acknowledge my presence until they notice that I am watching something move from the water of the ditch up to the bank and into the grass. But from the distance, they cannot tell what.

There are already hundreds of tiny frogs climbing in the grass by the time Tulok snuffs out his cigarette and gives Bika a conspiratorial look. Bika nods. With deliberately slow and draggy motions, they step off the bench in unison and walk over to where I stand admiring the march of frogs. Tulok observes them with predatory curiosity.

"Are they not cute?" I ask. From the way they are observing the frogs, I am worried that they may commit a vicious act, but I can't imagine what it might be.

Tulok tilts his head one way then the other, making a production out of trying to find the beauty I have assigned to the frogs. Then, with a sudden kick to my shin, he brings me to the ground. I try to get up. Tulok knees me in the chest. Bika jumps onto the procession of frogs. With twisting motions of his feet, he keeps squashing them. Tulok joins him in a demented dance.

"Don't kill them," I plead, which only encourages them to trample and twist all the faster. I run head-on into Tulok to push him away, but it is like butting my head into a sack of potatoes. I fall back on my ass.

That is when Mother appears. She looks first at me and then at Tulok. With a derisive grin, he reaches to his crotch and makes an obscene gesture. In another lewd gesture, he licks the cigarette stuck to his upper lip. His teeth are yellow and as big as those of a horse.

Mother nails him so hard with a right hook that his chin jerks sideways and his smug smile turns into an expression of shock. He flails his arms in an effort to regain balance. Mother shifts her weight from one leg to the other and suckers him with another punch. Tulok falls, touches his mouth, and stares at the blood on the back of his hand. Mother wipes her hands in her apron as if to remove some contamination.

"That was for the baby frogs," she says. Tulok gets up and steadies himself. Mother kicks him in the crotch that only a minute ago Tulok had been offering with that obscene gesture.

"And that was for my son," she says as she watches Tulok fold over. She takes my hand with a grip so strong it almost hurts, turns, and leads me home.

"I'm proud of you," she says, without explaining why. She closes the gate. I stand with tears trickling down my face and imagine myself doing to Tulok and Bika what Mother has just done.

I was surprised to see Mother, whom I have always thought of as warm and tender, act with such fierce violence in defence of the frogs and her son. I will understand only later—when I find out that she rowed, played tennis, was on her school's gymnastic team, besides being a member of the *Sokol*, a youth movement dedicated to self-improvement, founded in the old Czechoslovakia and adopted by many Slavic countries.

"Everything's OK with your health?" Krizsik asked. His mouth was smiling but his eyes were not. They issued flickers of malignant intensity from under his sloped forehead. He looked up, squinting in ice-cold appraisal, scanning for signs that would reveal my mental state. With his pen, he pointed at the chair in front of me, indicating that I should sit down. I ignored it. I threw my head back and contemplated the white ceiling. "I mean the surgery," he said in a malicious tone. I continued to study the ceiling.

I remembered the words of Tabody and Mateos. Their advice had been, "Be as passive as possible. Don't let him engage you. Krizsik is a vulture.

He circles and hovers and lands only when he sees you are ready to be picked apart."

"He's in no hurry." warned Tabody. "You are young and would be a precious asset with the promise of a rich harvest. A prized stool pigeon with a longer shelf life than us old farts, far beyond our usefulness. Ignore his jabs. He will tease, he will provoke; and if you engage him, he will chew you into pieces."

I didn't know where Krizsik wanted to lead me by asking about my health. I kept my eyes on the ceiling, inspecting it square foot by square foot, as if I was looking for cracks in the plaster. I could not have been more passive and less engaging than that. He began to tap the desktop with his pen.

"Your neck has been repaired, I heard …"

"Yeah," I muttered. Found a small crack above the window and watched it as if I was expecting something to crawl out of it.

"I don't see anybody up there," I heard Krizsik say. "Who are you talking to?"

"To you, I guess."

"Look at me then!"

I glanced at him briefly. The thin, caterpillar moustache above his lip began to twitch. I moved my eyes back to the ceiling and continued mapping it. Without wanting to, I must have unnerved him, because all of a sudden, he dropped the pen and banged his fist on the desk so hard that the pen and ashtray jumped in the air.

"When I ask questions," he seethed, "I want normal answers."

To this day, I do not know what got into me. I looked him in the eye and said, "I don't have time for chit-chat." His jaws slackened with astonishment. He sprang from his chair, as if he had been bitten by a scorpion. I was surprised and at the same time satisfied that I had gotten under his skin. I worked hard to suppress a smug smile and remain poker-faced.

"Chit-chat?!" he yelled with such force that the words exploded, one after the other, and pulsed in the air before they reverberated throughout the room. The skin of his neck and his face was suffused with dark purple-red. He wiped his mouth with the back of his hand. I was about to duck, but he lowered his hands onto the desktop and leaned on them with arms extended and locked out in such rigid immobility that I expected them to snap. The potbelly protruding above his belt heaved like a separate animal.

"You say 'chit-chat?'" he asked with irascible astonishment. Sweat broke from the pores of his face, still purple-red. He peeled its beads off with a jerky wipe of his curled forefinger, then began to walk around the desk toward me. I noticed he had a limp. He stopped right in front of me, as if to make sure I could see nothing but him.

"The Commander," I explained, "came to the Translation Office with someone from the Central Committee. I was given a book to translate." Krizsik stepped back and knit his eyebrows together. He appeared perturbed. "I must translate it as fast as possible," I added.

Krizsik picked up the cigarette holder from his desk, opened it, and slowly extracted a cigarette. Cigarette in mouth, he reached for his lighter, then lit the cigarette and drew on it with eyes half closed. He stepped to the window—I was able to confirm that he walked with a limp of the right leg—where he stood, studying the floor as though carefully thinking something through, processing information before commenting on it.

"That's what I mean when I say I have no time for chit-chat," I elaborated dryly, taking advantage of his lapse. "I would rather do some serious work than talk about my health."

Krizsik looked at me—or rather, looked through me—with his eyebrows still knit tight together. My casual mention of the Commander and the Central Committee was a blasphemy in itself. For a political operative in charge of undermining the minds of prisoners, it was as though an atheist had joked to a priest about taking a walk with the Creator. At the same time, he knew for a fact that I worked in the Translation Office. He must have known that I was translating an important book. But he hadn't expected that I would use that as an excuse for some intolerable insolence. Still baffled, he stepped back to his desk, plucked the cigarette from his mouth, and spoke slowly, almost absently, cutting the sentence up and announcing each word with grave import.

"Then. Go. Back. To. Your. Work." He picked up the phone. He spoke a few words in a low, almost defeated voice. By the time he put the receiver back onto the cradle, Apeman was already at the door. With eyes begging for illumination, he turned his flat, illiterate face at Krizsik, sensing that something had not gone quite well between the political officer and me, but unable to discern what. When Krizsik said, "Take him back," Apeman saluted stiffly with a loud "Yes, Comrade Captain." He watched me walk to the door with suspicious side glance, and I had a lurking feeling that, sooner or later, he would take revenge on me for upsetting his boss. My relationship with Apeman never improved after this incident.

The entire office was astonished to see me back so soon. They looked at me as if I was an apparition. Tabody and Matheos rose in unison and came to my desk.

"What happened?" Matheos asked. "Ten minutes and you are back?"

"Krizsik is fucked." I announced bravely and regaled them with what had transpired, injecting the encounter with more drama than it had actually had.

"Fuck it, fuck it, I can't believe it!" Matheos laughed and slapped his thighs.

"He will check himself into the *dilihaz*," I said with a laugh. "For some sedation and a sponge bath."

Tabody shook his head. He raised his hand and pressed it against the dome of his high, wide forehead. "He will make you pay," he said gravely and gazed out the open window. It was spring and the world visible beyond the bars was waking. Swallows cut through the sky, and doves carried twigs in their beaks. "Don't be in too much of a hurry translating this," he said, laying his hand on *Between Two Ages*.

Geresdy got up from his chair. He had been watching the three of us from behind his typewriter. He walked to the window and made a production out of inhaling the fresh air as if it was the sole reason for his presence. "Then Krizsik asked me about my neck," I said. Tabody winked at me.

"How compassionate!" Matheos grinned and walked away, conversing earnestly with himself.

Still waiting to board my connecting flight, I close my eyes and let my mind drift. I fold the letter I've been reading, walk to my carry-on and briefcase, and pull out another.

September 20, 1969

Dear Mother,

Thank you for your letter. I'm glad you like your new place. You must have already informed the prison authorities. I will still remind them to send my letters to your new address.

I'm glad you liked The Caine Mutiny. *I went back to the classics.* The Grapes of Wrath *and* Of Mice and Men *by John Steinbeck. I like them both better than* East of Eden, *which is not to say that I don't think highly of it. But after* The Grapes of Wrath *and* Of Mice and Men, *it seems too monumental, too intricate and perhaps a bit contrived.*

I can't get over Steinbeck's ability to describe a person, a character. Just like I could see, hear and smell the sights, sounds and the fragrance of the Salinas Valley when I read East of Eden, *I felt I knew Tom Joad, Ma and Pa Joad or George and Lennie, that mean little Curley, Candy the old ranch hand and Crooks, as I was reading* The Grapes of Wrath *and* Of Mice and Men.

I also read three short novels by Albert Camus: The Stranger, The Plague, *and* The Fall.

I think Meursault, the main character in The Stranger, *was a psychopath: no compassion, no empathy, no conscience. I found* The

Plague *a very serious novel of the human condition which is as absurd as it is in Kafka's* Trial. The Plague, *at least, left me with the impression that there is more to appreciate than to despise about humans.*

I must tell you that I failed to understand The Fall. *I found the series of monologues perplexing. When I talked to the fellow prisoner who recommended it, he made a serious effort to explain the history and philosophy behind the setting of the novel which left me with serious doubts about my education and my ability to comprehend philosophical issues. I must learn more and must say goodbye.*

Love You,

Mityu

I think of Camus, I think of Sartre. I liked Camus right from the first page of *The Stranger*. I thought I would like Sartre as well, and Simone de Beauvoir, but was disappointed to find them to be among those Marxist intellectuals whose minds were irrevocably organized around junky, old doctrines that made intellectuals out of them. They clung to their beloved ideology even after the horrors of Stalinism had been exposed, after they had learned about the Gulags, and even after the events in Budapest and Prague. Their mental inclination seemed immune to reason and facts. Or, given Sartre's shrewdness and his tendency to plot with Simone de Beauvoir, they were super-speculative. In their estimation, liberal democracy was either on its way to total decomposition or collapse in the face of a brutal attack on its principles and institutions, and they wanted to be advantageously positioned when it happened.

It is a bright summer day, and the river is flowing under the hot sun like molten brass. We climb out of the water and look for flat stones for skipping, my brother and I. Each time we find a good one to throw, we count how many times it jumps, planing over the surface of the water. After a while Andrew gets tired of it and, squatting on his heels, draws silly symbols in the sand with his finger. Further up the bank, Mother is gathering wildflowers. She always does that when we go to the river. She takes them home in a large basket on the front of her bicycle and makes a dozen bouquets, which she hangs upside down to dry under the eaves of the verandah.

It is quiet, except for the lapping of the water and the cheerful hum of bees buzzing from one flower to another. A tight little flotilla of geese appears from under the willows at the bend and moves down the river like a small raft, talking among themselves as they float close to the bank. The one in the lead, whose long neck ends in a white chin strap, seems larger than the rest. When I move, it honks and warns the rest.

Vicious intent comes over me. I tumble the gleaming, striated pebbles from my throwing hand into the other and pick up a big, shiny, wet stone from the sand. My fingers arrange themselves around the flat body; I throw it, and it skips in the direction of the birds. The leader honks again. My stone falls into the water somewhat short of the geese, who begin to break formation, veering away from the bank and treading water. I find another large stone and am about to throw it when they start to lift off.

"Stop it right now!" I turn to see Mother standing on the bank with her arm full of milkweed, thistle, and cattails. "Leave them alone," she says with a shake of her head. I drop the large, flat stone on the sand where my shadow huddles between my feet and toe the sand around it with anger. I watch the geese thrashing the water with their wings. They struggle for a while, then rise above the river. I kick the stone and hurt my toe. I hiss. I am mad at Mother.

They call for boarding. I grab my briefcase and carry-on, and join the passengers surging toward the counter where two attendants check our travel documents. On the plane, I find my seat, put my bag in the overhead compartment, sit down, and open my notebook. I should write down my memories before they melt away. I open another letter instead.

December 20, 1969

Dear Mother,

I hope my eyes will endure all the reading. If they do, by the time I get out of here, I will have read most of the good books in the library.

I just finished reading two novels. Erich Maria Remarque's All Quiet on the Western Front *and Graham Greene's* The Power and the Glory.

Remarque's description of war and the suffering it brings upon people is beyond anything that I have read or seen in movies. It felt like being in the trenches with those young boy-soldiers who died terrible deaths and listening to those who survived but whose lives were destroyed forever. But I do not think you should read it. You went through the horrors of war during the siege of Budapest.

If you have not, you should read Graham Greene's The Power and the Glory. *I wish I could give you an account, a review of this novel. However, it is just too much and too powerful for me to write more about it than that it takes place in Mexico, the country that I would avoid after reading about it. The novel has the mood of Hemingway's* For Whom the Bell Tolls. *The creation of the character of the mule-riding whisky priest alone is enough to make the book great literature. I started reading it Sunday morning and read it until the light went out in the evening.*

If you have happened upon more good books lately, please let me know and if they are available from the library, I will read them.

Hope You and Judith are well.

Love You,

Mityu

By chance and circumstance, the books I translated had become a firewall between me and Krizsik. By the fall of 1971, I had already finished *Between Two Ages* and was "busy" translating articles from *The Statesman*, *The Economist*, and *Foreign Affairs*.

One morning, Commander Klucso and the same civilian as before marched into the Translation Office. Geresdy jumped up as usual and looked at them beseechingly, like a dog. The civilian handed him a book. There was a brief exchange of words I could not hear, but I saw that the conversation was accompanied first by impatient gestures, then by dismissive ones. After they had left, Geresdy stood by his desk in the corner and stared at us helplessly.

Counter-clockwise from where he stood by his desk in the corner were Cserbakoi, Varga (aka Mahorka), Gabi, Uncle Andy, Tabody, Matheos, and I. With Akos in the *dilihaz* and Földes released after serving his lengthy sentence—for reporting human rights abuses in Hungary to the United Nations Commission on Human Rights in Geneva—our number had been reduced from ten to eight, with no future supply of prisoners in the pipeline.

Outside the prison, goulash communism had reached its zenith. The state had relinquished its absolute control over the economy, and everyone became busy taking advantage of the new opportunities. When the Party declared that "those not against us are with us," and directed its cadres to display a more laissez-faire, live-and-let-live attitude, even the diehards found little reason to protest against the regime. In the state-controlled newspapers, self-deprecating articles appeared, and the authorities not only let twist, rock and roll, and soul music be played on the radio but also allowed homegrown rock and roll bands to perform in soccer stadiums. Long hair and blue jeans ceased to be symbols of opposition.

The Political Police, with little else to do in this thaw, renewed their hunt for war criminals—mostly uneducated peasants who had served in Horthy's army as low-ranking soldiers, or proles with long-expired memberships in the bottom ranks of the Arrow Cross. Without any skills or education, they ended up in the shop where prisoners refurbished old army boots. The boots were trucked out to the prisons of the Hungarian Gulag.

Because the literati or intelligentsia had more government-infused goulash than blood in their veins, the Translation Office appeared to be condemned to a slow death. That was my diagnosis at the time (which proved to be wrong).

"Who wants to translate this book?" Geresdy asked. He tried to read the title, but gave up. "Someone in the Politburo wants to read it in a hurry."

Gabi stood up, walked over to Geresdy, took the book, and glanced at the title. "Count me out," he said. "I hate French."

I had been out of touch with the language for three years—and my French had not been great to begin with. I had learned basic grammar and vocabulary in the gymnasium, and I had battled my way through the obligatory classics as far as Montesquieu at university. Though I liked the language, I thoroughly disliked the professors who, unlike the ones in the English Department, were stiff, formal, and terribly pretentious. "Let me see," I said. Geresdy came to my desk.

"Here," he said, handing it to me. The title was *Ils Ont Tué Ma Foi*. To my surprise, I saw that the author was Hungarian, but I didn't have a clue who Georges Aranyossy was. I was happy with translating articles from *Foreign Affairs*—my English was good enough that I could produce the mandatory ten pages a day in less than three or four hours. With no books to be urgently translated, I spent the rest of my time reading or talking with Tabody, Matheos, and Gabi. I was not looking forward to difficult work, but I was curious about the author. I wanted to know who he was and what he could have written that had made the Politburo so interested. I didn't mind getting a bit ahead in my French either. I decided to let the magazines lapse and improve my French on the job. "I'll do it."

I had another reason, perhaps more important than satisfying my curiosity and upgrading my French. The time I was going to spend translating the book would extend my immunity to Krizsik's evil schemes. I hoped it would continue providing me with the protection that I didn't have when translating a few articles from *The Economist* or *The Statesman*. (That was the second prediction of mine that proved to be wrong.)

According to the introduction, Aranyossy had been a lifetime communist cadre who had risen in the ranks until he became a member of the Central Committee, the board of directors in the great enterprise of the dictatorship of the proletariat. But, having seen right in the kitchen how the communist soup was concocted, he lost his appetite for the feast. He became disillusioned when the Prague Spring was crushed by Russian tanks in 1968. He claimed he had had doubts during the Stalinist purges and show trials, but that his faith in communism prevailed and he toed the party line. Despite the fact that it was fought by workers and students, he accepted and believed the official version that the revolution of 1956 had been a *counter-revolution* incited by Western powers and staged by the enemies of the working class.

I found it unbelievable that an intelligent person, high in the echelons of the Communist Party, would claim that he had been ignorant of the barbaric cruelty of the ÁVO, the indiscriminate persecutions, and the farcical trials. That he didn't know that the crowd of one hundred thousand demonstrators who assembled in front of the buildings of the Parliament had been peaceful. That he could seriously believe the lie that the students and workers protesting against the abuses of a dictatorial regime and demanding free elections had been *agents of imperialist powers*—when in fact, all they had wanted at that first popular rally was that the government composed of dyed-in-the-wool Stalinists be replaced by more liberal communists.

But the old guard's distrust of any manifestation of liberty was innate—they could not have gotten rid of it even if they had wanted to. They not only denounced the demonstration, they ordered its immediate dispersion. When the crowd refused to move, ÁVO units hidden on the rooftops opened fire with machine guns. With that, all hope for a negotiated transition from hard-core communist dictatorship to socialism with heart and soul disappeared. What had started as a peaceful demonstration turned into a popular uprising. Members of the dreaded ÁVO shed their grey uniforms and went into hiding.

Because they could not rely on the Hungarian army, the hard-liners of the Communist Party called the Kremlin, who had installed them in the first place, for help—which came. The Russians intervened and the fight began. It was an unequal struggle: factory workers and students, some of them mere teenagers, faced the invading armoured columns. They had small arms and Molotov cocktails; the Russian had tanks and machine guns.

It seemed to me that Aranyossy had to be willfully blind to history in order to claim ignorance about the massacre at the Parliament, which was followed by the bloodiest suppression of any rebellion against the Stalinist yoke in Eastern Europe. In Budapest alone, several thousand died fighting the Russians. They were defeated within a few weeks, and János Kádár—who had betrayed the revolutionary government he had been part of only a few days earlier—and his makeshift cabinet entered the grounds of the Parliament in Russian tanks.

Didn't he know that Nagy Imre, who was a communist, and members of his government were executed together with hundreds of others? That tens of thousands were imprisoned and two percent of the entire population of Hungary became refugees? That the ÁVO was reorganized as the Workers' Guard. I had known about all this when I was in high school and found it beyond belief that an active, high-ranking member of the Party didn't. For me, he was not much different from those who pretended they didn't see and didn't know that their countrymen, because they were Jewish, were being deported and murdered by the Nazis.

My revenge against Aranyossy's claim of ignorance was that, by stretching the meaning of every French word and sentence, I made the Hungarian version more hard-hitting than he ever intended. His "disapprobation" of the party's strong-arm tactics against the nascent demands for human rights became a "condemnation" of the oppression of the people's desire for basic human liberties. His "incertitude" about the integrity of his ex-colleagues in the Central Committee was cranked up to his "conviction" that most of them were dishonest and corrupt. The "incapacity" of the communist leaders to recognize the obvious shortcomings of the regime transmuted into their stubborn refusal to admit the fact that it was bankrupt. His "dislike" became "disdain," his "aversion" became "detestation," someone lacking a broad-minded attitude was turned into a "bigot," and when he talked about the one-sided approach of party members, I made them "dogmatic morons." Each time I managed to increase the heat of his belated criticism of the regime he had once served faithfully until his defection, I imagined his ex-bosses in the Politburo cringing as they read it.

By the early seventies, some liberal-minded members of the party who wanted to remain communists even after the brutal repression of the Prague Spring decided that even the more benevolent ways of goulash communism were too harsh. They also refused to submit themselves to the periodic lobotomy required to toe the party line and accept the doctrines emanating from the Kremlin. Mother, at one of her biannual visits, took advantage of the inattention of the guard and told me about the Budapest School. In Budapest, a group of communist professors started a movement that openly criticized several party dogmas. They went so far as to declare that the suppression of the Prague Spring—*socialism with a human face*—had been a mistake. What Mother didn't know at the time was that this movement was not going to last. Following an *ukaz* from Moscow, its members were soon to be expelled from the Party and fired from their jobs, and some of them were even going to be arrested and prosecuted like the ones who had dared to demonstrate on the anniversary of the March 15 Revolution. Although goulash communism was still on the menu the government offered the people, it was soon to be diluted and the meat in it would all but disappear. Under strict directions from Moscow and with the full approval of the hard-liners of the Hungarian Communist Party, the hunt for *counter-revolutionaries* (meaning people showing sympathy for the events of 1956 and 1968), *cosmopolitans* (meaning Jews), and *revisionists* (meaning reform communists), and everyone who resented living under the hobnailed boots of the Russian Army resumed. All human activity had to be performed in service of the purest ideals of Marx and Lenin. And in case people entertained funny ideas about exactly what that meant, the propaganda apparatus drove it home to the masses with renewed brainwashing, with all the former Stalinist intensity. It was left to the Political Police to pick up those who were slow to turn their thinking back to the dogmas of the fifties.

In practical terms, this meant that workers did not labour to provide for their families but to fulfil their duty and obligation to satisfy the quotas set by the Planning Committee and to drive, with each hammer blow, a nail into the coffin of capitalism. Arts and science were not to be for some useless intellectual inquiry or curiosity. The duty of artists and intellectuals was to promote the party line by raising the consciousness of the people and to steer their mindset in the right direction. If there was any questioning, it was to be done by those in power, who not only demanded, but constantly cast doubt on, the absolute loyalty, dedication, and sincerity of devotion of intellectuals. The duty of scientists was nothing less than, by inventing and developing new technologies, to prove that the socialist way of production was superior to that of capitalism. Which meant that individuals, after enjoying a short-lived period of supervised play in the sandbox of goulash capitalism, were reduced again to mere pawns on the great chessboard of an ideological battle in which the two opposing camps, each claiming to possess the true vision of how societies should function, fought against each other with propaganda and violence.

What Mother did not tell me—she did not want to make me feel bad—was that soon after my arrest, the police had come to her house and taken her passport. When she wanted to visit Grandmother in Yugoslavia, they refused to give it back. Grandmother was very ill. Mother begged the police chief to let her go to be with her mother, all to no avail. When Grandmother passed away, again, Mother went to see the chief of the local police and asked him to return her passport so that she could go for the funeral. She was told that her "crime" was to have raised a son like me and the punishment for it was being "grounded." "Be glad that you have not been fired from your job," the chief said. Mother went to his boss in Szeged. Finally, she was granted a temporary passport on the condition that my sister not accompany her.

I was halfway through translating *Ils Ont Tué Ma Foi* when, one summer morning, a new addition arrived at the Translation Office. Joseph was a high school kid who had pinched a dozen red flags from the Liberty Bridge and thrown them into the Danube. He turned eighteen while in custody, so he was sentenced as an adult. His arrest and imprisonment was another sign that the party had hardened its line on all manifestations of dissent and resumed its commitment to forge the malleable masses into the *socialist type of men*. Those who resented this historic thrust and refused to morph from person to type were to be weeded out.

Cut off from the outside world for more than three years, I hung on Joseph's every word. Even more than politics, I was interested in the new rock and roll bands, like Led Zeppelin and Blood, Sweat & Tears. He talked about Jimi Hendrix. His solo guitar in "Voodoo Child" and "Hey Joe." He tried to teach me the tunes of "Whole Lotta Love" and "You Make Me So Very Happy." Between translating pages from *Ils Ont Tué Ma Foi*, we hummed "S t a a a a a i r w a i i i i way to Heaven," standing by the window, staring out into the prison yard. But, in a few weeks, we were deep into plotting against the regime and, in case that didn't work out, planning our escape from Hungary.

The paranoid security apparatus, fearing that an aging and totally infiltrated prison population might be the source of a nationwide conspiracy, wanted to make certain that channels of information between prisoners and the outside were severed. Letters between the inmates and their authorized contacts were censored and limited in both length and content. The brief visits were supervised, and any talk about politics and current news was even more strictly banned. The issues of the prison newspaper, which we called *My Ass and its Environs*, was totally devoid of any real or current news. Besides running the usual stories of reformed enemies of the working class and *mea culpas* from those whose souls were not yet saved but were well under repair, it announced in July that the winter was over and in December that the summer harvest was done. There was a loudspeaker in each cell. Government propaganda and brainwashing filled the air, alternating with exhortations to observe the prison rules and to respect and obey the schmassers.

I was lucky to be able to read *Foreign Affairs*, *The Economist*, and *The Statesman*. They gave me insight into global affairs, but Hungary and Hungarian society were not among the issues they dealt with. I knew less about current Hungarian affairs than about Sino-Soviet rivalry, the Middle East or the nascent European Union.

Cut off from outside news and having socialist propaganda administered daily into each prison cell, like IV drops into a vein, prisoners would have lived in a world of idle gossip born out of idle wits, had it not been for a few tiny radios in circulation. These were made in the special shops of the so-called Smaller Jail, where prisoners skilled in electronics made all kinds of gadgets—from listening devices to coding and decoding equipment—for members of state security. When the schmassers supervising them weren't looking, they also built radios that were as small as an earplug. If you attached their antenna, which was a thin, insulated wire, to the metal frame of your bunk bed, you could listen to Radio Budapest. Allowing inmates to circumvent the ban on news with these self-made receivers was perceived by prison authorities to be a security risk. The possession of a miniature radio was punishable with twenty days in the dark cell. Informants were to report anyone who managed to obtain and own one.

Like all prisoners, I received a small "salary" for my work at the Translation Office which was credited to my "account." It was barely enough to purchase a piece of soap, a tube of toothpaste, a toothbrush, and twenty packs of *Munkas* (Worker)—the cheapest brand of cigarette, made of the harshest, most barbaric tobacco grown on the planet. Ninety percent of the prisoners were heavy smokers. The twenty packs they were allowed to purchase were never enough to satisfy their appetite for nicotine. This imbalance of supply and demand made the *Munkas* the standard unit of exchange in the primitive barter system that allowed me, after the release of Földes, to persuade the prisoner in charge of book distribution from the library to give me the works of Twain, Hemingway, and Zola instead of those by Marx, Engels, Lenin, and Mayakovsy and other representatives of the Hungarian and Soviet propaganda literature of *socialist realism,* stocked in great abundance in the prison library. If I slipped a pack of *Munkas* to the prisoner in charge of clothing, I got a pair of pants with legs reaching to my ankles instead my knees. If Mengele refused to prescribe vitamin C for scurvy, I could get it from prisoners working at the hospital. If I wanted the dental technician, a prisoner himself, to freeze my mouth before pulling a tooth instead of offering me two tennis balls to squeeze if the pain was too much, five packs did the trick.

With the help of Tabody and twenty packs of *Munkas*, I became the owner of a receiver. On the first night, after the schmassers had turned off the lights, I pulled it out from under the corner of my straw mattress. With the help of a band-aid, I secured the end of the wire that came with the radio to the heating pipe that ran under my bed. I plugged the tiny unit, about half an inch in diameter, in my ear. I heard a few faint, spooky crackles. Marconi could not have been more excited as he stood on Signal Hill in Newfoundland, waiting to see if his radio waves could make it all the way across the Atlantic to England. I pressed my finger onto the band-aid to make sure that there was contact between the stripped end of the wire and the heating pipe. The voice of the announcer came through the static. It was Radio Kossuth, Budapest. Even if what he said was of no consequence, my heart beat faster with each word that came from the outside world. Then came the news, censored and spiced with the usual comments reflecting the party line, but at least it was current.

It became my habit to listen every night—making sure that I removed the device before I fell asleep. One great benefit of this set-up was that I could also listen to music other than the traditional workers' movement songs that blared from the speakers at the beginning and end of each prison propaganda session. I could hardly believe my luck when, one evening after the news, they broadcast Arthur Rubinstein playing the Beethoven piano concerto that, after Bach's *Goldberg Variations*, was Mother's and my second-favourite piece of classical music.

I gaze out at the wing of the plane that will soon put an ocean between Mother and me, and open another letter. Looking down at my handwriting, I remember a spring afternoon. The lilacs were in full bloom. On my way home from school, I saw Mother walking a few blocks ahead of me after her shift at the post office. I began to run and caught up with her just as she was opening the door. Once inside, she opened her bag and pulled out a set of old records that Grandmother had sent from Yugoslavia. "Once," she said, holding up a recording of Beethoven's Fourth Piano Concerto, "I wanted to play this, to prove that a woman could play it as well as a man."

We put the record on the cheap East German gramophone. As I listened to the opening chords, I couldn't understand why such simple chords in the tonic key would be a challenge for a woman—or for anyone—to play. It was only when the rhythm accelerated and became restless with energy that I recognized the sheer masculine force of the music, so physical that not even the great Annie Fischer felt herself strong enough to play it. In my mind's eye, I saw Beethoven, crazy with passion, breaking strings faster than his assistants could replace them.

June 19, 1970

Dear Mother,

Thank you for your letter, and thank you for recommending Thornton Wilder. The Bridge of San Luis Rey *was a great read. It would be nice to believe that the beginning and the end of a person and everything in between is somehow a part of a greater blueprint, a master plan, but I can't. In my opinion, there is no cosmic answer to what and why a certain, rather than a different, thing happens to us at a given time as opposed to another time. Wilder makes a good case, but I am inclined to think otherwise.*

I just finished reading Robert Musil's short stories entitled after one of his novellas, The Confusions of Young Törless. *It reminded me of William Golding's* Lord of the Flies. *I wonder if Golding was inspired by Musil.*

I look forward to reading his The Man without Qualities, *not available here. When Thomas Mann was asked to name the best novel of the century, he cited Musil's without hesitation, ahead of Proust and Joyce. I found out that all his works were banned as "degenerate" in Germany and in Austria under the Nazis, who demanded that the mind, instead of playing with thoughts, should join with others and create large columns to goose-step in a straight line to the drumbeat of slogans and rejoice in the impersonality of subscribing en masse to the master ideology.*

There is not much else to write about. I'm fine and hope you are not worried about me. Besides doing my work, which I like, I read a lot, exercise and feel great.

I Love You.

Mityu

One morning, before we were escorted to the Translation Office, I pushed my finger into my half loaf of bread (that was the allotment we were allowed to take to work with us) and sank my radio into it. After a bit of touch-up work, the crust where I had drilled my finger into the bread showed no more than a small, hardly visible crack. "How does it work for you?" Tabody asked when we arrived at the Translation Office.

"Fantastic!" Although Radio Budapest didn't play Jimi Hendrix or Led Zeppelin, the classical music I listened to each night after the evening news was an addition to the books and good friends, like Tabody and Joseph, that took the edge off the grindstone of prison life.

Taking the radio to work became a daily routine. Once in the Translation Office, when Geresdy and Gabi were not looking, I would remove the radio from my bread and put it in my pocket. I timed my visits to the washroom to the top of each hour. There, I would attach the antenna to the water pipe with a piece of half-chewed, sticky bread and sit on the toilet with the radio plugged in my ear. In case of a sudden *hippish* (frisking), I could flush the radio down before the schmasser could get to me. At noon, Tabody, Matheos, and Joseph would gather at my desk for lunch and my daily press release. Not for long.

Our noontime conferences must have drawn the attention of the resident informants, Geresdy, Mahorka, and Gabi. They could not have failed to notice that something fishy was going on. Gabi was a great actor and a smart operator. He was serving a life sentence, which meant fifteen years with no chance of parole for good behaviour. He said he had been convicted for spying for the Americans, and he certainly talked and acted as if he was the resident CIA agent. He entertained us with all kinds of scenarios for Hungary and the world, all of which ended with nothing less than the fall of communism. He was so convincing that he managed to con even some of the older prisoners into believing that he had a visceral hatred of Krizsik. As it was discovered after the fall of the regime, which event he must have dreaded, he was not only one of Krizsik's most valued informants, but an *agent provocateur* as well.

His tactic to discover what we were up to was one of feigned nonchalance. "Hey," he would say, stopping by my desk in a casual manner, as if a spontaneous thought had occurred to him. When I stopped my press release, he would say, "Keep going, I just want your opinion about a sentence I'm trying to translate."

I would say something like "Let's finish your sentence then. It's only my usual lunchtime tirade." Then Gabi would invent a problem and after dispensing advice on grammar, I would continue with the events of the day. With each reconnaissance mission, Gabi managed to catch a word or two and must have become more and more certain what our lunchtime conferences were about.

Geresdy was a *besugo* of lesser calibre and did not possess half of Gabi's inventiveness and outgoing personality. He would just study us from his perch in the corner, straining his ears—funnel-like mushrooms growing out of his head and moving like motorized antennae to catch every word spoken.

I had long paid off the twenty packets of *Munkas* when one morning, instead of one, four schmassers came to escort us from our cells to the Translation Office. One of them was the usual cranky old Cuccos with his dull, sallow face and its finely weaved web of wrinkles scrawled all over it that gave his complexion the appearance of a cocoon. During my time in the Gyűjtő, I had learned that Cuccos had earned his nickname, which meant "stuff," because of his habit of stealing the prisoners' cigarettes from their cells while they worked. That morning, he stood puffy-eyed before us (probably from too much brandy the night before), holding a small piece of paper.

The other three schmassers with Cuccos were Apeman and two young goons I had never seen before, most likely freshly recruited staff on an apprentice course. Their eyes moved between Apeman and us, and whatever Apeman did, they copied. When Apeman stood with his legs apart and thumbs stuck in his belt right behind the buckle, so did they. When Apeman shifted his weight from one foot to the other, they did the same. The scene reminded me of Tulok, my childhood bully, and his bum boys.

Cuccos regarded me with a long, sad expression, as if I was a son who had disappointed him. "XA 53 84," he read from the paper, adding, "Stand aside."

In my early days in prison, I would have asked him why. But now, almost halfway through my sentence, I had become used to strange things that happened unexplained and kept quiet. Cuccos glanced at Apemen and his underlings and made a helpless grimace, as if he wanted to disown the situation. Then he turned to Geresdy, and with Geresdy leading and Cuccos closing the rear, the translation group started to move in the direction of the stairs. As he walked past me, Tabody stopped. "Take it easy kid," he said.

"Move on!" barked Apeman.

"Fuck off, Apeman," said the hussar priest. He stopped at the landing and gave me the thumbs-up and a glance that was encouraging and restraining at the same time.

I was certain that something bad was going to happen, but I didn't know what. Apeman nodded to the goons, who marched into my cell. "Your bag," he demanded. I gave him my side bag. From the noises filtering through the door I knew that the *hippish* had begun inside the cell.

Apeman held my side bag for a moment. "Where is it?" he asked.

I stared at him blankly.

"You know very well what," he growled. He considered me for a while, deep furrows in his forehead, as if he had to dig up words buried in the dark cleft of his memory; words he once knew but had long forgotten.

"The receiver," he stuttered.

I shook my head. "I don't have a clue what the fuck you are talking about."

"The radio!" he said. "And watch your goddamn mouth."

"Radio?" I repeated after him, as if wanting to make certain we were talking about the same thing. "That one?" I jerked my head in the direction of the speaker of the prison radio mounted above the cell door. "The Red Parrot?"

"How dare you?" he snapped. "Watch your mouth!" His eyes bore into mine, telegraphing that he would prevail, no matter what. I glared back just as hard, sending him the message that I would not submit—not ever.

He tore my bag open and turned it upside down. My half loaf of bread, my dictionary, my pens, a pot and a spoon; they all fell on the floor. The pot started to roll. Apeman blocked it with his boot. He shook the bag hard and turned it inside out. He felt every square inch of it with his fingers, then held it open right side up.

"Pick up your shit. One by one. Start with the bread." He gave it a kick and, with a contemptuous air, watched it roll on the floor. "Got a little dust on it. Adds to the taste," he cracked.

"Fuck off, asshole," I said. "You eat it."

"You refuse to obey my orders?" His voice was shrill, bordering on the hysterical. "You fucking deaf? Not just stupid?"

Apeman dropped my bag, stuck his thumbs into his belt and towered above me in furious immobility. The veins of his necks bulged and throbbed. Our duel had become serious, and shots would soon be fired. He fixed me with a hard gaze to elicit my quick retreat, and when it didn't happen, he slowly removed his thumbs from his belt, squatted, and picked up the bread. He frowned at the half loaf, turned it over, and threw it into the bag. I slowly let out the breath I was holding. He leafed through the dictionary, shook it, and inspected its spine. Stuffed it into the bag and went for the pen, for the pot and spoon. He shoved the bag against the wall and stood up.

"Strip," he said. "Boots first."

I wanted to tell him he could take my boots off if he wanted but, thinking of my bread with the radio in it, kicked off my boots and unwound my foot cloths. He gazed at them for a while as if he had expected them to levitate up into his hands. When neither the boots nor I moved, he bent over and picked them up. He shook them, probed their insides with his hand, and threw them aside.

"Your shirt." I pulled my shirt off and handed it to him. He shook it and fingered it thoroughly.

"Get out of your pants." I dropped my pants, stepped out of them, and left them on the floor. He stood dumbly until he realized that I was not going to hand them over, picked them up and went through the pockets, turned the legs inside out, and felt them along the seams. "Drop your shorts to your knees." He inspected my shorts.

"Bend over," he barked. I almost suggested he could take advantage of the opportunity and lick my ass but, again remembering my radio still snug in my half load of bread, bent over without a comment. I looked back and saw Apeman's gargoylish head looming above me as he examined me from behind with one eye closed, as if I was on the glass slide under his microscope.

"Get dressed." He looked at my stuff on the floor, inspecting the items one by one with his weasel eyes. One of his apprentices emerged from my cell, visibly frustrated. Then, with eager eyes, he looked at Apeman, hoping to glean some knowledge from his superior. Finally, as if he had achieved sudden enlightenment, his face lit up. "Why don't we make him tell?" he asked, looking at me as he brandished his baton. He was clearly taken by the beautiful simplicity of his suggestion. For a moment, Apeman just stood there, natural stupidity oozing from his eyes and seemingly at a loss as to what to do with his authority over his subordinate. Then he narrowed his eyes, shook his head, and gave him a surly look that sent the minion back into the cell. Apeman followed and closed the door. I heard him talking in an angry, strangled voice, but could not make out the words. Whatever they were, they were followed by an outburst of profanity, then a long silence.

I pulled up my shorts and stepped into my pants. I was buttoning up my shirt when Apeman reappeared. Through the open cell door, I could see the other two leaning over my bed. "They can *hippish* the cell forever," I thought when, with a slow, sly smile, Apeman went straight for my bag. He grabbed the bread, dropped the bag, and began tearing the half loaf into pieces. My radio was snug in the end, right under the crust, which I hoped would hold. But, with a tiny, sickening thud, the radio fell to the floor. A look of ugly satisfaction crept over Apeman's face. He picked up my treasure, sank it in his pocket, and yelled for his acolytes, now deep in my straw mattress.

The next time I saw my radio, it was displayed on the desk in the staff room where Klucso held his weekly disciplinary hearings. He pointed at my tiny source of news from the outside world and read the label attached to it. "Twenty days in the dark cell," he said. "Reduced meals for showing disrespect to prison personnel."

My neighbour arrives, a short, bulky, middle-aged man with a resigned, melancholic expression. He takes a book from his briefcase and puts it on his seat with the front cover down. It is a small paperback, could be no more than two hundred pages. "I should go back to my notebook," I say to myself, "and write down my memories. Write them down before the growing spaces of oblivion swallow up the last stretches of recollection."

March 20, 1971

Dear Mother,

Another three months have passed and I like this place more and more. I am not joking. Everything from my work, the people I meet and their stories, to the books I read—I cannot find words for the experience. I do not think my life would be complete without it.

Thank you for recommending The Forty Days of Musa Dagh *by Franz Werfel. I must confess that I did not know anything about the terrible things inflicted on the Armenians. My ignorance probably made reading the book a more shocking experience than it otherwise would have been because I was not prepared for it. What a century! Homo homini lupus.*

Then I read The Little Prince *by Antoine de Saint-Exupéry and it restored my faith. The Hungarian translation was excellent, but one day I would like to read the French original.*

I just started reading Marcel Proust's In Search of Lost Time *for the second time. I don't think I appreciated it at university—in fact, I found it boring. Now I cherish every sentence, every paragraph and every description. I think one has to reach a certain level of maturity to enjoy such a refined piece of literature. I would have never read Proust again as a free man—one has to be locked up to pick it up for the second time.*

I hope you are well. If you come upon more good books, let me know. I will always keep you updated about my readings.

Love You,

Mityu

We hit some turbulence and the plane shudders. The seatbelt lights begin to flash.

It is late fall. I wake up to the scent of toasted bread wafting through the kitchen door. The sun is up, and the bare branches of the cherry tree throw intricate patterns onto the wall. I jump into my clothes and run to Mother, who is busy flipping slices of bread on the stovetop. Andrew soon arrives. We take our seats at the table and watch Mother pour milk into the *cikoria* coffee steaming in our cups. We watch as she sinks a cube of sugar into each and stirs the brownish brew until the sound of the spoon tells us that the cube is no more.

"Wait for Father," she says when I lift my cup. She goes to the pantry and comes back with a jar of applesauce. She gathers the golden pieces of toast from the stovetop, spreads some butter and applesauce on each, and cuts them in half.

Father walks into the kitchen wearing his pyjamas. He dumps himself on his chair and digs his fingers into his hair, sending squalls of his nasty mood over the table with his eyes. He is broodier than I have ever seen him. His wordless disapproval of everything, his all-encompassing gloom pervade the kitchen and crawl into my stomach. The coffee and buttered toast lose their taste, the applesauce its sweetness.

(Later on, I will come to worry that I might have Father's nasty mood and his dark, murderous looks when I grow up, and I ask Mother if she thinks so. "What do you mean?"

"Like the way he looks—always black."

"Not a chance," Mother will answer, smiling and laughing off my concern. "How could you have black looks with your blue eyes?")

Thick shoulders hunched, Father glares with contempt at the buttered toast Mother has placed on his plate, as though finding fault with its shape or colour. He turns to me and gives me the same look. "What are you waiting for?" he demands.

I almost ask him what *he* is waiting for when Mother says, "For you, Stephen."

Father rolls his eyes and, in an exaggerated display of disgust, pushes the plate away. "Tea?" he grunts.

"Not a pinch left," says Mother. "Can't get tea anywhere. Here is the coffee and here is the sugar," she says, consoling. "Want some milk?"

Father glances at Mother as if she had proposed something outrageous. He pushes back his chair with such force that it falls, and he heads for the closet. He reaches into the chest pocket of his coat. Mother stands the chair back up. Father comes back with a flat bottle of rum and pours its contents into the cup of hot coffee.

We gulp down our breakfast as fast as we can to escape Father's smothering presence. We excuse ourselves from the table, slip out to the verandah to leave the task of taming the beast to Mother. We hang about close to the door and listen. I wish I could be part of the floral pattern on the wallpaper and see and hear it all. Except for the clatter of cups and plates in the dish bin, I hear nothing.

We are about to step inside to pick up our school bags when the door swings open. Glum, unshaven, taking a drag from the cigarette hanging from his lips, Father appears. His windbreaker is open, and he stomps out so fast that the straps of his aviator hat stream behind his neck. He stops at the shed, pushes his motorcycle off its stand, spits the cigarette to the ground, smashes it with his boot, and is about to raise his foot to the motorcycle when the neighbour's rooster breaks out in a victorious cock-a-doodle-doo. "Shut up, rooster," Father groans. But the rooster repeats his morning song with such a crescendo that it fills the entire back yard. We try to hold back our laughter, but can't.

"You too!" barks Father, scowling. We duck behind the rickety rocking chair that Mother has bought at the market for one of her restoration projects. Knowing that Father's squalls of anger are often followed by a good beating, we huddle in silence. Inspired by the rooster, the neighbourhood dogs begin to bark. Father lets fly with an angry swear word and kick-starts the motorcycle. We stay squatting on our heels until the sound of his Csepel putters out.

We are about to stand up when Mother steps out. We must look scared, because she raises her hand to her mouth and shakes her head. "My God," she says. She gestures for us to stand up. Soon her expression changes, and she motions with her hand like a conductor inviting a choir to sing.

"Cock-a-doodle-doo, the rooster sang," and we sing cock-a-doodle-doo with her.

Perhaps all the dark cells were occupied or booked, for it took more than a month for Apeman to come to my cell with the necessary transfer form. He stood in the doorway and read out my sentence, halting like an illiterate between the syllables.

The punishment section was in another wing of the prison. Through a series of gates, Apeman led me to a large receiving room. He saluted the old sergeant who sat behind an ancient desk reading a paper, placed the transfer form on the desk, and stood waiting for his presence to be acknowledged. A minute or so passed in silence. Apeman cleared his throat. The sergeant glanced at us and dismissed Apeman with a slight nod of his head. Apeman hitched up his belt, saluted, and left. The sergeant folded his paper, reached for the transfer form, adjusted his glasses, and began to read.

"Radio," he murmured and shook his head without looking up. When he was finished, he slowly turned his head in my direction and cast a pair of sympathetic eyes at me. "Well," he said inspecting me more with pity than curiosity, "you will have to navigate these twenty days in the dark cell in radio silence." He opened a large tome, booked me, then pulled a sheet of paper from one of the file holders. "I will read you the rules," he said and in a gravelly voice rattled off the sentences, one after the other: "Respect and obey the staff. The light will be off in your cell at all times except for the ten minutes allowed for the meal. Knock on the door each time you need to go to the washroom ..."

He picked up the phone and spoke in a low voice. Before he could return the receiver to the cradle, a huge guard with the arms of an orangutan arrived. I wondered if he was Apeman's twin brother. He switched his baton from his right hand to his left and saluted the sergeant, who gave him a slip of paper and sent us off with a wave of his hand.

In an adjacent room, I was given a horse blanket and a new set of prison garb. No shoelaces in the boots, pocketless pants, and a short-sleeved shirt. Orangutan watched me change with the predacious curiosity of a sadist. Long arms dangling, he led me to my cell. "Be quiet," he barked in a hoarse, raspy voice. "Don't give us trouble." He unlocked the door, whose monstrous hinges creaked as he pushed it open with his boot. He flipped the light switch and pushed me inside.

Except for a wooden plank the place was bare: no window, no toilet, not a chair. The door was shut behind me and the light went off. It was so dark that an owl would not have been able to see the tip of its beak. Except for the jumble of images in my head, everything was pitch-black. I didn't trust my balance. With arms outstretched, I felt my way to the plank bed. Sitting on its edge, I pulled my legs to my chest, embraced them, rested my chin on my knees, and pondered the twenty days ahead me without light. It was so quiet in the dark that within a few minutes, I could hear my own heartbeat, the water flowing in the heating pipes, and the cockroaches crawling on the floor.

"To pass the time," I figured "and to prevent me from going nuts, I must occupy myself with whatever I can."

I started with mental exercises. In alphabetical order, I went through the past participle of every irregular English verb I could think of. Then came the plurals of such nouns as "cactus," "oasis," and "corpus." The young ones of animals like swan and sheep. When I got tired of the oddities of the English language, I began to recite Keats, Shelley, and Blake.

I got up and paced out the cell, drew my hand along the wall and calculated distances: the length and the width of the cell. Standing on the plank bed, I reached up and touched the ceiling. I made up my mind that I would exercise as much as my reduced diet would allow.

Each day, to keep track of the passage of days, right after my ten-minute march in the prison yard, I chewed a small piece of bread and rolled it into a tiny ball. I stuck it on the underside of my plank bed. When I was uncertain of how many days were ahead of me in the dark cell, I counted the balls.

I invented a game. I tore the top button off my shirt and threw it against the wall. For the first couple of times I went through the entire cell with my hands, acting like someone long deprived of most of his senses. My hearing improved in the dark, and soon I could follow the sound of the button from the moment it bounced against the wall. Tuned my ears to its faint clatter as it rolled on the concrete floor. After a few days, I was able to pick it up right where its journey ended. My hearing improved to the point that I could hear the schmassers walking along the row of cells, moving like cats in their soft-soled shoes. From the sound of their footsteps, I could time the very moment when they would draw the shutter from the keyhole to my cell. I put my hands up over my eyes before they could flip the light switch.

It was one of their sadistic games. They would guffaw when I was blinded by the light, which burned my eyes and sent a stabbing pain to my head—I'd swear and scream "Fucking pig!" Finally, I managed to turn their game around. I deduced from the various stealthy sounds exactly when the shutter would be drawn. When I knew that the schmasser's face was right against the peekhole and his finger ready to flick on the light, I would bang on the door as hard as I could. "You bastard!" the schmasser would roar and let out a torrent of stammering curses.

"Let me go to the washroom!" I'd roar back.

There were exactly eight days left of the twenty when I heard a schmasser's sneaky footsteps in the distance. I noticed that he did not stop to peek into each cell—he was coming straight to mine. He flipped the switch without the usual prelude of barely audible sounds, but I was still able to get my hands up in time to shield my eyes. I peeked out from between my fingers and surveyed the cell: the white walls, the needle-sharp image of my plank bed, the details of the grey uniform in the doorway.

I was led to the sergeant's office. He gave me a tired grin. "Strip," he said. I slowly removed my laceless boots, my shirt, and my pants and waited. One by one, the schmasser examined the items of my prison garb and threw them back at me piece by piece. I dressed, then stood clueless. Either I had lost a few balls of bread from my secret calendar or I had lost my mind. "Is it possible that eight days have passed without me noticing?" I asked myself. "That my days in the dark cell are over?"

After the schmasser had led me through a few familiar steel gates and around a few well-known turns, I realized I was being led to Krizsik's office. "Good," I said to myself. "I haven't lost any bread balls from my calendar. I haven't lost my mind." With his baton, the schmasser gave me a signal to stand aside and knocked on the door. It opened immediately, as if Krizsik was standing right behind it, waiting. Paying no attention to the schmasser,

Krizsik stood and scrutinized me from head to toe, as if to let a pleasing, savoury sight seep slowly into his mind. He contemplated my pants and shirts with such curiosity as if they were designer styled and not punishment issue.

"Now that you have plenty of time," he said, after the schmasser had left, "we might be able to *chit-chat*." He blinked and pointed at the chair in front of his desk. With the slight limp he was unable to hide, he walked around to the other side of the desk, and slowly, robot-like, lowered himself into his chair. I remained standing as if I hadn't seen his gesture. He lit a cigarette, drew on it, and placed it on the ashtray. Slowly ejected two jets of smoke through his nostrils and stared fixedly into the resulting cloud. "How's life on the dark side?" he asked, when the smoke had cleared the space above the desk.

"Better each day." There was an almost imperceptible wince of irritation —as if the needle of my response jabbed into a sore spot. He took the cigarette from the ashtray, lifted it halfway to his mouth, and admired the smoke rising from it. Behind the mask of his blasé, impassive air, the gears of his mind were desperately searching for the right riposte. "Well, that's all I wanted to *chit-chat* about," he said. He lifted the telephone and called for the schmasser.

I wondered about the purpose of his staging this seemingly meaningless meeting. To see me broken, to confuse me, or to let me know that he had not forgotten about me and still remembered our famous *chit-chat*? Or to drive me crazy trying to decipher in the dark cell the meaning of our curious encounter? If I had not had my regular routine, I might have tried harder to comprehend the meaning behind that brief adaptation of Beckett's theatre of the absurd. I reached under my bed, found my button exactly where I had stuck it, threw it up against the wall a few times, and caught it rolling and sliding on the floor. Then I kicked my boots off and tossed my toy up the air. It hit the ceiling. My ears followed the whiz of the button spinning in the dark. The workings of my mind narrowed to a single beam of consciousness between me and the button. A ritual concentration to the exclusion of everything else. When the button and my body aligned, I jumped and felt I could float in the dark, vibrating stillness of the cell. It hardly bounced back when my hand snatched it out of the air. I landed in a deep squat, then stood up and, motionless, with raised fists, began to recite Blake: "Tyger, Tyger, burning bright, / In the forests of the night ..." I stood in the dark and was hypnotized by the words filling the cell. By the time I reached "What the hammer? What the chain? / In what furnace was thy brain? / What the anvil? what dread grasp, / Dare its deadly terrors clasp?" I was in my own, small piece of jungle in the dark.

I lean back in my seat and feel the hum of engines in the back of my head. The mantel of snow on the wing is breaking up into clumps, which begin to shift and, one by one, fall to the ground. I lean against the hull and feel the quiver of the plane reverberating in my head.

It is a summer morning in 1958, our second time at my grandparents' in Zenta.

We walk to the boathouse, right beside the ferry moored along a scaffold of heavy, old timber. Mother is pushing Grandmother's bicycle, with two baskets hanging from the handlebars. Grandfather's rowboat is tied to the dock, the oars padlocked to the seat with a small chain. Mother stands the bicycle against the scaffold, and we bail rainwater from the bottom of the hull. She places the baskets, one with food and one with towels and a blanket, behind the seat, and we climb in. Andrew sits in the stern, and I perch on the bow.

Mother has been rowing up the Tisza for almost an hour before she finds a spot that she likes. Here, the river is wide and shallow. Mother noses the boat in to shore, and Andrew and I jump into the water and horse around in the shallows while Mother moors the boat with a rope around a tree trunk. She spreads the blanket in the shade of a tree and sits down to read her book. Every now and then, she glances up at us as we scrape palmfuls of colourful pebbles from the river bottom. We build sandcastles and decorate their turrets with stones and shells, and when we get cold from the water, we lie with our bellies in the warm sand and let the midday sun cover our backs with a blanket of hot rays. We climb the tall poplar that stands high on the bluff above the river. From there, we watch the Tisza roll between dark walls of willow trees.

At noon, Mother calls us down from the branches, opens her food basket, and lays out a cloth on top of her blanket. We sit around it and devour our sandwiches. It is a quiet time; there is nothing to hear but the river lapping against the hull of the boat and up the sandy shore, the impatient chirping of the sparrows waiting for leftover morsels.

After lunch, we push the boat into the river and, with oars drawn in, glide lazily with the slow current, keeping close to the bank. We admire the turtles sunning on logs and watch them slide into the water. Frogs jump and plop into the river with sucking sounds, and bumblebees climb in and out of the upturned petals of wildflowers growing among the shrubs. A heron throws itself into the air with a sharp, admonishing call. Riding softly on motionless wings, hawks patrol the air above the treetops.

The river becomes narrower and faster about a mile above the old bridge; it was destroyed in the war, but parts of it still stand. The current spins the boat around a sharp curve, and the oars creak as Mother straightens our course. When we are close to the bank, I stand up and reach for the overhanging branches of willows. Yelling "Tarzan!" I seize one and pull myself up, allowing the boat with Mother and Andrew to slip away underneath. Then Andrew takes hold of another branch, and we both hang from the trees for a while before dropping into the knee-deep water. Running grotesquely in mud, water, and sand, we chase the boat to the sound of Mother's laughter echoing between the banks. "Get up and run!" she urges us when we stumble and fall. She slows the boat down with the oars so that we can catch up and grab the gunwale.

The wing is now clear of snow. Flakes are still landing, but they are unable to accumulate.

In the dark cell, when I was young, Blake's "Tyger" was my victory song. The path I walked seemed straight and pure. I felt that nothing could sway me from being a rebel in the slammer. Not Krizsik, not Mengele, not the dark cell.

There were brief moments when, pining for peace and rest, I toyed with the thought of putting an end to the constant strain of resisting the Big Machine and instead letting myself slide into its well-oiled system of nuts, bolts, and cogs and feeling as snug as a yolk in an egg. Occasionally, I pondered moving inside from the cold, straight into the cozy and protective nest of power. To be a lapdog, rather than a wild animal. As I gaze into the swirling snow, I recall how, as a teenager, I was tempted by the siren call of power.

It was not long after my first encounter with the police over my playing the Beatles over the sound system at the public swimming pool when the drama teacher announced a nationwide contest. It was the winter of 1963 and the seventy-fifth anniversary of the birth of Anton Makarenko, the father of communist education and rehabilitation. Students were to compete in writing a play "that would reflect how the collective spirit would finally guide a gang of rogues and turn them into the true socialist type of youngsters." Twenty finalists would be chosen from Hungary's nineteen counties and the capitol. The day after the announcement, gazing at the school bulletin, I could already picture myself the winner—at the Palace of Youth, sailboats on glittering Lake Balaton in the background, in a luxurious camp, sailing, playing soccer, and walking on the beach with big-city girls. It was a cold January day. "It could be a bit of all right to spend a few weeks at a place like this," I said to myself.

Right after school, I picked up a pen and started to write. It was easy for me to create the first act with a bunch of rogue kids doing all kinds of mischief. Had the contest been about nothing more than showing how good kids are at breaking the rules and antagonizing the entire system of school, parents, and police, I would have certainly won the prize.

When it came to describing their fall, I had no problem with that act either. One of them talked and bragged. Through their informants, the police found out about them, and they were caught and arrested. The part where a kid managed to escape but was hunted down by the cops and roughed up was a great scene. It might have been a bit biased against the police, but not so much as to stop my play from advancing to the finals.

When it came to the kids' eventual conversion, however, I discovered that my brain was not geared in that direction. I awkwardly tried to describe a scenario where they managed to see the bright light of the common good, got rid of their habits of doing mischief, and were finally reformed. I worked hard to cast them in such roles, but whenever I managed to charter their glorious march to the tunes of Makarenko's *Pedagogical Poem* and back to the warm embrace of the welcoming collective, my kids bolted and wanted to run to the beat of Sillitoe's drum instead. A few tried to run the entire race to redemption, but at the finish line, they tripped over their own characters.

I stare at the snow-covered landscape slipping backwards as the plane accelerates on the runway. Soon, we lift and ascend into a blanket of fluffy clouds. My neighbour is deep in a book. I try to read the title, but I can't.

The teacher opens the classroom door, but instead of entering, he holds it open with an air of ceremony. A man, dressed in a smart navy-blue blazer, sharply pressed flannels, a long, unbuttoned coat, and a fedora enters. The principal follows. The man stands for a while and studies the class from under his hat, scrutinizing us one by one, as if counting heads. The teacher helps him off with his coat, and holds it draped over his arm as he takes the man's hat.

The principal motions to the stranger, and the two of them walk slowly to the back of the classroom, from where they can observe the class in progress.

"Which one of you nice, polite boys would be so courteous as to take comrade supervisor's coat and hat and hang them on the coat rack?" the teacher asks, beaming as if he were acting in front of an adoring audience. Arms fly up, as if my classmates were string puppets. I sit and look from comrade supervisor, now walking between the benches, to the teacher, who glowers back at me as if I were a blot to be wiped off his class—which otherwise shines like polished crystal—with a resigned shrug. "He can go and hang it himself," I mutter. The teacher, who has overheard me, turns chalk-white, then red. The kids around me are grinning and staring at him expectantly. He cannot ignore what I have said even if he wanted to.

When the class is over, without being asked, the same kid who was chosen from among all the arm-waving, fetches the coat. The duo is leaving. The teacher jumps around them like a court jester. But then he closes the door and walks straight to my bench. "See you in the office," he says. "Bring your control book." The anger on his face melts into a smile, and his voice turns to honey when he calls on the coat fetcher to do the same. The control book is a small book in which the principal and the teachers make notes about our behaviour. Each time a note is made, it has to be acknowledged by a parent's signature.

I take my time going to the office, and by the time I arrive there, the coat fetcher is already leaving with a dumb, satisfied smile. "I am disgusted by your rudeness," the teacher hisses and snatches my control book from my hand. "You are lucky that comrade supervisor didn't hear what you said."

"But all I said," I protest, perturbed, "was that he could hang his coat himself. He is an adult, after all," I blurt out, in a doomed effort to reason with the teacher.

"Now you are lying," he wheezes. "What you said was something else. A lot worse." He narrows his eyes. "It must have been terrible for the class to hear something that bad. I don't want to repeat it. I can't even write it down," he says. The teacher sits down, opens the control book and writes two words in it. He throws it at me, backhand. Without giving me so much as a glance, he orders me to stand facing the wall in the corner of the office for the duration of the break. On my way back to the classroom, I open the control book to see what he has written: "Unacceptable behaviour."

When I give Mother the control book, she reads the laconic "unacceptable behaviour" and asks me what on earth I have done to make the teacher send such a cryptic note. I tell her that I refused to join the puppets practically falling off their benches for the privilege of hanging up the supervisor's coat.

"That was all?" she asks. "Do not worry about it." I am annoyed by her usual stubborn optimism.

"Then the teacher gave me a stupid look," I go on, not listening, never listening. The words are dancing in my head. "I said he could hang it himself. In his office, he told me I had said something else, something so terrible that he didn't want to repeat it. When I asked him what was so terrible about an adult hanging his own coat, he said I was a liar and that I had said something else," I say, almost crying and filled with an outrage quite out of proportion to what has happened.

Mother regards me and shakes her head. Then, as if she had given up on me, she reaches for the pen on the kitchen table. She ponders the "unacceptable behaviour" and signs her name under it. "Next time," she said, handing me my control book, "try not to think aloud and don't be so argumentative. You have to learn to hold your opinion."

"Don't be so argumentative," I mutter with sarcasm. I turn my back on her and leave the room. I am disappointed with Mother. I had expected her to be proud of me for not being one of those mindless puppets who jump up from their benches to compete in obedience. I despise my teacher and my principal for cowering in front of the supervisor. I hate them both for recruiting kids to a lifetime of slavery, where every opinion and every argument is to be stifled. For me, they are not unlike those beggars who maim their children so that they have no choice but continue the profession. The contempt I feel will slowly spread to encompass my school, Mother, and the entire world of adults.

Not long after I had stuck the twentieth ball of bread under my bunk bed, I heard the sound of the familiar footsteps. I recognized Apeman's twin brother by his gait and immediately closed my eyes to deprive him of the enjoyment of seeing me blinking blindly like a toad in a hailstorm. By the time he inserted the key into the lock—with great stealth—I was already facing the opposite wall, eyes closed and hands covering my face. I heard the click of the light switch.

"What the fuck are you doing there?" he barked. "Praying?" Blindly, I peeked into the light from between my fingers. "Back to work!" he hollered, banging his baton against the door frame. "Move!"

He took me to the office of the old sergeant, saluted stiffly, made his report, and left. The sergeant peered into my file and watched wordlessly as I changed into my regular prison garb. My pants hung loose; I had to hold them up. "Looks like you lost some baby fat," he finally said. "Must be hungry. I tell you something. Don't stuff yourself with food. Some feast as though there was no tomorrow. If you are not careful, the first meal you eat could be your last. Or you become damaged goods."

I was not hungry and felt anything but damaged. In fact, I cherished those solitary days without light and regarded them more as a reward rather than a punishment. But my face, my eyes, and my entire body must have showed signs of distress, because when the door of my old cell closed behind me, Matheos reached for his leftover bread. Suddenly, my empty stomach drew up in me like a fist. I took a small bite and chewed it well. Uncle Andy went to his bed, opened his bag, pulled out a small, stunted apple, and put it in my hand.

"I saved it for you," he said. "Just leave me the core—just for the taste."

I held the bread in one hand, the apple in the other, and bit a piece off one then the other. The scent of the apple filled my nostrils and its caustic-sweet taste filled my mouth. Uncle Andy and Matheos watched me eat for a while and then, true to form, Matheos began pacing and talking to himself as if he was alone in the cell.

After the last morsel of bread, I told them about all the fun I had had in the dark of the punishment cell. The exercises I had done to stay fit, the game I'd played in the dark with the button to amuse myself. I explained how I had kept track of time and how I had thwarted the sneaky moves of sadistic guards. I left my weird rendezvous with Krizsik for last.

"You did good, kid," Matheos laughed, and resumed his pacing: three steps forward, turn, three steps back. His mouth began to twitch, and he uttered a series of staccato grunts that became frequent and harsh until they sounded like links in a chain rattling faster and faster. When his private discussion with himself was over, he looked as though he had discovered something. "Krizsik wanted to see you broken. When he saw you weren't, he could not handle it. By the way," he said, reaching toward the shelf, "there is letter from your mother. It arrived right after you were taken to the dark cell."

Uncle Andy fixed me with his gaze as if he had suddenly remembered something important. "Where is the core?"

"What do you mean?"

"The core of the apple I saved for you."

I glanced at the table, confused, as though it should be there somewhere, then said, "Looks like it didn't have any."

I removed the folded page from the envelope that had already been opened and stamped by Krizsik. I held it in my hand, admired her familiar calligraphy for a moment, then began to read. Her words, as always, entered my head lightly as a soft breeze, soothing and comforting, but by the time I had finished reading the last line, their meaning was deeply engraved in my mind. I read it one more time, reached for my pen, grabbed a sheet of paper from the shelf, and began to write. I realized that she had been quite worried at not hearing from me at the usual time.

The plane is still surrounded with clouds. I try to remember the letter I wrote, the letter Mother never received. It was something like this:

Dear Mother,

Thank you for your letter. Thank you for recommending Anna Karenina. *I liked it more than* War and Peace. *The nineteenth-century Russian novel grabs the soul. I also read* The Kreutzer Sonata. *It left me conflicted. I loved reading each superbly written sentence—it was like watching a master mason hew stone with skilled hands and fine tools and lay each piece perfectly in its place. So masterful that I felt I was under some magic spell until I began to ponder the meaning they conveyed. The more I thought about their message, the more I detested it. I'm into Dickens now. Less soul, more of a diagnosis of meanness and depravity.*

You must be thrilled with your new puppy. It is a pity you cannot send me a few pictures. From your description, she must be adorable.

I'm well. In fact, I'm terrific. I am sorry that it took so long for me to reply. I hope I didn't make you worry.

The reason I didn't reply right away is that I was on a twenty days' vacation as a reward for good behaviour (don't worry, I'm not crazy). I spent the entire time on a special diet, completed a special exercise regimen, and received all kinds of therapeutic treatments—all in an exclusive spa designed and appointed for select prisoners. I feel like new.

I will be back working tomorrow. With all my energy, I can hardly wait for it. It was good to be away for twenty days of relaxation, but it is also good to be back to be with my old buddies.

Looking forward to your next letter.

Love You,

Mityu

In the Translation Office next morning, Tabody didn't seem to share Matheos's enthusiasm about my session with Krizsik.

"Don't delude yourself," he said gravely. His face, chiselled out of the whiteness of the wall behind, hardened. "Krizsik never gives up. You have not won the final round yet." He ran his hands through his hair. "He will go after you like a bloodhound."

"By the way," he said "your desk was searched while you were away. They took a few slips of paper from under your typewriter. Then they went to the washroom and found some more."

"My journal," I said.

"Well," Tabody said "they've been added to your file. Hope they don't find anything in it that can be used to press new charges."

I wake up from a dream and try to remember it while I can. With fluid lightness, almost floating, we were walking on the lovely, soft, surface of the earth, Mother and I. We arrived at a path that, under the shade of flowers tall as trees, took us to a portal whose bright columns fell like a plumb line dropping straight down from the pale blue sky. Beyond the portal, a huge empty space devoid of colour spread out before us. I gaze at the clouds below. "What path? What portal?" I ask myself. "The path of our joint lives? And what is that portal and the vacant, colourless space beyond?"

Out of the corner of my eye, I can see that my neighbour is closing his book. He is holding it with his forefinger between the pages and his thumb on the cover. I glance at the cover: *The Iguana* by Anna Maria Ortese. I read the book four or five years ago. I want to say something to start up a conversation, but I don't.

I arrive home late from school, ill-tempered and full of sarcasm. I throw my bag onto the kitchen floor. Cica jumps off the chair by the stove, mewing. "Shut up, Cica," I say, kicking my bag and sending it sliding under the kitchen table. When I raise my eyes, Mother is observing me from the other end of the table with her finger in her closed book.

"Hi," she says.

"Hi," I grunt.

"Soup is on the stove. I kept it warm."

"Stop stating the obvious."

"Something wrong?"

"That asshole history teacher gave me a detention."

"Why?"

"I told him that what he said about the so-called Hungarian Soviet Republic of 1919 was total nonsense. But who am I talking to? You are a communist. I guess you have been cured. Rebel no more. Look at what you are reading. *In Search of Lost Time*. Searching for the lost rebel in yourself?" Mother looks down at the book, then at me. "Someone once said that a young person who is not a rebel has no heart."

"What else did that *someone* say?" I ask, dipping my tongue deeper and deeper into the vile brew of sarcasm that I feel the need to taste and re-taste. Anger is smoking red in my head, and it is spreading and darkening my world.

"An adult who remains one has no brains," she says with a smile.

"The answer is to become a conformist?"

"No," Mother says. "The answer is to become an individual."

With patience, and perhaps knowing that her efforts are futile, she explains that I will have to go through this process myself. That just as she cannot eat for me if I were starving, she cannot think for me either.

I heard the clinking of keys outside and the door opened.

"Here is your letter. I guess it's 'return to sender.'" Cuccos was standing in the corridor with my letter in his hand. "Looks like someone didn't like your story" he rolled his eyes, shook his head, and handed me the envelope. It had a large red stamp on it that read "Declined for improper content." Underneath were a few lines written in a clumsy scrawl.

When Cuccos had closed the door behind him, I took another look at the envelope. Under the red stamp, with handwriting that carved furrows in the tissue of the envelope, someone had written "Privilege to reply to letter from contact withdrawn. If prisoner XA 53 84 breaks the rules of correspondence again, his right to maintain contact through correspondence will be withdrawn for the duration of his entire sentence."

Each time a Western delegation or political leader arrived in Hungary, rumours of amnesty spread through the prison. U.S. Secretary of State Rogers's visit to Budapest in July 1972 and the signing of the Consular Convention on cultural and scientific exchange between the United States and Hungary set off gusts of gossip, and the naive hope that Hungary would distance itself from Moscow and move closer to the West became a strong prophecy. "Freedom for all" seemed to be the writing on the wall when Tabody, who since 1945 had spent more time inside than outside of prisons, was suddenly released on December 29th.

It was a Friday. Tabody and I were eating our lunch at my desk. The door opened and Cuccos walked in. "Tabody," he said in an uncharacteristically lively voice, "pick up your personal belongings. You are a free man!" he said with authoritativeness, as if he considered himself not simply a messenger of good news, but the person who had personally granted amnesty to the hussar priest.

We all watched as Tabody stood up, turned his head to the open window, stared into the blue winter sky beyond the bars, and closed his eyes for a few moments. Apeman opened the door and stood beside Cuccos (who, along with the entire Translation Office, ignored him). I waited until Tabody turned his head back from looking outside, which he considered simply a larger prison. "Good luck," I said, and, desperately searching for the right words, stuttered, "You made my life in prison easier."

"That was not the intent," Tabody said. "I never wanted to make anyone's life easier." With a smile, he added, "Easy never builds character, and"—here he grabbed my shoulders—"character is your only defence against dissolution." He gave me a bear hug, went to every prisoner in the Translation Office, and said goodbye to each one with a handshake. The he picked up his Bible and, with long, unhurried strides, walked out the door.

As I look out at the clouds stretching endlessly below, I think of the man who led me through the complicated labyrinth of prison life. Had it not been for Tabody, I would have come away from my first meeting with Gabi with the impression that I had met not only the smartest but also the worthiest and most upright man in prison. It was Tabody who saved me from the invisible clutches of informants and, at the same time, he saved me from hating them. Had it not been for him, Krizsik would have won. I would have ended up either in his bag or in the *dilihaz*. Tabody was right: he didn't make my life easier. Standing straight is harder than falling to one side or the other.

I reach under the seat and pull another letter from my briefcase.

September 20, 1972

Dear Mother,

Thank you for your last letter. I hope mine finds you in good health.

There is not much new here, except that I read three books that you should also read unless you have already read them.

The first I recommend is One Hundred Years of Solitude *by Gabriel Garcia Marquez. It was translated by Vera Székács. I have never read anything like this: the story, the language, the characters are amazing. Marquez is the twentieth-century Cervantes. I wonder how many new talented authors will come from Latin America.*

Right after, I read his Story of a Shipwrecked Sailor. *Totally different, but just as great a read.*

I also read a collection of what is called "absurd drama." Dürrenmatt's The Visit, *Ionescu,* Rhinoceros / The Chairs / The Lesson, *Beckett's,* Waiting for Godot, *and Albee's* Who's Afraid of Virginia Woolf *and* The Sandbox. *I always appreciate the drive for something new and something different, but it should be done with some energy, with a robust imagination and by reaching "down to where all ladders start" as Yeats used to say. I like the effort, but the lethargy, the failure to find creative inspiration and new themes are disappointing. There is no "masterful set of images" in these jagged, nihilistic plays like in* One Hundred Years of Solitude, *only barren, bleak landscapes with a few neurotic, life-weary souls wandering aimlessly around their own ennui. Looks like the old, boring "épater la bourgeoisie" is still alive in the arts. But for all my doubts, I still found them interesting. With good actors, some of the plays might create a totally different impact than reading them on paper, which feels like scratching an itch.*

Anyway, I must stop here, getting close to the twenty lines allotted.

Love You,

Mityu

PS. The last few lines after the twentieth were cut off with scissors from the bottom of your letter.

Within a few weeks, perhaps to maintain a steady representation of the clergy in jail, two freshly sentenced priests, Hageman and Somogyi, joined the Translation Office.

They were different from Tabody. When I asked Tabody if one could be good without God, he looked me straight in the eye and responded in plain language: "You can be good or bad with or without. It's your business. As far as I am concerned, I do not want *to be without*, and to me that is where it starts and ends." Tabody's faith, the final and unquestioned abode and asylum of his soul, was absolute. His direct knowledge of God didn't need fancy logic. It stood as he stood: straight and upright, without need for support from masterful, rational arguments. After a total of nineteen years in prison, his *circus animals* had long deserted him. His faith did not need any intellectual *ladder*.

The new priests must have considered themselves the Hungarian descendants of Spinoza. They must have thought it was their duty to convert me with complicated ontological arguments. Building their heavenward ladder of pure reason and formal logic, they explained that God existed as the *only absolutely infinite, self-caused, and eternal substance*. No matter what we started to talk about, they always managed to shift and extend the subject into the realm of scholastic discussion.

They seemed all right, each in his own way, but the preciosity of their exaggerated politeness got on my nerves. I could never tell if their good-natured smiles were genuine or were put on for the benefit of something they wanted to achieve. I could not stand that they talked to the schmassers nicer than to fellow prisoners. If a thug of a guard messed with the "hussar priest," he just told him to fuck off. But if the nastiest asshole barked at the new priests for no reason, they would gaze at him with the soft eyes of a pious saint and say something like "I'm terribly sorry, but I didn't quite understand the entire meaning of what you have just said." Or if Apeman happened to be in good humour and gave them a half-hearted grin, instead of ignoring the stupid bastard, they would smile back with sugary intent, lips stretched practically from one ear to the other.

Tabody would turn his head when the guards hung red rags in our faces on communist holidays. The new priests, instead of ignoring the schmassers would smile at them like Cheshire cats. I knew that, in the grand scheme of things, these snippets of behaviour were insignificant; nevertheless, they legitimized my dislike of them.

Sometimes I thought that they were "peace priests," as the regime called members of the clergy who were turned into traitors and toads by the Political Police. Perhaps they had failed to satisfy the demands of their masters and were sent to prison to ponder their mission more deeply? Over time, I realized that I was wrong. It was indeed their faith that cost them several years in prison, not underperformance as agents of the regime. They were among the best people I had ever met. But it took me a while though to get used to their perpetual piousness and to be able to stomach the many smiles they flashed.

One day, when I had hardly finished translating *Ils Ont Tué Ma Foi*, Apeman opened the door and held it open wide to admit Klucso and an army colonel, a broad-bellied tower, who strode into the Translation Office, both fully conscious of making a dramatic entrance. Instead of going straight to Geresdy, who had jumped up and was standing beside his desk, they came to a stop in the middle of the room. The colonel looked around and inspected all of us with such unabashed curiosity that he might have been studying dead men's portraits in a picture gallery.

He was holding a book in one hand. After he took his eyes off Uncle Andy, he turned to Klucso. Wildly gesticulating with the hand that was not holding the book, he inquired about something in a low but intense voice. "Interesting duo," I thought. I was curious about the little theatre unfolding across the room, but I could not make anything out of it. With my eyes above *The Statesman*, laid out at an angle and propped up by my thesaurus, I kept glancing at the two whenever they were not looking in my direction. The colonel kept probing Klucso, who appeared to answer each question in an affirming, convincing manner.

It seemed that Klucso had finally made his point to the colonel. He regarded Geresdy sternly, the lips under his large, cauliflower nose twitching as he stared down the little question mark standing at attention with exactly the same pathetic smile he had immediately pulled onto his face the moment the Commander and the colonel had entered. By the time they arrived at his desk, Geresdy had already added his usual beseeching gaze to the subservient grin. When the colonel tossed him the book, I expected him to bend over and kiss his hand. Klucso nailed Geresdy with another relentless look and issued some commands. Geresdy kept nodding; with each nod he seemed to lose more posture until his shoulders almost met in front of his chest. He listened to Klucso and adjusted his expression to every word with the instant response of a mirror. When the performance was over, the two left Geresdy standing and marched out in lockstep. Geresdy slowly disassembled his face and straightened his back.

I was curious. Got up, walked to his desk, turned the book to see the title: *Warfare in the Enemy's Rear*. Geresdy swept it up with one hand and held it against his chest. "Will you do it?" I asked. He shook his head.

"I just started this," he said and, with the hand that was not clutching the book, pointed at a technical manual. "You can have it," he said. "But remember,"—and his grimace became a poor knock-off of the grim expression of Klucso's that he had endured and absorbed for a few minutes and now tried to reproduce (with pitiful results)—"you cannot *ever* disclose its contents."

Gabi was watching us from behind his typewriter. "As usual," I said, infusing the words with a dose of sarcasm. Geresdy unfolded his embrace, and with utmost care removed the dust jacket and handed me the thick volume with a solemn gesture, as if it was a gift.

Gabi got up from his desk and stretched his back. He stood for a moment with both arms extended, tense but calm, and if one hand had been holding a tensioned bow and the other an arrow he would have been archer. He lowered his arms and walked to my desk. I glanced at him, torn between caution and the desire to have an intelligent conversation. With Tabody and Földes released and Matheos conversing mostly with himself, the only person I could talk to was Joseph.

"What have you got?" As always, his voice, a pleasant baritone, was friendly. Not a hint of the ultimate intent that guided his speech, not one sign of the prying inquisitiveness one would expect of an informant. He stood by my desk comfortably, and even in prison garb he looked elegant, engaging, polished. His relaxed posture, his youthful face, his attentive blue eyes—his entire being radiated a magnetic charm. Had it not been for his grey hair, I could have sworn he was only a few years my senior. That was the happy surface of his persona: amiable, appealing, and inviting. An unfathomably deep ocean of Machiavellian character underneath the allure of blue waves. You swam in it at your own peril.

"May I?" he asked. I nodded. He picked up the book, glanced at the title, and leafed through to the table of contents. "Huh," he said. "Heavy-duty stuff. Sabotage, subversion, guerrilla warfare! By the way," he asked, glancing at me over the open book, "do you know where the word 'sabotage' comes from?"

"Not really," I said. For all my contempt of Gabi the *besugo*, I admired the intelligence of the man; he was interesting, entertaining, and well-read and could talk sensibly about almost every subject, be it politics, history, art, or science. Once he engaged me, even if I felt conflicted, I found it hard to resist the promise of a good chat. He had a way of teasing my curiosity with things I didn't know, and my desire to learn usually defeated caution. Although I knew well that with every word he was laying a trap, my inquisitive nature prevailed, and I didn't want to sacrifice, on the altar of prudence, the opportunity to learn.

"'Sabot' means 'wooden shoe' in French," he explained. "Afraid of losing their jobs to machines, workers used to throw their wooden shoes into the textile looms to break their cogs. The Luddites adopted it as an act of self-defence against their employers. Together with strike and slowdown, damage to property became a weapon in the eternal arena of class warfare.

In military terms," he said, closing the book, "it's the destruction of vital equipment."

"Thanks," I said with a nod.

"How about 'guerilla'?"

"Haven't got a clue."

"Means 'little war' in Spanish. When *you* wage guerrilla warfare against an army of professional soldiers and of superior force, *you* ambush it, harass it, frustrate it, and weaken it until it withdraws, frustrated," he explained, underlining each "you" with a knowing smile. "If you describe the origin of such terms as "subversion," "penetration," "disintegration," "infiltration," "fifth column," you can make the translation a lot more interesting. The perfect book for you," he said with a smile. He set it back on my desk with care and tapped it with his hand. "And you are the perfect guy to translate it," he added, watching me with the sly, insistent grin of someone in possession of insight into my thinking, into my entire being.

I took in his knowing smile, and for a moment, I felt an urge to wipe the slate clean between the two of us and tell him that I also knew something about him. Something more damaging than anything he might or might not know about me: that I knew him to be the exact opposite of the mask he was presenting. "Thanks," I said with more restraint than I expected of myself.

"One day, you might find it useful." He tapped the book again and winked as if he wanted me to understand that he knew all about me and there was therefore no point in my withholding anything. He gave me the thumbs-up and turned to leave, then turned back. "As always, I'm happy to help if you are looking for the right word. Remember, I have been translating such books for the *commies* for quite a while ..." I bit my lip to stop myself from asking him what else he was doing for the commies.

"It took me some time to master the art of translation," he said. You are still an apprentice."

What he had said about me being an apprentice was true, but it was insignificant compared to the truth I could level at him. I wanted to use that truth as a weapon to humiliate him or at least to see his confidence waver. I gave him a quick glance. "What do you mean?" I asked with a sudden jolt. My voice was peevish, irritated. "What do you mean by saying that I might find this book useful? What would I find it useful for, *master*?"

Gabi didn't pick up the allusion. He didn't flinch. Unflappable, he let it float away without a blink. He had played this game a thousand times in hundreds of variations, and nothing I could say would have surprised him. I was about to tell him that I knew very well that he was mapping me under the guise of helpfulness when I realized that, armed only with clues and lacking evidence, I would never manage to get him to even half admit he was working for Krizsik.

"You sound hurt," he said, consoling, and made a veering, retracting motion with his hand. I stared at him wordlessly, taken aback by his uncanny ability to ignore the allusive scorn in my voice. "I never meant to question your ability to translate that book." His voice had a humble, almost painful inflection as he pretended to admit something other than what he was accused of. "When I said 'apprentice,'" he purred, like a cat licking its litter and grooming me back into trusting him, "I didn't mean to belittle your abilities. Feel free to see me when in doubt." He snapped his fingers and regarded me with the innocent, and at the same time somewhat offended, expression of someone completely misunderstood.

I knew I was talking to a person who, in many ways, was a lot smarter than me, smarter than Krizsik and all his *besugos* together. That if I kept talking, my words would call up other words and I would say things that shouldn't be said. I knew if I continued fencing with words, Gabi would outplay me, disarm me, and win. "Thanks Gabi. I'll keep that in mind," I said. To make our disengagement final, I opened the thick volume and leafed through it.

"Would you be able to kill people?" I looked up from the book. "I mean to kill people on the other side of the barricade," he explained. "Or as part of a mission." I opened and closed my eyes, trying to concentrate on the question. It was spring. Through the open window behind us, the draft of velvety air touched my neck. "To kill an enemy," I heard him say. "In battle."

It was one of those situations where whatever I said, it could only be wrong—saying the right thing was not even an option. I kept turning the pages until Gabi's silhouette disappeared from my cone of vision.

The book started with the advice of an ancient Chinese general, who explained how to overcome a foe without a blow by undermining its morale, its will, and its ability to fight—achieving victory without openly engaging the enemy.

Otto Heilbrunn had written a textbook on various guerilla and commando tactics: how to cut supply lines to the front; how to ambush and destroy depots, communication centres, and headquarters; and how to breach and penetrate units, creating chaos—all without engaging the enemy with substantial forces. Once the enemy lost control, the regular forces could finish the job—if they had to.

Translating Heilbrunn's book, I often imagined myself a one-man commando fighting the Russians. One day I was a diver, the next a sniper, and the next an explosives expert. I cut hydro and telephone lines, sabotaged equipment, blew up ammunition depots, ambushed troops, and set fire to underground storages of fuel. By the time I finished the translation, the occupying forces had withdrawn from Hungary in total disarray. Swimming in fantasies without coming up for breath, I singlehandedly accomplished what thousands of freedom fighters could not achieve in 1956. Planning these imaginary attacks became something like drinking a potion that, instead of quenching my thirst, only increased it.

Despite my refusal to provide him with an answer as to my capacity for killing people, Gabi paid regular visits to my desk to draw me into places where, without noticing, I would reveal one more trait, one more component of the *psychological profile* he was completing for Krizsik. Even when he was simply sitting at his desk, I could feel his prying eyes on my back.

In my enthusiasm for the book, without wanting to, I must have offered Gabi a rich harvest. Krizsik must have learned from him that I talked a lot more than usual with Joseph—and not about rock, not humming Led Zeppelin at the window. Even if he didn't know that we had made a pact to escape from Hungary, and before that do something big that would shake the regime, Gabi must have gathered from the expressions on our faces that we were using Joseph's remaining days in prison to devise all sorts of actions against the police, the Workers' Guard, and what we considered to be the source of all evil—the Soviet Embassy in Budapest.

I remained under the spell of Heilbrunn and my pipe dreams until the next issue of *Foreign Affairs*, which woke me up to reality with its prediction that the Soviet Union would never be defeated by military means.

The lights go on and the captain announces that we are going to run into some turbulence. He asks us to fasten our seat belts. Outside the sky is dark. "Quo vadis?" I ask. I think of Mother lying in her hospital bed. Is she alive? I contemplate the night sky and have no sense of moving forward. I travel backward in my head instead.

Curious how thoughts and memories connect. In one of Mother's quarterly letters, she wrote that Father was in hospital with an advanced case of throat and lung cancer. That he was reduced to skin and bones and was unable to talk. Mother took the train to visit him once a week. Considering that they had been divorced for fifteen years, I appreciated the charity she showed by visiting my dying father.

Even though what little affection I felt for Father had long been extinguished by his drinking, and what I now felt was more compassion and pity than filial love, I thanked Mother for taking care of him.

March 20, 1973

Dear Mother,

Thank you for your letter. I'm glad that you and Judith are well. It is great that Andrew moved to Germany from Sweden. Even if he can't come home for a while, he is closer to you and closer to your cousin Imre. I am glad that he went to visit Imre in Switzerland right away. You must have been thrilled to see the picture of them together.

I am into my last semester at this very special university and will graduate soon with the best PhD. I know it sounds incredible, but I have learned more here than if I had six lives. The books I've read, the people I've met, and the things I have been through can't be replicated. I feel very lucky for having had the good fortune of going through these adventures. Looks like prison is the cauldron for me where I will mature faster than I would have otherwise.

Once you mentioned that Hungarian males come to their senses somewhere around sixty, but it is usually a temporary experience, because they lose it immediately. Looks like I'm ahead of the time designated for that special event and hopefully I will not lose it that fast.

I am very sorry about Father and ever so thankful to you for taking care of him. With Andrew away and me in prison, he has no one left but you. It must be awful for you to see him like that—a man who used to be strong and full of energy, even if of the wrong kind. Tell him to hang on and I will see him soon.

I read two exceptionally good books by Max Frisch: I'm Not Stiller *and* Homo Faber. *If you have the time for more reading, go for them. I enjoyed them as much as I did* The Alexandria Quartet *by Lawrence Durrell. I just started the* Tropic of Cancer *by Henry Miller.*

I think we have only one or two letters to write before we meet. I can't believe how fast the years have gone.

Love You,

Mityu

"Tell him to hang on and I will see him soon," I said to myself a few times as I read my letter before handing it to Cuccos. The recognition that I had less than a year in prison hit me. Joseph had been released a month before. Visions of freedom began to dance in my mind. "Gee," I said to myself. "If I don't do something crazy, I will be out of prison next May."

I was swimming in dreams about my approaching freedom. Sitting at my desk in the Translation Office, in my mind I was paddling down a river. Standing in my cell watching Matheos pacing up and down, uttering grunts like a hog or some unknown animal, I was running down a trail in the woods at night. At night, when the lights went out and Uncle Andy began to moan in his bunk like a seashell, I was dreaming about faraway places: oceans, mountains, and rainforests.

After a while, most of my dreams about freedom turned into nightmares. I would wake up with a start from a nightmare in which I was banging on my cell door on the morning of my release; the schmasser would come and tell me that I had an extra year to serve on charges of inciting a prison uprising. Or instead of being taken to the gate and set free, I was transferred to the *dilihaz* for psychiatric tests. In each nightmare, in one way or the other, I was told that my release wasn't going to happen. It was like flying in an airplane with the captain announcing that there will be no landing, because the earth has disappeared. I would wake up rolling about in my own sweat on the straw mattress, look around me, and yell "No!" exhaling so hard that I could feel my chest sink.

When awake, I often thought that my being in prison was a dream. I had to touch things to feel their form and shape, or touch my face with my hands and push my fingernails into my flesh to make certain that it was all real. There were times when I no longer believed myself able to exercise control over my thoughts.

It didn't help that my life in prison, which had once been devoid of boredom, had become flat and monotonous since the release of first Tabody, then Földes, and finally Joseph. Going through each day was like dragging my feet through muddy water. I found it harder and harder to talk to fellow prisoners—their mere presence in the cell annoyed me, and in the Translation Office they got on my nerves. I was on the way to becoming a confirmed solitary, even a misanthrope.

There was a brief respite. New books arrived in the library: Borges, Harper Lee, Lampedusa. We were allowed to borrow two books from the library every two weeks. Because Uncle Andy's dementia had reached a level where he forgot the contents of a page before starting to read the next, and he could therefore read the same book forever, I had three books to read every two weeks. I took them to work and read after translating my quota of ten pages, and I stayed up at night and read by the light of the moon and the stars at the barred window long after the schmasser had turned off the light. When my eyes got tired, I placed the open book on my chest and listened to the sounds of the night for a while: an owl hooting in the cemetery across from the prison, another answering the call; the vibrations of moths' wings; the footsteps of a schmasser down in the prison courtyard.

Mother maintained that books were a sanctuary for her soul. That when her mind entered their pages, they protected it from persecution. But even the printed word failed me. It gave me only brief relief, but as soon as I closed a book, the tedium of seeing the same faces and the terror of going through the same nightmares returned. I paced up and down in my cell—bumping into Matheos, who was doing the same—in an effort to clear my head, but without much success. Three steps, turn, three steps, turn. But my head wouldn't clear. I felt I was going crazy, like Matheos. I wanted a change. I needed change. And, through a strange incident, that's what I got.

"We redecorated your old cell," said the old sergeant, his face stern but his voice warm in an apparent attempt to humour. He ignored the form that Apeman placed on his desk.

I stared, not quite certain how to respond.

"Fresh paint job, new curtains on the window so that the sun does not bother your eyes."

Apeman's face lit up with the dumb smile of someone having fun without quite knowing why. "And a TV with a rocking chair—" he chimed in. A sharp look from sergeant shut him up.

"Corporal!" the sergeant said, and paused for a moment, "as soon as I need you to finish my thoughts, I will let you know." Apeman stood with his lips still formed around the word "chair." A perplexed expression spread across his face. He had expected an exchange of looks affirming comradely complicity but had received a stern rebuke instead. The sergeant begin to study the form that Apeman had placed on his desk. I stood poker-faced, trying not to reveal how much I was enjoying the scene.

"I charged him with assault," Apeman ventured, "but he got away with a lesser charge." He placed the paperwork on the desk. The sergeant took a thoughtful measure of Apeman then scrunched the paper up in his palm. Apeman wanted to say something, but he swallowed instead; his Adam's apple bobbed up and down as if he had an egg stuck in his gullet.

"You can return to your duties," the sergeant said in a casual manner and without looking up, as though he had forgotten and then remembered Apeman's presence. Humiliated in front of a prisoner, Apeman stood as if stabbed in the gut. He raised his hand stiffly, saluted, and left.

The sergeant waited until the door was closed, then lifted the form from his desk. Adjusted his glasses and began to read it aloud: "On April 12, 1974, Michael Fekete, prisoner XA 53 84, was charged with assaulting prison staff. On April 16, 1974, Commander, Lieutenant Colonel Klucso sentenced Michael Fekete, prisoner number XA 53 84 to twenty days in solitary dark cell confinement for showing disrespect to prison staff." He dropped the form with Klucso's chicken-scratch signature on the bottom and gazed at me inquisitively. "What happened?" he asked.

"It's complicated."

"Make it simple."

"I spilled a pot of hot soup on Apeman—I mean, the corporal ..."

"You can call him anyway you want. I don't give a flying fuck."

I told the sergeant that for days, each time when I reached through the opening of the cell door to get my dinner, Apeman would slam the door of the food hatch tight on my wrist. He enjoyed seeing me torn between two choices: dropping the hot pot of soup and losing my dinner, or holding on to the *tschaika*, the aluminum pot, and letting my hand burn. When he had had enough fun, he would open the hatch door all the way and watch me dance to the table, careful not to spill the soup. He'd laugh when I plunged my hand into the bucket of cold water we used to wash our hands, our dishes, and our utensils.

The sergeant nodded. With a pained expression, he put his palm on his forehead then ran his fingers through his grey hair. "Then what?" he looked up and made a motion as if to adjust his glasses, but ended up pointing at the chair in front of his desk instead.

"The last time Apeman did that to me, the soup was steaming hot. I could not hold it. I had to let the *tschaika* go, and the soup spilled into his face. I never heard him swearing so bad."

"No soup spills going up."

"That one did."

"You threw it in his face, didn't you?"

I didn't reply.

"That is an aggravated assault on prison staff."

"Apeman charged me with assault and disrespect. At the disciplinary hearing, Commander Klucso decided it was only disrespect."

"You have only a few months left," said the old sergeant. "Try to be quiet. Too much time in the dark cell messes up your brain. If it has not been messed up already," he added, dismissing me with a resigned motion of one hand while already picking up the phone with the other.

I would have liked to tell him that, on the contrary, I was looking forward to my time in the dark cell. That I would rather see nothing than those miserable vistas from the window of my shared cell or from the Translation Office. I would rather do nothing than turning those endless sentences, paragraphs, and pages from English to Hungarian. I wanted to explain that I was weary of the lukewarm routine of the entire prison, the siren call of my approaching release, and the nightmares associated with it. That I was bored with seeing Uncle Andy's face worn down by the years and by disgrace; tired of his apathy, his brooding, and the perpetual ventilation of his laments over his wrongful imprisonment. Tired of the mere sight of him—laid out on his bunk like a pharaoh in a sarcophagus, blinking occasionally, as if surprised to find himself alive after a momentary death. I wanted to clear my head of Matheos's incessant political ramblings and the impotent monotony of his grievances against the regime, gibbering like a chimp in a cage with lunatic brightness in his eyes. That I needed a break from the metronomic predictability of his grunts after each sentence produced by his rigid, inflexible mind. I knew he was fighting his demons. I fought my own. But did it in silence, without trumpeting it to everyone around. I was sick and tired of fending off Gabi's provocations, annoyed by the phoney, pious manner of the new priests and the permanently subservient expression on Geresdy's face. For me, another twenty days in the dark cell would be not unlike going from a cage in the zoo back to the solitude of the wild.

I had a plan. I would exercise. Special exercises, like rebound push-ups with a closed fist, landing on and bouncing back from my knuckles. Jumping up from a squat, touching the ceiling and falling back and spinning left and right in the air before landing. And of course, throwing a button torn from my prison garb at the wall or the ceiling and catching it in mid-flight.

I also planned to test and refresh everything I had learned. From music to history, from geography to biology. I would split my brain into two; one side would ask the questions, and the other would answer. I made a vow that I was going to get out of this place stronger and smarter. I owed it to myself and to all those who had died within these walls or were disgorged from it broken. I was not going to count the days, eager to know when I would step out from the dark. I was looking forward to spending time in a place where there was very little input from the outside—only what I put into it.

The dark cell seemed darker than last time. It was a black box. When the door slammed behind me, the damp February cold felt like a shroud. I staggered to the cot, wrapped myself in the horse blanket and curled up on my side on the wood planks. I lay with legs pressed together, knee on knee, ankle on ankle, heel on heel. Little by little, I felt in possession of the place. Not unlike in childhood, I listened into the darkness with separated perception of each isolated noise: my heartbeat, the creaking expansion of the cast iron pipes, the catlike steps of the guard on patrol, the scuttle of a cockroach, the distant moan of a prisoner sounding like a stray animal in terrible fear of not finding its way back to the herd.

The turbulence is gone. The quiet progress of the plane through the night sky reminds me of something, but I can't tell what. "Dante, Machievelli, Giordano Bruno, Galileo Galilei, Caravaggio, Michelangelo, Tintoretto, Leonardo da Vinci. How melodic Italian names sound. I enjoy saying them over and over. When I walked to the place right by the Spanish Steps, the very house where John Keats died in Rome in 1821, on the plate he was "poeta Giovanni Keats." A most befitting name for the poet who maintained that "a thing of beauty is a joy forever." I think he also said, "Beauty is truth, truth beauty." Or *"Bellezza è verità, verità è bellezza."* If I had a choice, I'd rather be an Italian, with an Italian name, like Michele El Negro. I wish I had learned more Italian when I was in the refugee camps in Italy. I suddenly remember what our night flight reminds me of.

I lay on the cot in the dark and let my mind wander; each moment existed on its own. My stomach grumbled, but I didn't care. I was sailing and flying, back and forth, flitting among events, places, and times and trying to evoke everything I knew about them. Troy, where Achilles slayed Hector; Athens, where Plato wrote his *Dialogues* and Pericles delivered his speech on democracy; Lycurgus's Sparta and Pheidippides's Marathon; Rome and Carthage. Forward in time to Genoa, Venezia. Campania in the kingdom of Napoli, where Giordano Bruno was born and wrote the *Ars Memoriae*. I follow the voyage of Vasco da Gama.

In twenty days in the dark cell, I took inventory of everything I knew about history, art, science, and brutality. Of kingdoms that had disappeared and peoples that had vanished. Of cities that had been destroyed and cultures that had perished. I was already in London during the Blitz when the light went on and the cell door opened. Apeman's twin brother stood grimly on the catwalk. His left hand was positioned on his hip, and his right clutched the baton nervously.

"Move!" he barked and slapped the baton against his boot shaft.

"What?" I asked.

"Term's over."

He took me to a room where I changed back into my regular prison garb. Soon, I was back in the office of the old sergeant, who dismissed my Neanderthal guard with a wave of his hand and glanced at me from above his glasses.

"You OK, kid?" he asked.

"I'm fine."

He picked up the phone and requested an escort to wing Left 3.

"Don't want to see you back," he said. I nodded.

"You will be free soon." I nodded again.

"Good luck on the outside."

"Thanks."

Old man Cuccos walked in. "Vacation's over?" He grinned. He and the sergeant exchanged some pleasantries before Cuccos escorted me back to my cell.

"The Art of Memory," I say to myself and stare out the window into the dark. Mine is getting sketchier by the day. I'd better write down a few things while I can still remember them. I pick up my notebook and fall asleep before writing a word.

The *Washington Monthly* was added to the list of publications—which included *The Statesman, Foreign Affairs,* and *The Economist*—from which I had to translate selected articles. It dealt exclusively with the affairs of America's government, its culture, and its institutions; exposed a wide range of social problems; and suggested ideas on how to solve them. The leaders of Hungary seemed to be showing more and more interest in the West—particularly in America.

One day in the fall of 1973, I was translating an article in *Foreign Affairs* on the strained relationship between Canada and the United States. The author compared the actions of the two countries to those of two rowers in the same boat who start beating each other up with their oars. He portrayed Canada's case with more sympathy—for me at least. Right or wrong, I had the impression that Canada was being bullied by a more powerful neighbour, and this gave me an additional reason, besides the ones I already had, to emigrate there if I ever got out of Hungary. I was almost finished with the translation when Cuccos opened the door, walked to the middle of the room, and pointed his finger at me. Like most of the older schmassers, he was a heavy drinker. That morning he must have knocked back a few shots of brandy to get him through the day. Matheos had told me that while the pathologically sadistic guards thrived on attending the daily hangings and hearing the moans of tortured souls, those who regarded being a schmasser as merely a job relied on drinking as the only way to dull their minds to the cruelty they witnessed daily. Although the torture and hangings had long stopped, the schmassers' drinking habits went merrily on. Cuccos stood and motioned at me with his crooked finger.

"What?"

"Come," he said, clicked his keys and cocked his head to one side. "Nowadays you are quite popular."

"What is it?"

"Someone wants to see you. Don't be so damn curious."

"What is it?" I asked again.

"Your buddy," Cuccos finally said in his usual laconic manner. He squinted one puffy eye in baleful feigned humour.

Krizsik greeted me as if we were old friends. "How's everything?" he asked, beaming with fake friendliness. He extended his right hand in the direction of the chair in front of his desk.

"Fine."

"How do you like your new colleagues?"

"Sorry?"

"The priests," he winked and gave me a comradely grin.

I shrugged and stared blankly ahead, as though what he said had no meaning.

"Strange bunch, those priests." He pulled a cigarette from his cigarette case, rolled it a few times between his fingers and lit it. "I don't know what to make of them."

I didn't know either, but I stuck to the rule Tabody had made absolutely clear: never engage in any talk about fellow prisoners. You make a seemingly innocent comment about someone. It leads to an exchange of opinions about the character of that person. At a certain point, the Rubicon is crossed and, without your noticing, you are walking on the other side of the river from where there is no return. I chose to ignore his comment on the priests. Expectant, he waited, then drew on his cigarette and blew the smoke up into the air.

"Look." he said. He put the cigarette in the ashtray. "I think I know you." He gave me a look that seemed to imply more than what he said.

"You think so," I thought and continued my blank stare.

"I will be very straightforward," he said. I suppressed a smile and watched the unthinking and impassioned movements of his fingers on the desktop. They moved as if doing so on their own. "This is the deal," he said, licking his lips as though what he was going to say meant food to him. "Your term is soon up. You can go back to school. You can do whatever you want as long as ..."

"I don't understand," I said, pretending.

"Others do."

"I can only use my own brain, and it doesn't."

"OK," said Krizsik. "Let's stop beating around the bush." With great care he inserted his little finger into his ear and concentrated on wiggling it around for a moment. "You sign an agreement of cooperation and you can go back to university and have a good life after all this time in prison."

"I will also be straightforward," I said, looking him squarely in the face. "I knew that sooner or later we would come to this. I know about the deals you are offering. I cannot say that I haven't given them some thought. If I were not who I am, the deal you are talking about would have already been signed, but I can no sooner be your informant that I can change the colour of my eyes or reverse the flow of blood in my veins." I looked Krizsik in the eye and tried not to show the force of my feelings. "I would rather shovel shit for the rest of my life," I said in a level tone, as if making a simple statement, "than to spit in the mirror each time I see my face. My sentence is over soon, and I do not want to replace it with a life sentence of infamy and shame. No deal. I pay the full price," I declared with finality in my voice. I felt the sweat gathering under my arms.

Krizsik took my refusal to play in the most unruffled manner. He picked up his cigarette, twirled it a few times between his fingers, contemplating. He drew on it, slow and long, and blew the smoke up toward the ceiling. His face remained calm, almost bemused. But the occasional glint in his eyes betrayed that beneath it all, calculations were being made and remade until he arrived at a solution.

"Fair," he said. "I will see you before your release, in case you change your mind. The offer stands. Think it over carefully," he said and adjusted the ashtray, the lighter, and the pen on his desk as if they were figures on a chessboard. He inhaled deeply, as if he wanted to gather enough air for what he was going to say. "You must admit that your choices haven't always been for the best," he said, talking to the smoke swirling up in the air and with fake empathy, as if my habit of making poor choices saddened him. He put the cigarette onto the ashtray.

He raised his hand, thumb extending from his fist. "In high school," he said with a pitying look, "you embraced the destructive ideas of the enemies of the working class and let your brain be infected by them." His index finger followed his thumb. "At university, you chose to be a troublemaker, an agitator, a piece of scum." His middle finger snapped up in anticipation of the next bad move of mine to be announced. "You destroyed the symbol of the international working class, our cherished red flag." Then his ring finger sprang up. "In prison, instead of renouncing your criminal past, you befriended our most ardent ideological foe and became a hard-minded enemy of the working class. You broke the rules, and you assaulted prison staff, for which you spent time in the dark cell," he concluded, shaking his head as if the enumeration of my bad choices had saddened him.

"And now, when given the chance to start a new life, just when you're due for some good luck," he said, contemplating his open hand, "you refuse to walk the right path. Think about it. Think hard," he said, without anger and looking exhausted and disappointed. He drew his fingers back into a fist and reached for the phone. "Pick up for XA 53 84."

There was a knock on the door and Cuccos appeared. "How did it go?" he asked, once we were out in the corridor.

"It didn't go anywhere."

I wake up to the rhythmical rocking of the plane. I remember what Tabody said before his release: "If Krizsik feels that he can't get you through threats and promises, he will try to get you through your own weakness. He will try to get you through the ones you love. Be prepared."

At her next visit, Mother told me that Father had died. That he had been buried in a simple grave in the cemetery close to the old farm. I did not know what to say, because I didn't know how I felt. Perhaps, I didn't feel much more than a final acknowledgement of the end of a life—a life that could have been that of a father, had the fatherhood in him not been slowly but inexorably leached out by brandy. As I stood looking wordlessly at Mother standing on the other side of the wire mesh, vague images of Father—some good, some funny, and a few ugly—flashed through my mind. Father on his motorcycle with Grandmother in the sidecar. Father singing, Father playing Othello in the garden. And Father sitting in the pub drunk, his head tilting forward more and more, until it dropped onto the tabletop.

I finally said something that made me wince as soon after the words left my mouth. "Perhaps it was better for Father to die." Once I said it and realized how awful it was, all I could do was to qualify it by stating the obvious with a terrible remark: "He must have suffered ... " It was so bad, I could not even finish it. Instead, I told Mother that, with only two visits and four letters left, we had better stop exchanging meaningless letters and staring at each other from behind the wire mesh for twenty minutes. Mother stood, perturbed, and stared at me in disbelief. I told her it had nothing to do with Father, with her or even with me, I wanted to stop it because it simply didn't make any sense to me. In fact, it made a lot of sense. It was part of my plan of deception I had been working on since my last encounter with Krizsik. The schmasser tapped me on my shoulder, indicating that the visit was over. I said goodbye to Mother and turned very slowly as if I didn't want to break the thread of her gaze. Back in my cell, I picked up my pen.

December 20, 1973

Dear Mother,

I'm sorry to have reacted to Father's death the way I did. There is no explaining. I hope I didn't hurt you when I told you that we should not write and should not see one another. But that is the way I felt and feel.

This will be my last letter. All I can write about is a few books I read. The Collected Short Stories *of Jorge Luis Borges you recommended are not available in the library here, but I decided to read again* To Kill a Mockingbird *by Harper Lee. A truly great book. Everyone should read it. If everyone would read this book when young, with a mind that is not set in one way or the other, and with a heart and soul not yet hardened, they would be immune to the calls of prejudice and hatred that seem to be able to unite people more than love and understanding. The Hungarian translation is excellent, but I would like to read the original one day.*

I also read a very interesting book by Giuseppe Tomasi di Lampedusa, The Leopard. *It was written in the sixties and it reads like a nineteenth-century novel. Lampedusa put the ingredients of* War and Peace *and* Gone with the Wind *into his cauldron, added the most exquisite spices and cooked the most delicious Italian dish. The descriptions of the land, the buildings, and the characters are so rich, so decadent and nostalgic that after having read the novel, I would have, if I could, immediately set sail for Sicily to see the sky, inhale the air, walk the streets and watch the people going about their lives unaffected by modernity. Interestingly, there is a Hungarian relation: the author spent some time during World War I in a Hungarian prisoner of war camp, but escaped and made his way back to Italy.*

Mityu

I glance up at the screen tracking our progress; we're flying over the Atlantic. My head feels like it is drowning in old, fragmented memories. I glance at my neighbour, still deep in his book. I still feel the need to talk to someone and decide that, if the chance arises, I will say something about the book. A memory springs up in my head.

It is a Saturday morning. I am riding my bike, returning home from my first paddle of the season. It is my second year in the local canoe club, and I was waiting all week for the coach's note in the mail that finally set the date for what we call the "Icebreaker." I was so excited that I didn't sleep a wink last night, and I left home early without breakfast. Things didn't turn out to be as great as I'd expected. The coach made us clean the clubhouse first. Then he checked every boat, every paddle, and every life jacket before lecturing us endlessly about safety and paddling etiquette. Finally, I got onto the river, which was flooding and full of fast-moving eddies. At a sharp turn, my kayak tipped and I fell into the freezing water. There was no heat in the clubhouse, and when the coach saw me shaking and shivering, he sent me home. I mounted my bike and felt the cold wind cutting through me like a knife. It had been raining all night and there were pools of water in the depressions in the road. When I tried to avoid one, I swung out in front of a truck; the driver leaned on the horn, then shook his fist. I almost rode my bike into one of the road construction machines standing like prehistoric creatures in the mud between two piles of gravel.

The road leads uphill, and I ride standing on the pedals. The entire bike is creaking and ready to fall apart. The wind gets sharper. I pass one side street after the other, all of them with tree names—Poplar Street, Chestnut Street, Elm Street—without a tree in sight on any of them. I got my bike from a guy down the street in exchange for repairing a wrecked kayak. He said the bike could be fixed, so I had high hopes for my vehicle and wanted to paint it in the bright colours of my club. But it keeps breaking down faster than I can fix it. Whenever I repair one part, another one breaks—I have sort of given up.

Now, just as I get to the top of the hill, the chain falls off. My hands are numb, and I am cold and wet and hungry and mad. I decide to leave the chain hanging and coast down the hill with one foot on the pedal. I almost crash into the gate. I kick it open, leave the bike on the grass, run to the verandah, and open the door.

Instead of the usual cooking smells, the air in the kitchen has a strange, cool fragrance. Mother is standing at the table with a bundle of white and pink flowers in front of her. Some are standing in a vase. There is peace, a calm elegance, in their long faces. I take a deep breath and say "Hi" to Mother, who merely picks up one lily from the bundle, snips a piece from the end of its long stem with her scissors, and places it in the middle of the vase. It is very tall, with long, linear leaves rising from a strong, straight stem ending in three smooth flowers, all fully opened. I am annoyed by her fussiness, the way she iss focused on arranging her flowers. She says, "Hi" absent-mindedly and arranges the rest of the blooms around the tall white lily in the centre.

"Anything to eat?" I ask, swinging my arms in exasperation. I am annoyed by Mother's indifferent serenity, her casual acknowledgement of my presence. She picks another flower and admires its half-open pink petals. "It's a stargazer," she says.

"Anything warm?" I make an impatient gesture in the direction of the stove.

"I can warm up some soup," she says, as if talking to the lilies.

I walk over to the stove and spread my hands above it. They are still numb. "But it's cold," I inform Mother with a good dose of filial scorn. Over the vase, Mother glances at me with weary resignation.

"Get some wood and start the fire," she suggests. I look back at her, practising my angry masculine glare.

"Nice," I say with a smirk.

She looks at me for a long time, longer than I can bear. All of a sudden, I realize how abruptly I have shattered her calm. I feel a flood of guilt invading my heart. "I'm sorry Mom," I sigh, grasp the wood basket, and go to the shed. When I come back, the flowers are standing in the vase, perfectly arranged—the ultimate reproach. Mother is nowhere. I feel terrible. Then I hear the sound of pans and pots in the pantry and see Mother coming with the soup. I crouch in front of the stove and, by way of asking for her forgiveness, I place the sticks of kindling, one by one, on the cast iron grate.

I must have slept for a while. The screen shows our plane still flying above the Atlantic. I glance at my neighbour. He is reading the last pages of his book.

I was reading an article in *Foreign Affairs* on the impending collapse of the comatose socialist economies and was looking for the best Hungarian words still within the intended meaning of their English equivalents only more merciless than the original. All of a sudden, dressed in civilian clothes, Commander Klucso stormed into the Translation Office. He slammed the door behind him with a vicious backhand motion of his right hand. It bounced back on its hinges and if Cuccos hadn't caught it, its edge would have crashed into his wrinkled face; the old schmasser stood with a puzzled, bewildered look, holding the door with one hand and scratching his head with the other.

Klucso strode in, propelled forward by his own sense of importance, and stopped in all of his majesty in the middle of the room, where he stood motionless, taking a census of us from over the top of his glasses, as though reviewing his possessions. He looked cross. I noticed a miniature red flag pinned to the lapel of his blazer. My eyes went to the book he held in his hand.

The typewriters had stopped clattering. Cserbakoi buried his head in his dictionary. Mahorka stared dumbly at the latest Mercedes Shop Manual as if it was written in Chinese, and the two priests pulled piously smiling masks onto their faces. Cuccos stood in the gap and leaned against the door jamb as if he was tired.

Geresdy scrambled from behind his desk and rushed to report to the Commander. Klucso cut him off by stabbing the book against his caved chest. "I want this translated," he barked. "Quick! I don't care if everyone drops everything else." With a look of helplessness, Geresdy held the book in his shaking hands. He opened his mouth, then closed it without saying a word. He might have wanted to ask Klucso how to go about this order. To ask for another seven copies? Or tear this one into eight and give everyone a chapter or two? Perhaps request the arrest of a few English teachers?

"We have only one English translator left" he croaked, glancing at me sideways. "He has little time left ... "

"He will have a lot more time," hissed Klucso—there was a wry, meaningful grin on his face—"unless he translates this book as fast as he can." And with this, he left Geresdy standing in the middle of the office and marched past Cuccos, who held the door wide open, rolling his eyes as Klucso stormed out.

Geresdy walked to my desk and dropped the fat book onto my desk as if he had no energy left in him. "You heard the Commander," he intoned. I picked it up and studied the dust jacket. *Inside the Third Reich: Memoirs* by Albert Speer. I didn't have a clue who Albert Speer was. Perhaps a British spy? I opened the book and began reading the jacket. It was the autobiography of Hitler's architect and Minister of Armaments. Speer had been sentenced to twenty years in Nuremberg in 1945 on charges of using slave labour. He wrote his memoirs while in Spandau prison.

I shook my head. I was not interested in translating one single sentence. In my mind, Nazi Germany had been a grey, monolithic collection of programmed robots moving in unison to the drumbeat of Hitler's *Mein Kampf*. In the end, however, I consented and found that Speer's book turned out to be a fascinating description of the Nazi leadership, a collection of demented, megalomaniacal thugs. After reading Solzhenitsyn's description of Stalin, Zhdanov, Yagoda, and Beria, the similarities between Hitler, Göring, and Himmler and their bolshevik counterparts was astounding. All psychopaths, obsessed with power, bent on ruining and destroying the lives of millions, without conscience and without any remorse whatsoever.

Speer made it clear that, as in Russia under Stalin and in France during the Terror, the Nazi leaders could have never achieved such a degree of mass psychosis without the active participation of the population: "The herd bellowed and convulsed to the beat set by Hitler and Goebbels. But their leaders were not the true conductors. It was the *herd* that ruled. To allay their sense of misery, hopelessness and frustration, the nameless lynch mob wallowed and rejoiced in their obsession, savagery and licence. Their general despondency was fast replaced by a frenzy that demanded a scapegoat on whom to lay the blame for anything and everything that went wrong."

Krizsik kept his word. A week before my release, Apeman opened the door of the Translation Office, one hand hooked into his belt and tapping the knuckles of the other on the door jamb. He rarely stepped inside—with all those books, dictionaries, and typewriters, the place made him feel uncomfortable. Except for Geresdy, who immediately rose from his chair, and the new priests, who nodded and gave him their saccharine smiles, we ignored his presence.

Geresdy rushed to him like a lackey. He stood twisting the sleeves of his shirt with his fingers. Apeman's large, bent frame towered over Geresdy's small, crooked, solicitous figure. He spoke a few words to Geresdy that I didn't understand, except "XA 53 84," which he spat out like a curse. I wondered what kind of a parting gift he was going to give me before my release. Like a trained dog sent by its master to fetch something, Geresdy hurried to my desk. "The master corporal wants you," he stuttered with urgency in his voice.

"Master corporal?" I asked, glancing at Apeman. An extra star on his epaulette indicated that he had been promoted. "The corporal can go and fuck himself." Geresdy half turned his head and rolled his eyes, as if it was awful for him to listen to such blasphemy. I relished the effects of my profanity on him for a few moments before getting up from my chair; then I folded the issue of *Foreign Affairs* I'd been working on and closed the dictionary, both for no other reason than to make Apeman wait for another minute.

"What?" I asked, pokerfaced.

"Still don't know how to report?"

"Don't give up on me, Apeman," I said. "I have one week left to learn." I could not resist the temptation. "You still eat cabbage soup without a spoon?"

"It's not over yet," he wheezed, creaking like a rusty hinge. This was the first time he had heard me call him "Apeman" to his face. There was a sense of desperation, urgency in his voice. With my impending release, his mad quest to hurt me was nearing its end. "That way," he barked with impotent rage and pointed his baton in the direction of the empty hallway behind the door.

He didn't have to tell me which way to go; I knew where we were heading. Apeman first knocked on, then opened, the door to Krizsik's office. Krizsik was standing by the open window, lowering the blinds. When he was finished, he turned around and showed me the chair in front of his desk. Once I was seated, he picked up his cigarette and began pacing behind me, from wall to wall and back again, without saying a word.

I tilted my head to one side and pretended to be asleep.

"A week," I heard him say, "and you will meet your mother and your sister." I knew where he was going and kept faking somnolence. "I will wait you out," I said to myself in a manner of encouragement. Krizsik must have realized that talking to me from behind my back was not working. He walked into my cone of vision, went to the window, and pulled up the blinds. The sun invaded the room. I opened my eyes and blinked a few times. Krizsik turned away from the window and stared at me with a look of disbelief. He shook his head, stepped to his desk, and pulled the chair under his ass. "You were sleeping," he stated with an incredulous expression, his tone of voice making it more of a question than a statement. To doze off in the presence of the political operative was an act of ultimate insolence.

"Was I? I asked, still blinking.

"Looking forward to seeing your mother, your sister, your friends?" he changed his voice back to normal. It was obvious where he wanted to steer the conversation. In his place, I would have been ashamed of such a poor spin. I hoped that I would play this game better than he did. I wished that Tabody could hear and see how his apprentice duelled with the devil. I felt that my entire stay in prison was a rehearsal for this final battle.

"Not really," I said, and blinked some more. As if a drop of vinegar had fallen into his expectations, his eyes contracted in disapproval as he recoiled and wrestled with the information. His face then slowly hardened, like wax in a pot under which the fire had gone out. I wanted to tell him "I know very well where you want to go, you motherfucker. That Mother will lose her job, my sister will not be able to go to university ... and all the bad things that will happen to them if I do not take the deal you last offered."

Instead, I said, "I do not look forward to seeing them at all," in a voice like that of a stranger.

"Why?" he asked, stunned. With the sudden stalling of his mind, the large sponge of his face shrank and became vacant, as if the juice in it had suddenly leached out through the crater-like pores of his skin.

"I've hated my mother ever since she divorced my father," I said gravely, as though I was making a confession. "I could not stand my sister from the day she was born." I added, extending the immunity from any potential retribution to Judith. I knew he was well aware that Mother and I had stopped writing letters and she hadn't come for the last visit. "I told Mother a year ago that there was no point in us talking or writing letters."

Krizsik looked at me with his chin lowered. He parted his lips and blinked rapidly, as if a powerful light had been switched on and its glare was hitting him in the face. He blindly reached for his lighter, but only pulled it closer to him on the desk.

"The only person I loved in my life," I said, my voice cracking, as though it was hard for me to open my heart to a stranger, "was my father."

"Sorry about your father" he mumbled as if he was not quite sure what to make of what he had heard. His words sounded like a recorded speech played at the wrong speed.

"You bastard," I thought. "You knew that Father was dying before I did. You opened and read every letter Mother wrote, long before I could cast an eye on them." I was worried that he would get up and offer a clammy hand, but he didn't.

"Well," he said. He pushed his lighter back and forth with his crooked forefinger, "Good luck." He waited for me to say something. When I didn't, he picked up the phone and called for Apeman.

My neighbour marks his place in the book with what looks to be his boarding pass. Closes it and slowly puts it on his lap.

"How do you like it?" I ask, with an awkward attempt at a smile.

"I like it a lot," he says. "I have only a few dozen pages left. You can have it when I am finished. I'm Tony, by the way, Tony Abeles. Or Anton."

I am not sure if Anton means "Just leave me alone and let me finish this book. Please read instead of bothering me." But the directness in his voice allays my worry that he might mean the opposite of what he's saying.

"I'm terribly sorry, Michael. Michael Fekete.

"From your accent, I gather you are Hungarian."

"I was born in Hungary, in fact, in Yugoslavia. The borders kept shifting and the town of my birth changed ownership a few times. I read *The Iguana* a few years ago. It was recommended by the owner of my old bookstore, Writers and Company. It's since closed, like many. It's a shame."

"Indeed. My wife gave me her copy," he says, tapping the cover with his finger. "She told me that every women's book club reads it. First, I thought it was an attempt at a fairy tale, but it turned out to be a lot more. Now I wish I had been there when my wife and her friends were talking about it. What do you think?"

"Don't get me started. Neither of us will sleep until Montreal," I say, but I feel grateful to Anton for the question.

"I was sort of baffled," he says, evidently not to be dissuaded by my warning. "Halfway through the book I thought that besides the language and some weird symbolism, there wouldn't be much more to it. The acceptance of slavery as one's fate. Or a devotion to a skewed relationship, a Manon Lescaut in reverse?"

"But Ortese takes it further," I point out. "The prince keeps offering Iguana the chance of freedom, but she rejects not only the opportunity to be freed, but also to be loved, respected and appreciated. If I remember well, this option was never offered to the Chavelier des Grieux—or at least not in such a forceful manner. I was astounded, and at the same time irritated, by Iguana's stubborn refusal of a beautiful offer and her acceptance of abuse as her ordained lot. Her explanations drove me crazy." I add, "I hope I'm not spoiling your reading," realizing as I speak why I am so upset with Iguana: her resigned acceptance of her fate reminds me of Mother.

"Not at all. I'm past that. I have only a few dozen pages left."

"It will not get any better," I say. "The fact that the offer of freedom comes from a most attractive man who declares his love for her makes it worse. It made me sad and, at the same time, mad. When I read it, I happened to have read a few books by Roberto Calasso. I had the idea that

Ortese had fashioned the character of the count after him. I wrote Calasso a letter and asked what he thought of it."

"Did Calasso reply?"

"In fact, he did. He told me he didn't think so, because when Ortese wrote the book, he didn't yet fit the character of the count. But at the same time, he didn't think it was impossible, because *time moves back and forth*. That things we think of as being in the future might already have happened, and that things we consider to be in the past are, in fact, still ahead of us."

"Time moves back and forth," says Anton, "Time moves back and forth." He repeats it, as if he wanted to underline the sentence in his head. He nods with an empty gaze into the space ahead of him.

"That's what Calasso said."

"Do you believe in conscious choice?" he asks.

I hope my face does not reveal my initial shock. This is the kind of question we used to ask in high school and at university, when we babbled on about existentialism and Camus, or maybe in prison, when we entered the realm of metaphysics with the priests. But asked on an airplane, it sounds as if the captain had just announced the loss of one of our engines.

"I do," I say, hoping my face and voice don't reveal how unprepared I am for the segue from *Iguana* to certain beliefs I might or might not have. "The opportunity for a conscious choice of some consequence is quite rare, though. Someone once said that the only choice of consequence that really matters is deciding to end one's life."

Anton turns on his seat and observes me with a curious glint in his eyes. "Have you ever made a choice of consequence?" My eyes widen in astonishment. Five minutes ago, we were complete strangers and now Anton is asking me another intimate question.

"A few, I think."

"Meaning?" Anton adjusts the book on his lap.

"When I was in prison," I say—Anton's eyebrows rise almost imperceptibly—"I made the choice not to be an informant of the political police."

Anton's jaw drops. "Tell me!"

"It was not a difficult choice. I knew all along that I would resist the pressure and reject the offer, whatever it took. The difficulty was in finding a way to do it in such a way that I would not harm myself and others. I must admit, I had some help. From a priest."

"Are you religious?" Anton asks with the disarming directness of a person who hides nothing of himself.

Again, for a moment, I do not know what to say. I can't even blame Anton asking me a question that I am unprepared for. After all, I am the one who started this conversation. Had I kept my mouth shut, he would be happily reading Ortese and watching the drama unfold between Daddo and Estrellita instead of cross-examining me on matters of faith.

"No, I'm not. At least, I do not think I am. But I must admit that that priest left a civilizing mark on my animal brain."

"When did you go to prison?"

"1968."

"For what?"

"I burned a Russian flag."

"In 1956?"

"No, I was only nine years old then and too young to be sent to prison. The flag burning happened in 1968."

"Oh, a revolutionary!"

"Rather, a juvenile obsessed with grandiose delusions. Took me some time to learn to get my point across quietly instead of shrieking it from the rooftops."

"How did you manage to escape?"

"I didn't, not from prison. I don't know of anyone who managed to do that. I served my prison term. But yes, I did escape eventually—I mean from Hungary. I swam down a river at night to Yugoslavia. From there I went to Italy. I spent six months in refugee camps in Trieste and Latina. From Italy I went to Canada."

I glance down at the book in Anton's hand and remember that night in August.

Lights off, my friend Cimbi and I rode his motorcycle down a narrow dirt road, into the dusk. To the right, behind the levy, the leaves trembling on the top branches of poplars caught the last, fiery crimson rays of the dying sun, which had already lost its warmth. To the left, there was a long stretch of overgrown pasture that had not seen grazing sheep or cattle for months. Here and there, from among the stunted crabapple trees dotting the roadside, a pheasant rose with a loud clatter of wings and disappeared into the evening. Rabbits would pop up from nowhere and race us, running zigzag, then jump into the dark clumps of tall grass. I tried to keep an eye on the levy winding along the edge of the Tisza, so that I could spot any jeep headlights in time and avoid running into the advance patrols checking the border zone for intruders. Those who didn't reside in the area or didn't have a permit to enter it faced arrest if caught.

Cimbi shifted down and we rode slower. We were close to the place where I wanted to enter the river and swim all the way down to Yugoslavia. The Tisza, flowing from north to south, from Hungary to Yugoslavia, was my only chance of escape. The border was tightly closed. With tripwires attached to flares that shot up into the sky to light up the terrain and German shepherds trained to sniff out, track, and bring down anyone who tried to escape on land, any attempt to cross the border other than swimming down the river would have been insane. Besides, water was my element. I had grown up paddling on the river and knew it like the back of my hand.

It was dark when I spotted the ramp I was looking for. In my kayaking days, that ramp marked the limit of how far we could paddle down the Tisza without getting into trouble with the border guards. That is where we would pull our boats ashore, dip into the water to wash off the sweat, take a leak, walk up the levy, and stretch. We'd fill our T-shirts with crabapples and paddle back to the club.

I pressed my thumb against Cimbi's back. He nodded and cut the engine. We dismounted, pushed the motorcycle into the tall grass, and climbed up the ramp. The large face of the August moon rose above the poplars, and the light spilling among the trees licked the leaves with every breath of wind. We stood on top of the levy for a moment, then walked down on the river side into a thick growth of wild berries. The sweet scent of decaying vegetation rose from the ground as we pushed our way through dense foliage. After a few minutes' walk on soundless moss, we arrived at the bank and stood under a dark willow, which bowed like a consenting witness, its delicate leaves tracing themselves against the evening sky. I dropped my knapsack onto its exposed roots among clumps of dry mud, leaned against its moss-crusted trunk and took off my shoes. Here and there, a gleam of moonlight would dart through the branches to light up a small patch of ground. The shadow of a branch cut a dark slash across Cimbi's face as he stood and took my clothes one by one, folded them, and put them into the waterproof bag. He added a few pieces of small steel rods for weight and pressed the bag against the tree trunk to squeeze the air out of it. Then he sealed the bag and placed it on the willow's roots. A lonely frog began to croak. Soon it became a duo, a trio, a quartet.

Cimbi took a flat box from the inside pocket of his jacket, opened it, and handed it to me. I rubbed the thick grease all over my body, then gave it back to him. He put more on my back. I was going to spend several hours in the river and wanted to insulate my body against the cold as much as possible.

"Good luck," Cimbi said when he had finished strapping the bag onto my back. "Swim slowly. Let the current take you. Look for that watchtower. It'll be on your right."

"Hey," I said.

I entered the river and began to wade into the deep. Under the moonlit sky, the Tisza shone like a wide streak of molten silver, and the leaves of the poplars glistened like nighttime eyes. Except for a few wisps of cloud obscuring the moon, the night was clear. An owl hooted. Another one answered. A fish leaped, and the sound of its splash made my heart skip a beat. I took a deep breath to restore my calm. I turned and waved at Cimbi—or at least in the direction of where I thought he stood in the dark of the willows lining the bank. I gave myself up to the cold embrace of the current and floated motionless until it took me to the middle of the river. Once there, I began to swim in complete silence with long kicks; my arms stretched out in front to avoid making ripples that could have been seen or heard from the bank. I felt that I was not swimming in the river as much as I was resting in it. My body floated under the night sky like the reflection of a happy cloud until I arrived at a slight bend, where I had to kick harder to resist the current's strong, sideways drift, which wanted to push me against the right bank. After the bend, as far as the eye could see, the river rolled soft and straight between its dark banks. The moonlight hung in the air like fine dust, and the stars were bright in their configurations, the Big Dipper right overhead. With streaks of light between them, the smaller stars spread as far as the eye could see, and the sky ended where they fell into the river. The sky was so clear I could have been looking through a telescope right to the end of the world.

Except for the gentle lapping of the water against the banks, the breeze rustling through the leaves, and the occasional, choked shriek of a night heron, there was hardly a sound to disturb the quiet. The vague outline of the two banks fringed with poplar and willow slipped by in silence. The moon faded behind the first clouds drifting above the right bank. The water turned into a dark mass of liquid glass. I let it enter my mouth, drank from it, and felt its taste rising from my mouth to my nostrils. "Everything will be fine," I repeated to myself. "Everything will be all right."

Cimbi had told me that somewhere down the river, close to the border, above the right bank, there would be a watchtower with powerful searchlights. He knew about it from having once accidently missed the ramp to the levy and unwittingly paddled too far south. He was stopped and held by the border guards, who let him go only after he convinced them that he was a member of the local kayak club and was simply paddling outside the usual training hours. While being questioned, he had taken a good look at the tower and the area.

An hour passed. I decided to take a rest from swimming and simply drift with the current. I peered into the dark to see if I could spot the tall silhouette of a watchtower. Cimbi had said I would see it rise above the treetops, but now that clouds streaming from the north had completely obscured the moon and the stars, the Tisza and the trees along its banks had lost their distinct shapes, forms, edges, and outlines and turned into a continuous gradation of dark. Had I not known that the current was flowing south and that I was to swim with and not against it, or had I relied on visual cues alone, I might have lost my way. Anxiety crept over me, and I felt somewhat unsure of my chances of escape. "OK," I encouraged myself. "If I happen to fail, it would not be a tragedy. Just a brave attempt that did not work out." I maintained my position in the middle by dead reckoning. Little by little, my eyes got used to the dark.

Another hour passed. I was drifting down on a long, straight stretch when suddenly, just behind a bend, a floodlight streamed down in front of me onto the surface of the river like a comet streaking across the night sky. It was coming from above the right bank. Blinded, heart hammering against my ribs, I stopped, treading water against the current. The cone of light moved slowly across the wide stretch between the willows lining the banks. Wherever it went, it shed a light a hundred times brighter than the pale candle of the moon peeking from behind a thin shroud of cloud. I didn't know whether I had swum faster than I estimated or the border was closer than I had thought. Either one could have been the case or not have been the case; it didn't matter. What mattered was that I had miscalculated. My plan had been that upon sighting the structure, I would swim very close to the left bank, possibly under cover of willow branches hanging over the water.

The searchlight went out as suddenly as it had appeared. I began to swim hard in the direction of the left bank. The hostile silhouettes of the tall trees stood like sentinels above the tangle of shrubs, ready to topple into the river. When I got close enough, I grabbed a large, overhanging branch of a willow. I hung on to it and waited, keeping my eyes on the vague, dark outline of the watchtower looming over the opposite bank. Without the moon and a clear sky, I couldn't see much. I was beginning to feel the cold seep into my body, and I had to clench my teeth to stop them from chattering. For a moment, I toyed with the idea of proceeding on land, but fear of being detected by foot patrols with German shepherds pushed that thought away.

I was about to let go of the branch when, a short distance away from where I was, another beam of light jumped onto the surface of the river. Like the previous one, it swept between the two banks then went out again. This happened a few times, always at about the same interval. Each time the light went out, I counted to about ninety or a hundred before it was turned on again to wander back and forth between the banks for a minute or so. I decided that I would use that period of darkness to swim as fast as I could to get beyond its reach.

When the wide circle of light shimmering on the water came too close to me the next time, I let the branch go and submerged. Eyes open, I watched the light linger above me, then move away. When I popped up to take a breath, I found myself drifting away from the branch. The light went out, and I began to swim hard, away from the bank and down the river. Either I had made an audible splash or it was mere bad luck. Suddenly, I found myself right in the centre of a bright beam of light. Without time to take a deep breath, I dove under and swam with eyes open, watching the surface above me shine like a mirror. After a minute or so, my lungs began to cry for air and my ears began to pound. With powerful kicks, I swam with the current as fast as I could. To be able to resist the urge to surface for air, I reminded myself that my destination was ahead of me—not somewhere below, with a bullet in my head. It was more a fight with my starving lungs and my eyes, which wanted to pop, than a contest with the border guards tracking my underwater glide. I kicked harder and went as deep as I could. "I endured a broken neck, arrest, interrogation, the dark cell, and Krizsik, I must hang on for another minute"—I held back the breath that wanted to escape my chest—"or I endured all that for nothing. I'm on my way to freedom! I can't let myself be sucked backwards, all the way to prison."

They must have lost me, for the light lingering above veered away. I kicked, surfaced, exhaled the old, reused air and took a long, deep breath. I was in the middle of insanely intense breathing when, before I could submerge, the beam of light swept back and blinded me. Someone barked commands. "Halt! Halt!" Then I heard the crack of the warning shot. Then another, followed by their echoes bouncing between the banks. With a circular motion of my arms, I dove as deep as I could and kept swimming down the river and away from the light, which became paler and paler with each kick of my legs and with each wide sweep of my arms. My head emerged from the river for another breath, and before I submerged I could hear the noise of an outboard coming from the direction of the watch tower. My head kept popping up and submerging until I reached the shallows of the left bank, where the water sat like molasses. My feet touched then sank deep into the muddy bottom.

I waded out of the river. The bushes on the bank were a surging mass of black. I was dizzy and fought to regain my balance after stumbling and falling in the shallows a few times. Sliding in the mud, I managed to climb up the bank. Once on dry land under the cover of trees, I began to run, staggering among shrubs matted together by creepers. I stayed close to the river so that I could dive back into it in case I encountered a patrol with German shepherds. After a few minutes, I arrived at a place where the land was bare of trees. I lowered myself to the ground and crawled along the grass. Occasionally, I stopped and listened. I could hear the sound of a motorboat up the river as it approached the left bank. To my right, I saw streaks of light in the dark sky. I was about to get up and run when something I didn't see pushed against my shoulder.

Suddenly, a yellow streak appeared on the left and streamed up high into the sky; I had touched a tripwire. When the flare stopped climbing, it hung above me for a while, turning the night into day. Commands and the impatient barking of dogs rang out in the distance. Flat on the ground, I waited until the fireworks above had ceased. Then I began to run back to the river, hoping that I would get there before the dogs caught me. Against them, I would have no chance. I was still running when the moon moved out from behind the clouds. I raced my shadow all the way to the bank.

When I stopped at the water's edge, I saw that the beam of light from the watchtower was focused on a point about a hundred yards upriver, at the place where I had climbed out of the river a few minutes earlier. In the moonlight, I saw the vague outline of a motorboat and the border guards, who were pointing flashlights and guns. I slid into the Tisza and dove under. I swam downriver as long as my lungs would let me stay beneath the surface and came up only to take a long breath. I did this a dozen times, then simply floated in the middle of the river, looking back with my eyes above the waterline. Upriver, I saw two teams; one in the motorboat and the other standing up on the bare bank above, pointing their flashlights in various directions. I saw the silhouette of a German shepherd moving on the bank where I had re-entered the river. It seemed as if they could not decide where to search: on land or in the water.

The current took me farther and farther down the river. When I thought it was safe, I increased the speed of my drift by kicking with my legs and holding my arms tight against my side. When I passed a curve in the river, they all disappeared from sight: the boat, the guards, and the dog. I was shivering with cold and could hardly move my arms and legs.

I managed to get back to the left bank. I stood for a while in the shallows to regain my balance, climbed up, and began to run. The earth under my feet suddenly turned soft. I looked down and saw a wide track in the moonlight, ploughed and raked smooth and running from the riverbank into the distance on the left. I knew that this was the so-called track zone. I also knew that I was about a hundred yards away from escaping Hungary. I kept running, sinking to my ankles into the soft earth. When I thought the border was far enough behind me, I stopped. The breeze was cold against my skin, and I realized I was standing naked; my clothes were in the bag strapped to my back. With shaking hands, I opened it and pulled on my jumpsuit. I put my muddy feet into my shoes, tied the shoelaces, and began to jog. With the moon behind me, my body cast a huge, bobbing shadow on the ground.

At dawn I came upon a boat sitting snugly on the bank, chained to the trunk of a willow tree and secured with a large padlock. I slackened my pace and halted. The boat was heavy, and when I tried to lift it, my stomach muscles strained at the effort. I dragged the boat until it slid into the river; then I kicked away from the bank, jumped in, and grabbed the gunwales. The chain snapped, the skiff glided away from the bank, but an eddy curled it back. I pulled up the seat, a two-by-six plank, sank to my knees, and began paddling to catch the current, which soon dragged me downstream. The horizon turned pink, and by the time dawn heaved itself into day, I was sound asleep in the bottom of the boat, deep into Yugoslavia.

Anton is full of questions. "What was it like in the refugee camp?"

"You mean, what was it like in Italy?" I ask. I never felt as if I was in a refugee camp. I was free to go anywhere I wanted. The camp was like a hostel with free meals—an address, a place where all the paperwork was done. I loved Italy and loved Italians. After my paperwork was done, I found work with a stonemason, for whom I worked during the week. On weekends I would take the train and travel from Latina to Naples, to Rome, to Pompeii.

I look out the window, into the night. I remember my first telephone call from the refugee camp. I called the post office where Mother worked and asked for her. When I told her I was in Italy, there was silence. Then she began to cry. Later, she told me that on the very night of my escape, she had had a bad dream. A nightmare. That I was being shot at and wounded while trying to escape.

"Where do you live in Canada?" Anton asks.

"Toronto. I have been living there since I arrived from Italy."

I think of my first years in Canada—perhaps the happiest in my entire adult life. I found a job as a construction worker. Twice a week I went to the University of Toronto for evening courses. I cleaned an office building at night and slept four or five hours in the elevator room before walking across the street to the job site where I wheel-barrowed concrete, shovelled gravel, and hauled lumber. On weekends I took the ferry to Ward's Island to paddle with my new friends, Chris, Jeremy, and Graham. The Toronto Island Canoe Club became my new home, its members my family, and after such a long time, kayaking was back in my life.

"How about you?" I ask.

"Montreal. I live in Montreal and do business in Prague. I would say, I live between Montreal and Prague. Sometimes I don't know which one is home." He pauses to consider. "Perhaps Montreal. My parents live there, I have family there. Yes, it's Montreal," he finally concludes, nodding. "For my parents, it's definitely Montreal. St-Bruno-de-Montarville, to be exact. Except for a brief visit in 1968, they never went back to Prague."

I gaze at him quizzically. "I would have thought otherwise. Those who arrive in a new country late in their lives find it difficult ..."

"My parents left Prague young. Right after Hitler annexed the Sudetenland in 1938. They had just got married. They grabbed what they could and took the train to Zurich. From Zurich, they went to London. They stayed in England till the end of the war, when they moved back to Prague, where I was born. They stayed only four years. Four sad and disappointing years."

"How so?"

"Soon after their return, they found that most of their family—my grandparents, uncles, and aunts—had been killed. Only a few friends had survived."

"What was called "liberation" and, for most of them, was indeed liberation, soon turned into terror. The Muscovites took over and from Nazi rule, the country fell under a bolshevik dictatorship. Show trials, persecution, suppression of every freedom. Not even the solace of a happy marriage and the birth of a child could cancel out the lack of grandparents, uncles, and aunts who vanished, or their disappointment and their despair over the direction the country was heading." Here, he paused. "But of course, what am I saying? You already know all about that. Anyway, when I was three years old, my parents managed to obtain passports and took the train to Vienna. From Vienna they went to London, thinking they could pick up where they had left off. But they were worried that the Iron Curtain would soon be drawn over the rest of Europe, including Britain. They wanted an entire ocean between that crazy violent continent and themselves. They decided to move to Canada."

The flight attendant is pushing a cart down the aisle. I glance at the screen showing our altitude, speed, and location—we're over Newfoundland.

"I was thinking along the same lines," I smile. "Once I realized that I could not beat them, and I knew that I would not join them, I wanted to put as much distance as I could between the commies and myself. Sometimes I wonder what will be the next calamity to fight or to run from."

"I tell you," says Anton, "it's upon us and there is no escape from it."

"Oh?" I ask, wondering if he means bigotry, intolerance, terrorism.

"The Nazis were defeated. The communists have lost the Cold War. But their mercilessly efficient over-organization of human existence has won the day."

Without waiting for me to process what he said, Anton fixes me with his gaze, as if he wanted to hypnotize me. "Blinded by the hard glare of technology," he announces, "we have become machines attached to machines, big and small. Machines programmed to eat junk, drink junk, breathe junk, listen to junk, talk junk, and read junk. Our world has become a work world. The reward for our efforts is garbage. Huxley was right."

I open my mouth to reply, but Anton is now clearly on a roll; he takes a deep breath and ploughs ahead. "According to his calculations," he says as, if he was talking to the book, "at the rate we are going, places of peace and quiet, together with our hodgepodge civilization, will disappear in a few decades. If you want to find tranquility, you have to dig deep for it, like an archeologist. Have you read *The Illusion of Technique?*"

"Huh," I say, "you sound like one of those Slav nihilists."

"Maybe a realist," he replied. "Less and less happens according to the laws of nature, according to the norms of decency. And more and more happens through mechanical control and greed. What I see is a world of cheap appeals and cheap prods, life hollowed out and turned into a thirst for superficialities. Politics? A democracy, in which the party that succeeds in deceiving more people than the other governs? … I better stop preaching. Tell me about the Canada you found."

I shut my eyes and try to think of how to respond. For me, to live in Canada, to be a Canadian has always been a great piece of luck. But I want to cheer up this bitter man with my first, ridiculous impressions of Canada. Like how I wondered why people gather dog shit on the streets into small bags. Why all those coloured women were pushing white kids in prams. I want to talk to him about my introduction into spoken English by Willoughby, a Cockney, my first boss on the construction site who yelled, "Gimmi mi hamma an a nile" and became upset when I stood shaking my head in total ignorance. "Fuck," he would say, "another one who does not speak the white man's language. Matzaal put the kettle on, have some tea and see what the fuck I can do with you."

I did not have the clue what "mi hamma" and "nile" was meant to be, and it took me a month to figure out that "matzaal" meant "might as well." After his tea, Willoughby broke out in a long and furious sentence: 'The fucking safety inspector just dragged his ass onto the site. Clean up after the fucking bricklayers, then go inside and clean up after the fucking plumber who leaves his shit behind like a fucking dog. "Gee," I said to myself, "what a sexually overheated nation!" From inspectors through bricklayers to plumbers down to the last dog. It was coffee time. I imagined the bricklayers having sex with their girlfriends behind their pick-up trucks, the plumbers doing the same in the bathtub. Only after I bought my first banana from the caterer, who pulled onto the site, horn blaring, did I finally understood that "fucking" on the construction site was a permanent adjective stuck to everyone and everything, like "fleet-footed" to Achilles or "cunning" to Odysseus. As I struggled to figure out the best way to peel the banana, Willoughby interrupted scornfully, "Even a fucking monkey knows how to open a fucking banana!" He grabbed from me, held it by the stem, and whipped off the peel—much to the delight of the trades, who were rolling with laughter by the time he handed it back to me, peel dangling.

"Beautiful," I end up saying, with a glance at Anton. I keep it to myself that I never saw, and still do not see, any hollowing out of life; my world never became that of cheap prods and superficialities.

"Beautiful," is what I told Mother when I called her from Canada. "The grass is greener, the lakes are cleaner, the forests are incredibly larger. The people are nicer."

As if I were a river
The harsh age changed my course,
Replaced one life with another,
Flowing in a different channel
And I do not recognize my shores.
—Anna Akhmatova, Russian poet

It is a hot summer afternoon. The cottage feels like the inside of a furnace. With the windows closed and the shutters blocking the sun, Mother sits in her armchair, trying to read a book in the half-light. David is lying on the kitchen floor, legs splayed. His arm is resting on Small Dog.

I step out. If there is any movement in the air, it is the rise of dazzling heat from the scorched ground and from the flat rocks covered with dry lichen. Instead of the usual, happy summer concert of birds, all I can hear is the loud shrill of a cicada and the whirl of insects around my head. Only the tiger lilies growing wild by the steps leading down to the dock seem to enjoy the heat of the day. Except for a buzzard making lazy circles high above the marsh between Black Lake and Otter Lake, the white, hot, tin dome of the sky is vacant.

"Otter Lake," I murmur to myself as I walk back to the cottage.

"Let's paddle to Otter Lake," I say in the doorway. "It's better on the water."

Mother looks up from her reading. David sits up, and Small Dog tilts her head as if she wanted to hear me say it again. Mother smiles, marks her place in the book, and places it on the sofa.

"Let's go," she says. She walks to the kitchen counter and fills three bottles with water. She puts on her sunglasses and her wide-brimmed hat.

With Mother sitting in the middle and David and Small Dog in the bow, I'm paddling up Black River. Under the shade of trees lining the right bank, we are barely moving against the slow current. Mostly birch, maple and willow, the canopy of their branches reaches almost halfway across the river. The mesh of their roots runs down the bank and into the water. Frogs catapult into the air and plunge into the river, then disappear among the thick web of dark weeds. Small schools of fish patrol the shallows, shifting and splitting in ever-changing formations. Around the canoe, swarms of water bugs skate on the surface. Mother watches them in a sort of rapture. When the bow hits their small flotillas, some surf alongside the canoe and ride the wake.

We pass by Gumigan's cabin, huddled between two large willows. The current is faster here; it spirals around the rocks and logs. I widen my strokes and paddle around the bend. Soon, we are on the narrow and shallow channel that runs all the way to Otter Lake between thick forest on the right and marsh on the left. Whenever I try to plunge my paddle in deeper, I hit the bottom and see mud rising to the surface.

The long stretch of marshland left of the channel is covered with lily pads. A muskrat cuts through their maze, reaches the channel, and dives under when it sees our canoe blocking its way to the right bank. Dragonflies hover above the water, hunting for insects.

"Dad," says David, and points at the tall, dead tree ahead of us. Like the mast of a sunken ship, it towers above the reeds and bulrushes stretching behind the sea of lily pads. A young osprey leans back and forth on a short branch sticking out of a trunk that has long lost its bark. There must be wind blowing up there; its nape feathers are ruffled. The bird turns its head, inspects us for a moment, then jumps into the air with a high-pitched, whistling cry. It hangs above the marsh for a while, peeping, before veering off in the direction of Black Lake. I stop paddling and we watch it until it completely disappears.

It is late afternoon when we arrive at the end of the channel. The sky becomes soft and mellow as the sun moves further down on its path to the distant line of treetops in the west. David picks up his paddle. We adjust our strokes, and the canoe picks up speed. The channel widens as it turns and we are a few paddle strokes away from Otter Lake. Small Dog lifts her paws onto the gunwale and pushes her head up in the air. Her nostrils twitch faster and faster as we get deeper into open water.

The breeze that ruffled the feathers of the osprey now brushes my ears and cheeks. Mother stretches her back. She pushes her hat up and turns her face into the wind. With the countenance of someone expecting something good without quite knowing what, she looks at the small island with a few stunted pine trees rising from the red rocks glittering in the last rays of the sun. Their shimmery needles dance in the breeze, which brings the scent of resin to the canoe. David turns around, lays his paddle cross the gunwale, and watches Mother gazing at the island. I stop paddling, so as not to break the spell, and let the canoe glide softly until it stops in the lee of the island, where all is still. The shapes of trees against the lake and the sky freeze in their arrangements, as if for one moment stillness held this small part of the world together. Even the colours have stopped changing in intensity and remain constant.

"How beautiful," Mother says.

The current turns the canoe, and with it, all is set in motion again.